CONTENT OF THE *Curriculum*

ASCD

1988 ASCD YEARBOOK

of the
Association for
Supervision and
Curriculum
Development

Edited by Ronald S. Brandt

Executive Editor: Ronald S. Brandt
Manager of Publications: Nancy Carter Modrak
Associate Editor: René M. Townsley
Editorial Assistant: Scott Willis
Art Director: Al Way

Printed in the United States of America
Typeset by Scott Photographics, Inc.
Printed by Jarboe Printing Company
ASCD stock number: 610-88008
ISBN: 0-87120-150-X
Library of Congress
Catalog Card No.: 87-72734
Price: $14.95

Content of the Curriculum

Foreword

Content of the Curriculum addresses the concerns of educators and society for what should be taught in schools today. It presents recognized experts' thoughts about the content and organization of each discipline and answers questions about what students should learn at each level of schooling. These answers provide fresh perspective because they are in a social context that recognizes current conditions as well as possibilities for the future. Also, because the authors are concerned with the continuing search for strategies that promote learning and thinking, they have considered what is known about how youngsters learn and have related that knowledge to the nature of curriculum content. The authors maintain that the curriculum must be rethought periodically to ensure that what is taught and how it is taught are both accurate and relevant.

This book presents cogent, concrete, and discipline-specific material in a way that should enable curriculum decision makers to translate the recommendations into a workable curriculum. Other decisions appropriate for individual states, districts, and schools must be made with respect to implementation strategies, time allocations for each discipline, and specific topics within a discipline. The interrelationships among the disciplines and the possibilities for integration are also left for local consideration, as are plans for staff involvement and preparation required by a new curriculum.

Content of the Curriculum offers a framework of discipline-specific concepts that can be revised or expanded in response to community expectations and needs of particular students. It is a starting point for local curriculum leadership.

MARCIA K. KNOLL
ASCD President, 1987-88

1. Introduction: What Should Schools Teach?

Ronald S. Brandt

THE TOPIC OF THIS YEARBOOK—CURRICULUM CONTENT—IS both timely and timeless. It is timeless because the task of deciding what students should learn, and what schools should teach, is never complete. In fact, the authors of two chapters—those in science and home economics—describe a current effort to redefine their field. Most of the other authors, even those where opinion leaders generally agree (mathematics, foreign language, and technology, for example) describe a program that they concede exists more in the professional literature than in actual practice in most schools.

A book on content is timely because curriculum leaders are faced with an unusually potent challenge to their credibility. Two best-selling books and a well-publicized national report have not only made a strong case for study of more classic literature and traditional history but have attacked curriculum workers for intentionally engineering neglect of these important subjects.

The first salvo in this one-sided battle was fired by E.D. Hirsch, Jr., who contends that the main reason many students—especially those from low-income homes—do not read well is not their lack of skills but their limited background knowledge. In *Cultural Literacy: What Every American Needs to Know* (1987a), Hirsch argues for a curriculum that systematically and as early as possible teaches the information and ideas that are the foundation of our national culture. He cites research on artificial intelligence, which he interprets as proving that intellectual skills are integral to particular bodies of knowledge and therefore not transferable. Most educators, he claims, believe otherwise; hence their current interest in teaching critical thinking and their disdain for "mere facts" (Hirsch 1987b).

An even gloomier portrait of American education is painted by Allan Bloom (1987), whose devastating critique of higher education indirectly indicts elementary and secondary schools as well. American students had never come to college with the book learning of their European counterparts, he writes, but the fresh curiosity of these "natural savages" constituted a large part of their charm (p. 48). Even that openness to ideas was lost, however, when in the late 1960s the universities capitulated to "the various liberations" and gave up all pretense of requiring a liberal education. As a result, "today's select students know so much less, are so much more cut off from the tradition, are so much slacker intellectually, that they make their predecessors look like prodigies of culture" (p. 51).

Bloom marshalls all the power of his considerable eloquence to urge upon his readers the gravity of the situation: "To repeat, the crisis of liberal education is a reflection of a crisis at the peaks of learning, an incoherence and incompatibility among the first principles with which we interpret the world, an intellectual crisis of the greatest magnitude, which constitutes the crisis of our civilization" (p. 346).

The crisis Bloom refers to is the inability of colleges and universities to define a core program of studies for all students; to decide what it means to be an educated person in this society. "These great universities—which can split the atom, find cures for the most terrible diseases, conduct surveys of whole populations and produce massive dictionaries of lost languages—cannot generate a modest program of general education for undergraduate students" (p. 340).

Bloom's implied criticism of elementary, middle, and high schools—schools that he claims had formerly produced "natural savages" and are not now doing even that—is made more explicit in three publications that analyze results of the first national assessment of high school students' knowledge of history and literature. Writing in *What Do Our 17-Year-Olds Know?*, Diane Ravitch and Chester Finn, Jr. (1987) report that large numbers of adolescents could not tell the half century in which the Civil War occurred or who wrote "Leaves of Grass." Concluding that "our eleventh graders as a whole are ignorant of much of what they should know" and roundly condemning this "shameful performance" (p. 201), Ravitch and Finn demand much more time for instruction in history and literature at all levels.

In a more balanced treatment of the same data, published by National Assessment itself, Applebee, Langer, and Mullis (1987) write, "Although lack of student knowledge about some historical topics is a matter for serious concern, about two-thirds of the questions were answered correctly by more than half the eleventh graders. The performance on the literature assessment was slightly lower, perhaps in part because some of the questions asked were about specific works and authors not included in the curriculum until after the junior year in high school, if at all" (p. 3). These views are probably closer to those of most practicing educators, who, though they may be equally disappointed by results of their efforts, are acutely aware of the many barriers in the way of greater effectiveness.

Content vs. Process

What makes it difficult to consider critiques such as Ravitch and Finn's more objectively is their seemingly gratuitous attacks on educators. For example, they charge that "there is a tendency in the education profession to believe that *what* children learn is unimportant compared to *how* they learn; to believe that skills can be learned without regard to content; to believe that content is in fact irrelevant, so long as the proper skills are developed and exercised" (p. 17). These unnamed educators are not only wrong-headed; they are lazy and even cowardly. For example, they "could not or would not make the effort to show how traditional and modern literature together can . . . help us better understand ourselves and our society" (p. 10). Moreover, the reason they have chosen to teach skills rather than content is that it is "easier."

> Unlike skill training, teaching the humanities requires people to make choices. Deciding what content to teach risks offending some group or individual, those who prefer a different version of history or different works of literature. How much easier, then, to teach social studies as skills rather than as history, offending practically no one; how much easier to teach the skills of language arts, to fill in blanks and circle words, rather than to bear the burden of selecting particular poems, plays, short stories, and novels and to have to figure out how to make them meaningful for adolescents (p. 8).

In a separate broadside published by the National Endowment for the Humanities, which funded the Ravitch-Finn study, Lynne Cheney (1987), chairman of the Endowment, lays the blame for students' sorry performance at the feet of "education specialists." In her largely undocumented attack, Cheney charges that these villains ignore curriculum content because of their infatuation with process (p. 8), which she does not define. She recommends that school districts hire fewer curriculum directors and supervisors and use the money to hire teacher aides for humanities teachers instead (p. 29).

It may be true that some educators are so concerned with skills and processes that they consider content "irrelevant," but most probably believe that both are important, and that stating the issue that way creates a false dichotomy. If so, they are in agreement with Cheney and with Ravitch and Finn, both of whom make that point. Educators do hold varying views about the purposes of education and the way curriculum should be organized to achieve them. In all fairness, however, these differences can be ascribed not to laziness or cowardice, but to deeply held convictions about what is best for children.

Rather than responding in kind, educators should conserve their energies for the continuing struggle of deciding what schools should teach. Curriculum leaders do not make organizational decisions by personal decree;

they manage a give-and-take political process in which the views of teachers, board members, parents, and others are heard and considered. The ideas of outside authorities may carry special weight, but only to the extent that local educators judge them reasonable. Most existing school programs are an amalgam of progressive and traditional practices, the best that can be achieved under the circumstances but not fully satisfactory to anyone. The point is made most poignantly by Sizer (1984) in *Horace's Compromise*, which conveys the frustration and despair of a contemporary English teacher.

Knowing this, we may regret the hostility expressed by Ravitch, Finn, Cheney, and other critics, but we must not disregard their position. These capable, informed scholars have not only succeeded in placing their case persuasively before the American public; they have raised legitimate questions that must be answered anew by every generation. Their views, and the views of those who disagree with them, can perhaps be more readily understood and compared by making the underlying assumptions more explicit.

Conflicting Conceptions

A useful scheme for "analyzing the implications of an otherwise confusing body of arguments" was developed by Eisner and Vallance (1974, p. 2). In *Conflicting Conceptions of Curriculum*, they identified five orientations that could be discerned in the educational literature of the 1960s and '70s. These orientations, which with some variations remain valid today, reflect competing notions about the role of schools in our society and therefore differing perceptions of the goals, organization, and content of education.

In the Eisner-Vallance scheme, Ravitch and Finn represent *academic rationalism*, which they describe as "the most tradition-bound of the five orientations." Academic rationalists seek "cultural transmission in the most specific sense: to cultivate the child's intellect by providing him with opportunities to acquire the most powerful products of man's intelligence. These products are found, for the most part, in the established disciplines" (p. 12). Adherents of this orientation are generally opposed to having practical subjects such as driver education, homemaking, and vocational education in the curriculum because doing so "dilutes the quality of education and robs students of the opportunity to study those subjects that reflect man's enduring quest for meaning" (p. 12).

Eisner and Vallance noted a new approach to thinking about the disciplines aimed at determining "what it is about their respective content that distinguishes them from each other" (p. 13). Because advocates of this *structure of knowledge* orientation continued to assume the validity of subject matter divisions, Eisner and Vallance considered it a subcategory of academic rationalism, although they pointed out that its focus on "the logical and structural bases" for the disciplines adds "a new dimension to this orientation." For example, it brings a "sophisticated concern with process [to] a traditionally content-saturated conceptualization of education." Because this approach is so different from traditional academic rationalism, I believe it should be regarded as a separate category.

Another conception of curriculum emphasizes *development of cognitive processes*. Advocates of this approach are "primarily concerned with the refinement of intellectual operations . . . the development of independent cognitive skills applicable to a variety of situations. . . . The interactive relationship between the learner and the material is of prime concern." According to Eisner and Vallance, these educators rarely concern themselves with curriculum content, "focusing instead on the how rather than the what of education" (p. 6).

A fourth approach also focuses on process, but in this case it is not the student's thinking process but the educator's process of instructional design. Those who view *curriculum as technology* are concerned with the way "knowledge is communicated and 'learning' is facilitated." They assume that learning occurs in "systematic and predictable ways and that it can be be made more efficient" if it is properly controlled. The curriculum worker's problem is a practical one of "packaging and presenting" the material to learners (pp. 7-8).

Proponents of *self-actualization* see things quite differently. They believe that education should help "the individual discover things for himself" and that curriculum should provide "personally satisfying consummatory experiences for each individual learner." They insist that education provide "integrated experience" and "a liberating force" by "enter[ing] fully into the child's life." They are very concerned with the content of education, which they consider "an end in itself" (pp. 9-10).

A final orientation is *social reconstruction-relevance*, which is concerned with "social reform and responsibility to the future. . . . The social view of schooling examines education and curriculum in terms of their relation to the social issues of the day." It has two branches: the adaptive approach, which "views social issues and change as a crucial context for personal development," and the reformist approach, in which students are educated "to intervene actively to shape the changes" (pp. 11-12).

These are not the only possible conceptions of curriculum, and they are not necessarily representative of the actual views of particular individuals. Most people's views, in fact, are probably combinations of several of these positions. Moreover, the descriptions reflect the biases of Eisner and Vallance. Their distaste for the "curriculum as technology" approach, for example, is evident in their characterization of it.

The point is that discussions of curriculum necessarily proceed from assumptions about the nature of knowledge and the purposes of education.

In their portrayal of at least two of these approaches (cognitive development and curriculum as technology) and perhaps a third (social reconstruction), Eisner and Vallance agree with Ravitch and Finn that the proponents are concerned primarily with process rather than content. Yet content is a crucial element in education, as ASCD recognized several years ago when we decided to prepare this book.

I began planning for the book by asking educators familiar with the various subject fields to recommend prospective authors. When I had contacted the authors, I asked them to consider the classic influences on curriculum—the nature of society, the nature of today's youth, and the nature of knowledge in their subject—to help decide what should be taught. The responses are quite disparate and in some cases unexpected. For example, Paul Lehman, author of the chapter on the arts, concentrates not on self-expression but on specific outcomes to be achieved by students at each level of schooling. Linda Bain, author of the chapter on physical education, examines the social context of education and stresses the importance of critical reflection. Charles Suhor, who writes about the English curriculum, defines content not as "that which is to be taught," but instead as "that which is to be processed," thereby placing the content vs. process issue in a different perspective.

Variations such as these stem partly from individual preferences and partly from differences among the disciplines, but mostly from differing conceptions of curriculum. From the academic rationalist standpoint, these authors do not deal with curriculum *content*, because they do not mention Mozart, volleyball, or Melville. Needless to say, the authors, all experts in their fields, believe they are indeed talking about content. As you read each chapter, you might try to identify the author's conception of curriculum and his or her view of the relationship between content and process.

References

Applebee, Arthur N., Judith A. Langer, and Ina V. S. Mullis. *Literature & U. S. History: The Instructional Experience and Factual Knowledge of High School Juniors*. The Nation's Report Card, Report No. 17-HL-01. Princeton, N.J.: Educational Testing Service, 1987.

Bloom, Allan. *The Closing of the American Mind*. New York: Simon and Schuster, 1987.

Cheney, Lynne V. *American Memory: A Report on the Humanities in the Nation's Public Schools*. Washington, D.C.: National Endowment for the Humanities, 1987.

Eisner, Elliot W., and Elizabeth Vallance, eds. *Conflicting Conceptions of Curriculum*. Berkeley, Calif.: McCutchan Publishing Corporation, 1974.

Hirsch, E.D., Jr. *Cultural Literacy: What Every American Needs to Know*. Boston: Houghton Mifflin, 1987a.

Hirsch, E.D., Jr. "Restoring Cultural Literacy to the Early Grades." *Educational Leadership* 45, 4 (December 1987b-January 1988): 63-70.

Ravitch, Diane, and Chester E. Finn, Jr. *What Do Our 17-Year-Olds Know? A Report of the First National Assessment of History and Literature*. New York: Harper & Row, 1987.

Sizer, Theodore R. *Horace's Compromise: The dilemma of the American High School*. Boston: Houghton Mifflin, 1984.

2. Social Studies: The Study of People in Society

Donald H. Bragaw and H. Michael Hartoonian

Here each individual is interested not only in his own affairs but in the affairs of state as well. Even those who are most occupied with their own businesses are extremely well informed on general politics. . . . We do not say that a man who takes no interest in politics is a man who minds his own business; we say that he has no business here at all.

Pericles, 431 B.C.

IN 1982, JOHN NAISBITT IDENTIFIED THE SHIFT FROM REPRESENTATIVE democracy to participatory democracy as one of his ten megatrends. His opening statement of that chapter provides a central rationale for a public policy-oriented social studies curriculum:

> The ethic of participation is spreading bottom up across America and radically altering the way we think people in institutions should be governed. Citizens, workers, and consumers are demanding and getting a greater voice in government, business and the marketplace (p. 175).

Naisbitt follows that with the axiom that "People whose lives are affected by a decision must be part of the process of arriving at that decision" (p. 175). This axiom is rooted in the traditions and practice of our nation's heritage from the town meetings of colonial New England to today's ballot boxes. Included in this tradition are two fundamental principles:

1. A clear commitment to democratic ideals that are constantly developing through public discourse and action; and
2. An understanding that such development occurs when the people are educated to the responsibilities and processes of acting on personal and public issues.

Social studies, then, is the study of how citizens in a society make personal and public decisions on "issues that affect their destiny" (Cleveland 1985). The keys to that study lie in providing students with significant experiences in the disciplines of history, geography, economics, and the other social sciences.

Education directed at preparing knowledgeable, active citizens with the goal of developing personal and public policy requires a conscious and deliberate social studies program focused on recognizing, analyzing, and acting on problems or decisions that affect an individual's, group's, and nation's well-being. From student decisions regarding homework, hallway behavior, and school dance regulations to public policies of a global dimension, the focus is the same: How do I as an individual—and as part of many groups—learn how to identify and respond in a civilly responsible manner? A democratic society demands no less.

And it demands more. According to Robert Bellah and his associates, "Citizenship is virtually coexistent with 'getting involved' with one's neighbors for the good of the community" (1986). That involvement ranges from talking—"talking" is doing in a democracy (Matthews 1985)—to direct political or social action.

Social studies is the school-based subject with the best potential for helping students put their citizenship all together in preparation for a lifetime of holding "the office of citizen" (Tussman 1958). In the new century students will confront significant developments in science and technology requiring of all people skills greater than reading a newspaper, viewing a television news program, or casting a ballot.[1] Technology will force more rapid policy decision making and greater concerns for the ethical, social, economic, and political nature of those decisions. Students will need to be able to more firmly commit themselves to the ideals of civic obligation and action in both their personal and public relationships. In any age, such a relationship constitutes the social contract all people must make in order to survive. "One of the keys to the survival of free institutions is the relationship between private and public life, the way in which citizens do, or do not, participate in the public sphere" (Bellah et al. 1986).

The study of people in society (social studies) should involve students in studying how people go about the business of governing and conducting the affairs of a dynamic society. In this sense, knowledge not only illuminates the past, it can also enable people to make their lives better and more meaningful. Thus, the twin goals of social studies are to make people aware of and maintain their cultural heritage and to empower them with knowledge and skills to make *new* commitments to create a world of better tomorrows.

---

[1]We recognize the substantial literature on decision making, problem solving, and reflective thinking as related to citizenship; by placing the emphasis on personal and public policy making, we hope to add a civic imperative for which social studies instruction has a primary school responsibility.

The Nature of Knowledge in Social Studies

Almost everything about the social world is more complex than we lead students to believe. Instructing students on how the world works always carries the dilemma of the proper relationships among information, knowledge, and reality, and there is a significant difference between information and knowledge. Information is one-dimensional: linear or horizontal, fragmented, and quite useless in and of itself. On the other hand, students gain knowledge about regions, for example, when they can take information about places on the earth and structure it to show relationships among those pieces of information and use it to form their own concept of region. Once formed, the student's concept of region can be refined and used again and again, each time with greater clarity and analytical power. It is the structuring and use of information that becomes knowledge. Information provided by a teacher or textbook is generally, and wrongfully, perceived as knowledge. Such collections of information, structured according to frameworks designed by the text or constructed by adults, remain information, not knowledge. Knowledge is something *created* through a process of personal involvement that allows for complex relationships between the learners (including the teacher) and the text and context of the classroom, even when that classroom includes the larger community (Raskin and Bernstein 1987).

The challenge for teachers is to promote the use of information from the several areas of the social studies, as well as from the humanities, science, and mathematics, to help students create knowledge for themselves. For this creative process to work with integrity, the most powerful content-based concepts must be used, for they are the best ideas available for helping students formulate personal and public policy decisions. Content ideas such as justice, equality, freedom, and diversity become powerful when students grasp principal relationships within and across subject areas and use these ideas to conceptualize reality, deal with causality and validity, and create meaning.

While it is important to select information and knowledge from the humanities and from mathematics and science as well, this type of interactive social studies curriculum is grounded in history and the social sciences.

The nature of this knowledge, however, must be seen from the vantage point of two interrelated questions: (1) What content should be selected to best serve students in their search for understanding the human condition? and (2) What abilities should students develop in order to engage in this search?

Operational Abilities

Content should help students study, learn, and use the powerful ideas from history and the social sciences. Whatever the program—whether focusing on history, expanding horizons, or concepts—the significant question is what students will be expected to achieve as a result. Those expectations should be centered around the following abilities:

1. *Students need to develop an information base in history and the social sciences and to make connections among previously learned and new information*. The most important attribute of this ability is the idea of "connections." A necessary condition of making informational connections that move one toward knowledge and wisdom is a sound factual base. But the sufficient condition comes with the extension of this information to areas that are new to the learner. Learning the facts about the needs that people have in societies A, B, and C, for example, is a necessary condition to learning about the connections between needs and social institutions. It may well be, as Hunt and Metcalf (1955) observed, that "there is only one role which facts can play in meaningful learning—to function as data in conceptualization. If they do not, they may, perhaps, be memorized and retained for awhile, but their meaning and future usefulness will be slight." This ability to conceptualize is, basically, knowing how to use data to make meaning. Marilyn Ferguson (1976) summed it up nicely:

> In most lives, insight has been accidental. We wait for it as primitive man awaited lightning for a fire. But making mental connections is our most crucial learning tool, the essence of human intelligence: to forge links; to go beyond the given; to see patterns, relationship, context.

The task of the curriculum leader, then, is to make sure that a dynamic factual base is built into each social studies program. However, those facts that are of most worth help us build connections and deal with *orders of magnitude*. For example, knowing the number of farmers in the United States is not as important as knowing the percent of farmers in the economy and their contribution to the gross national product. Knowing the size of the national debt in and by itself is not as powerful as knowing the magnitude of the national debt in relation to national worth, or the relationship between the resources spent on the world's war industry and the total income of the people of the world. Orders of magnitude also have historical and geographical worth. For example: How have income levels changed over the last 75 years in the United States? Where is the population center of the United States today? Where was it 75 years ago? Why has it changed? Curriculum designers can address the factual base of the social studies by introducing materials that raise questions about connections. That factual base that helps children best see relationships and connections in their own lives is the one to use; but students must realize that facts are constantly changing. Each grade level should stress different orders of magnitude and different fact clusters.

2. *Students need to think using different logical patterns and perspectives obtained through the study of history and the social sciences*. The content areas of the social studies can help students use different logical patterns and see cause/effect relationships. Causality means dealing with questions

of explanation, evidence, and bias. For example, older students can be helped to identify the political, economic, and historic rationales for active U.S. involvement in Central American affairs, and be able to construct arguments for and against such involvement in ways that reflect the patterns of thought and world views of the actors on all sides of the issue. This ability would involve using inductive, deductive, and analogical forms of logic. At the lower elementary level, this ability might be developed by a class establishing reasons that schools and communities have rules.

Logical patterns and perspectives of history and the social sciences must be understood within the time-space continuum in which we live. In this sense, history and geography are parts of the same whole. What does a map of the world look like with China at its center? What was going on in China or Alexandria (in North Africa) as compared to activities in Western Europe in 800 A.D.? The answers to these questions suggest that time and place orientations provide frameworks for thinking about issues, problems, and possibilities. Logical patterns and perspectives also have to do with the analysis of the social systems in which we live. This means attention to how reality is conceptualized, how these conceptions are explained and validated, and finally, how new concepts, generalizations, and laws are created. Students who grasp the essential meaning of the nature of the 15th and 16th century Renaissance (rather than just the names of painters or writers) will be more significantly served when they encounter the Harlem Renaissance in American history or the term "urban renaissance" in their daily newspaper. Thus, the ideas of perspective (time and space) and logic (the analysis of social systems) provide criteria for content selection by suggesting questions such as: Does this content and material allow students to "travel" to different times (past, present, and future) and places (near and far) in a way that allows them the opportunity to see connections? Does this content allow students to analyze institutions and systems in these times and places as a way of finding out how their own world works? Does this content allow students to "see" this multicultural, multi-ethnic world through "different eyes"—as well as their own?

3. *Students need to recognize that new knowledge is created by their interaction with new information from history or the social sciences.* Creating new knowledge means to develop and design new stories, explanations, models, pictures, dramas, music, or other modes of communicating extensions of previously learned knowledge to new settings, questions, and issues. In this context, students may, for example, design and build new model communities (in the third grade), write dramas about social institutions in different cultures (in the sixth grade), or prepare a position paper on changes in fiscal policy that could reflect serious thought about the economic health of the country (in the twelfth grade).

The most important element in the process of helping students become more creative in their ability to develop useful knowledge is the "pairing" of facts and ideas—that is, the bringing together of different thoughts, points of view, or rationales to form a reflective and new synthesis. For example, as third graders consider the traffic patterns in a community and talk with police and city planners, look at traffic patterns in other communities, and discuss the issue with people who drive cars and/or use other means of transportation, they can propose a new design to move people and goods. Students who pursue a study of peace or conflict resolution over the vast span of history (e.g., the Trojan War to the Camp David accords) might be able to develop some basic principles or axioms that appear useful in settling disputes. Such principles might then be tested by students to examine current conflicts and make judgments about the lessons of history. Learning such as this will need to be based on many different types of materials and resources. Curriculum leaders and teachers need to provide settings and resources that can help students consider different ideas and express their own.

4. *Students need to learn to communicate with others about the data and interpretations of history and the social sciences as applied to their studies and to the real world*. Communication skills such as reading, writing, listening, and speaking should enable students to convey and receive knowledge from history and the social sciences in ways that will communicate meaning and a rationale for civic behavior. They must be given opportunities to recognize different perceptions and to learn and practice how to negotiate positions with others with different perspectives. Additionally, they need to recognize that some people operate from an irrational base, which makes it difficult to either communicate or negotiate. What are some strategies and settings in which to study problem solving, bargaining, and the use of force in human decision making? Historical examples of this are frequently found in the causes of war.

In using *communication/negotiation* as a criterion for content selection, we must take into account two notions of human interaction. One obvious idea is that communication/negotiation is a matter of skill development in reading, writing, listening, and speaking. These skills are important to all school subjects, and the content selection criterion here is simply permitting enough time to allow students to write, for example, and teachers to guide them in their communication skill development process *within* the social studies program. A less obvious notion is the appreciation of the nature and necessity of going beyond personal experiences and sampling those ideas from the past as well as from contemporary societies that help us carry on a human dialogue, bringing meaning to persistent questions like: What is the good citizen? Can an individual be just in an unjust society? What is the proper relationship between positive and natural law? Can virtue be taught? How should minority rights be protected? What is justice? What is happiness? Understanding of these and other questions demands good communication and negotiation skills.

It is important that students deal with representative ideas that connect certain themes across the ages. It is equally important that students know how to sample the totality of information in the first place. Thus, the learning materials should use or have students use sampling and other methodological techniques, including how historians and social scientists collect, organize, interpret, and *communicate* information and knowledge.

5. *Students need to learn how to make enlightened personal and public policy decisions based on their knowledge of history and the social sciences, and by participating in meaningful civic activities.* Making personal and public policy decisions means that students can conceptualize a problem or issue, create a plausible sequence of cause/effect relationships between events and consequences, create alternative sequences, evaluate alternatives, and implement a decision that has as its base concern for the value of democratic society as well as individual well-being. These abilities can be discussed from the point of view of questions such as: Were people less concerned with environmental issues in the 18th and 19th centuries? What is your evidence? What should we teach about the social ecosystems in which we all live? How can we learn to become better inhabitants of the earth?

By policy making we also mean that students, through formal and informal learning and social relationships, begin to develop self-governance abilities (personal policies) that extend into the area of the various publics in which students find themselves. Creating civic actors from the early years onward requires that the social studies program include contemporaneous, historical, and literary elements that will help students increase their critical thinking capacity about all types of people making personal and public policy.

Such an orientation calls for developing social participation activities that focus on democratic, individual, and cooperative policy making such as:

- developing classroom and school rules (fairness),
- dealing with classroom and school incidents that call for adjudication through negotiation (justice),
- agreeing on and carrying out work tasks related to projects (responsibility),
- reading and discussing stories that pose dilemmas for their characters and give students opportunities for vicarious policy decision making (values examination).

Consider, for example, the issue of whether or not a state should build a new maximum security prison. An instructional unit that addresses the five abilities could first develop factual background on the issue and stress those data among which connections can be drawn. For example, what is the relationship between incarceration and state crime rates? How much will the prison cost? How will the money for the prison be raised? What trade-offs will have to be made in the state budget?

Second, students can look at the issue from different political orientations. They could role-play the different positions through a series of "public hearings," which provide opportunities for practicing communication and negotiation skills. Public policy positions could then be formulated based on the results of research and discussions. Student participation in government, business, or other internships would provide practical experience in observing how policy is derived.

Abilities Into Knowledge

The successful learning of these five abilities demands content and materials that deal with topics of public and private importance. Discussion, for example, of the New Deal, or the New Frontier, the location of a new school, or welfare programs become important when students can see the nature of the policies and their implications for their own lives. Content selection criteria should address settings and materials that help students develop problem-solving skills from hypothesis formation to using probability and statistics. These settings, resources, and materials should also include opportunities to engage in scenario development, case study analysis, philosophical reasoning, and the use of documents and stories (literature) that illuminate the lives of people—their intellectual, moral, physical, and spiritual courage as well as their corruptibility (Lynd 1940, Dewey 1927, Bayles 1950, Engle 1960, Newman 1977, Bragaw 1986).

When this content is used as a basis for the interactions between teacher and student, the result is social studies knowledge. By definition, then, the quality and self-correcting features of this knowledge are functions of the quality of the interactions among teachers, students, and content resources within the bureaucratic and ideological constructs of school. By considering knowledge in this way, it is also possible to more accurately develop an evaluation system that is both logical and fair. Students achieve more when they know what the focus of learning is. Program evaluation is also easier for the same reason. The five abilities can be considered not only as criteria for content selection but also for student and program evaluation.

Again, our purpose is to refocus curricular questions away from the coverage of information and toward helping students construct frameworks of meaning that are consistent with the nature of knowledge in the social studies. This will mean giving ourselves permission to let go of some information that we are now teaching and reallocate that time to deeper inquiries that will help learners build intra- and interdisciplinary connections.

Program Design

The constantly changing nature of society, the increased volatility of human interaction, and the dynamics of historical and social scientific information continue to promote multiple interpretations and questioning about the ordering of social studies content. The fundamental scope of the present social studies program took shape and has remained the same since the turn of the century, although heated discussions have raged about the relative emphasis of one subject or another ever since. Whatever the arguments among the scholars over the role and function and proportion of history and the social sciences, process versus content, national or international stress, and the merits of inclusion (or exclusion) of certain topics, the standard program since 1916 has consistently included American history, geography, and government (under its various guises of civics, problems of American democracy, citizenship, and political science). Less constant and far more subject to political and educational winds are world history, cultural studies, the various social/behavioral sciences as individual electives, and special topics such as the environment, law-related education, and so forth.

The present program *gestalt* in social studies took on its major synthesis—the widening world or expanding horizons notion—in the mid-1930s. Prescient for its day, it continues to hold out a logical formulation for students preparing for the new century. The expanding horizons format comes closest to bringing understanding to how the real world actually is and operates. Its acceptance by school people and the general public reveals its viability. Whether that expanding concept has history, geography, civics, or any other social science as its core, children must grapple with two major forces as we turn into the new century: (1) the irrevocable global interdependence of all people and nations, and (2) the creation of knowledge patterns that no longer fit neatly into Aristotelian and Germanic discipline structures (Raskins and Bernstein 1987). Both of these forces make it essential that education provide better opportunities for students to learn how to participate in the decisions that will affect their destiny. While the emphasis on citizenship is not new, the emphasis on policy studies within the total program is.

Such an emphasis must take into account some "constants"—topics essential to the perpetuation of this culture—as well as new phenomena brought about by the advances in science, technology, and new thought in history and the social sciences.

The Constants:

1. There must be a continuing emphasis on the principles and values of a democratic society, with an awareness of the nature and operation of policy making and implementation so that democratic participation can flourish (Dewey 1916, Butts and Cremin 1954, Giroux 1984).

2. There must be a continuing study of our national heritage, including the struggle to achieve the principles of the Declaration of Independence for *all* persons. The enactment of policies dedicated to those principles has enabled our constitutional government to progress and become strong (Burns 1982, Marshall 1987, Butts and Cremin 1954).

3. There is a continuing need to provide students with a common grounding in the fundamentals of history, humanities, and the social/behav-

ioral sciences to guarantee a sound determination of this society's cultural literacy (Wronski and Bragaw 1986, Boyer and Levine 1981).

4. There must be a continuing search for the best learning and thinking skills consistent with the development of children and the nature of the content so as to enable students to communicate beyond purely adversarial positions to stages of development that include mediational and negotiated agreements (Goodlad 1984, Denham and Lieberman 1980, Edmonds 1982).

But new constants must also take into account that:

5. Technology has permitted new forms of communication that have become the province of all peoples, forcing them beyond parochialism to consider new ideas and perspectives of geographic, political, economic, and social boundaries (Global Education Task Force 1987, Cleveland 1985, Boulding 1985).

6. Information growth recognizes the integrated and interrelated nature of all information, creating new configurations of hyphenated knowledge of the social and natural sciences (e.g., bio-ethics, psycho-history, socio-linguistics, etc.) (Raskin and Bernstein 1987, Cleveland 1985).

A policy-oriented curriculum is a synthesis for the new age. It combines the intellectual dimensions with action required by all citizens who will increasingly become aware of the nature of the political processes controlling their lives. The power of national and global televised public action and government operation will force such recognition.

Primary Years

In translating these goals into curriculum guidelines, the primary grades should concentrate on providing the student with a base of knowledge and skills built on appropriate history and social sciences, but also integrating language arts, literature, and science, where advantageous. A democratic policy-defining and policy-making overlay or governance would be introduced as part of each of the units.

Learning basic notions of history and historical method would be accomplished by investigating self, family, community, and state historical events. The goal would be to provide students with a sense of history, including introductory notions of time and place. Reading stories could reinforce the themes.

Because not all students' heritage and experiences are exactly the same, natural curiosity should arise as to why differences exist. Children should explore the very significant questions of diversity and possible conflicting values between and among individual experiences. In organizing such social studies components at every level, other questions should also be used to promote civic understanding: why a group of people chose to live in one area over another or why the school is located where it is. A number of well-planned field experiences, such as visiting archaeological digs and historical restorations, would help students to further grapple with notions of time, place and diversity.

Learning basic map skills, social and cultural features of place, location, and environmental change are all necessary components of the primary social studies program. Geographic knowledge is not just place location, but should encourage student analysis of the why and what of location decisions. These considerations can be examined in concrete fashion by examining the home, school, and city location, and by multiple experiences with many different kinds of maps.

Economic concepts of meeting basic needs in a world of scarcity should also be included in the program. Basic understanding of how an economic system operates can range widely from individual lessons. Experiences in operating classroom stores and participating in full-scale mini-economies (where policy-making choices become everyday experiences) can be used to integrate economic concepts into elementary programs. Merely talking about stores, or visiting them, will not help students realize how much their interaction with the economy depends on their choices in the marketplace. From earliest time, students need to deal with affluence, poverty, hunger, and employment, and major issues like welfare and well-being as part of local, state, and national policy (Joint Council on Economic Education 1985).

Skills of policy analysis and decision making should begin in the kindergarten. For example, do you think this rule is fair? Who makes rules for our city or town? How? How should we handle the playground dispute? In each case, the student learns by actual experience. Developing simple but worthy classroom, school, and community service projects would encourage early student recognition of policy outcomes: school improvement, antilittering, and safety campaigns could be organized and carried out by students.

An Integrated Year

Throughout their education, students move from one vertical experience to another. They briefly encounter (in 20-30 minute lessons) mathematics, reading, science, social studies, art, music, and physical education. (Mathematics and reading lessons are usually longer.) The day is a series of nonintegrated experiences requiring students to accomplish minor miracles of transition, critical thinking, and valuing that few adults are asked to do or can achieve. Students are taught subjects as separate entities in a world that is an integrated whole.

The third grade should provide a year in which students are deliberately helped to integrate and apply their knowledge in the development of two major units. The first of these units might be to develop an "ideal" community. The unit could be based on district-prepared or commercially available materials that call for information gathering from *all* disciplines, data analysis, and decision making that involves policy judgments.

Such a unit would center around a group investigation project. A variety of sources would be fair game, and each unit would be oriented toward reflective thinking or problem solving. This type of integrative approach would make writing, literature, language arts, art, science, health, and other subjects logical parts of the whole, thus encouraging students to experience the interdependence of knowledge. Mathematics could be taught separately or included in the integrated study. The most important outcome of the integrative approach would be helping students to see connections and to apply skills and ideas to the wholeness and continuity of life.

The second unit should be similarly developed but focused on a variety of issues broadly representative of various American geographic and sociocultural settings different from the students' environment. Again, group investigation using questions developed over the past three years would be appropriate.

Elementary Years

Applying the same approach to the later elementary program, the emphasis would be put on state, national, and world studies. The five perspectives of history, geography, economics, political science, and the behavioral sciences would be again brought to bear on the role the state, nation, and world play in students' lives.

Students should be able to distinguish between the responsibilities of state government as opposed to local and national government in, for example, the areas of taxation, property ownership, and laws of control. Students at this age are thinking about real and unreal subjects such as dinosaurs or time and space travel. "The State" is as unreal to them as a romantic voyage into fantasy; their learning needs to help them both in perspective (Bettelheim 1977). The organizational systems that are required in human interaction (family, government, economic systems) are keys to compare-and-contrast studies that help bridge reality and fantasy. Making real such notions as the United States and United Nations can be accomplished by examining Star Trek's Federation of Planets just as well as through examination of state legislatures, Congress, or the General Assembly. The history of the public policies that brought about such responsibilities should be a part of that learning.

Students need to develop geographic and historical notions of regionalism, political boundaries, and people interacting with an environment. They should examine the policy decisions that have affected their local political boundaries and the individual and state economic policies that have economically affected the area.

Student recognition of the cultural diversity that exists in the United States and worldwide is important at this level. Group migration decisions, national immigration policies, and the arrival of peoples from diverse cultural backgrounds would create a need for examining contrasting cultural and personal values and actions.

Continuing the governance thrust from the earlier grades, students should be introduced to more formal interactive communication and negotiation devices and principles. There should be in-depth learning about how a government, school, business club, or larger group goes about developing, enacting, implementing, and judging policy decisions. All rational and irrational aspects of negotiation are keys to helping students recognize skills in resolving conflicts.

Involving students in discussions of issues such as divisions of power, slavery, environmental dangers, hunger, poverty, capital punishment, nuclear concerns, or racial equality helps them see how various people and various levels of organizations or governments respond. Those repeated experiences help establish a model of action and response. This is especially effective when the classroom and the school practice democratic principles of the negotiated life.

An Integrated Year

Grade six, like the third grade, would become an integrative experience. After an introduction to global geography, students would deal with one or more cultural areas of the world, selected to give students a totally different exposure than their own heritage would provide. Depth studies should include historical background, geographic data, and the major cultural influences and developments. The progression from early River Valley civilizations to the present Middle East would be one such study; Ancient and Medieval Studies would be another. Similar treatments of Asian or African cultural areas would also be ideal. In each case, students should study the areas from the perspectives of the people living there, which would expose students to other value systems while reinforcing the democratic values of our own society. Teachers should try to arrange for native-speaking guest speakers or videotaped cultural exchanges.

Students should begin to develop an understanding of cultural diffusion, global connections, and the need for empathetic analysis of an area's economic and political development. Art, music, literature, religion, and world beliefs could be skillfully woven into the total program. For example, study of the Middle East could include science lessons focused on the history of science, aspects of climatology, and the flora and fauna of arid and semiarid areas. Technological development and its effects on people and culture are also appropriate issues. Other issues for study might include oil, migration of people, religious differences, or the role and position of women and minorities. Students could also be exposed to the languages of the area as well—perhaps with some audiolingual experiences in Hebrew or one of the Arab languages, learning the close relationship of language and culture.

Comparison and analysis of economic and political systems and everyday customs offer an opportunity to recognize the universalities of state (or provincial) and national functions, while still understanding that philosophical and operational differences exist. By the end of their elementary years, students should be able to make major distinctions among various economic and political systems.

The Secondary Experience[2]

In the secondary years, students should receive a good grounding in the history and government of their own nation, the culture of Europe, and the culture of several non-Western areas. They should also be exposed to and use the several social science disciplines. The placement of these topics and how they are treated should be made consistent with learning theory, the expertise of the teaching staff, and with community consultation. A balanced social studies program would allocate two years to United States history, two years to studies of the world (both European and non-European centered), and two years to personal and public policy issues that combine history and the social sciences.

To expand their civic memory and social conscience, it is essential that students have a firm foundation in the cultural values of U.S. democracy. In one interpretation, the history of the United States is the history of personal and public policy making at all levels of government and in private life. For example, Susan B. Anthony chose a personal policy of persistent pursuit of public recognition of women's rights. A major policy study might focus on constitutional development. Specific projects might include constitutionality of laws, child welfare, slavery, mental hospitalization, railroad regulation, conservation, and neutrality. Students would define policy choices and discover how people choose to resolve an issue through public discourse and action.

Additionally, a two-year study would delve more deeply into the values of U.S. society and how they change yet continue to influence our lives. For example, American individualism continues to hold its own alongside an abiding sense of community. The conflict of those two values frequently influences our history and is found in literature, art, and daily life. In many

[2]The middle school movement suggests that the years from 11 to 14, approximately grades 6-8, are significant transitional years in which flexibility and exploration should be key guides to program decisions. The authors believe that the crucial decisions at this school level are instructional not content. The program design recommended here can be adjusted to the social and intellectual needs of the students, and political decisions of the school and community. We would strongly recommend that the integrated personal policy year be included to provide for the students' psychological needs.

ways, such values also determine people's choice of personal and social behavior.

No attempt should be made to cover the entire scope of European history. That study should focus on major economic, social, and political ideas (justice, equality, liberty, capitalism) and events that have influenced the development of western culture. The evolution of representative democracy (English example, 1215-present), migration of peoples (Islamic peoples), and communication-technological development (ancient science through industrial revolutions to microchips) would be appropriate areas of investigation. The program should be developed to promote the public policy orientation and critical thinking.

The following questions could provide useful unit theses: What kinds of political, economic and social policies did the European nations make and carry out after the discovery of the New World? What effect did those policy choices have? What societal responses were made to the industrialization and intensive urbanization in the various areas in which it developed? What effect did the advent of printing technology have upon the intellectual and cultural development of Europe and the New World? How were various peoples or minority groups treated for their religious beliefs or by reason of their sex? What impact does the European common market have on the economy of the United States?

Again, the study of non-European cultures (representative studies from African, Asian, Middle Eastern, and Native American cultures) should include the perspective of the indigenous peoples (Banks 1977). Major ideas such as environment, imperialism, cultural development, nationalism, industrialization (to include technological development), and other major concepts should control choice of content and include compare-and-contrast connections to other cultures. Emphasis on universal values of justice, human life, and dignity should be stressed throughout all these studies.

Two of the six secondary school years have great potential for helping students integrate and apply knowledge. In the ninth grade, when students struggle to build an identity and search for ways to deal with crucial personal relationships, there should be an opportunity to identify, clarify, and propose alternative solutions to personal and public policy issues (selected from all levels: local, state, regional, and national). The second year (the twelfth grade is recommended) should concentrate on a similar pattern but address personal and global public policy issues. The program should provide direct training in public policy analysis; examine a variety of philosophical and ethical rationales; integrate the social sciences, humanities, science, mathematics, etc.; encourage some kind of public or community service (tied into the formal study), and, by so doing, help students see the benefits of the integrated nature of knowledge.

These two integrated learning years continue to stress the need for students to see the relationship between their learning and their continuing role in the broader society. By so doing, they are also exposed to the realization that knowledge can be organized and interpreted in a variety of ways depending on their world view and the world views of others. Change is the constant that they must come to understand. Such programs enhance the value of critical thinking for students, and require the use of different methodologies from the various knowledge sources. By using these tools, students reinforce previous learning about developing, communicating, and negotiating their own personal policies as well as those of national or international import.

Year 13: Public Service

If citizenship education, defined as learning to take "the office of citizen," is as significant and important as the vast majority of American people believe it is, perhaps it is time to revive an old but good idea: public or community *service* (Boyer 1983). Such service would make real the relation between thought and action to promote the public good, helping individuals apply the knowledge they have gained and practice their reasoning skills. Before a student goes on to college to focus on self-enhancement, a period of time given in service to others might encourage a greater sense of community. For those for whom getting a job after high school is the immediate goal, such a term of public service would also strengthen their commitment to the goals of society.

No such program can be successful if it is limited to make-work projects, or is merely a makeshift job created to fill the bill. Former President Jimmy Carter has publicized one kind of service: giving of time and skills to rebuilding or providing housing for the poor, using donated materials. Local services to the elderly, needy children, and other groups in need of support are other areas of possible service, as are public works, environmental improvements, and public surveys. Education projects such as teaching aides, tutoring, peer counseling, working with teenage groups, service to senior citizens, or serving on school board advisory groups are also creative uses of time. The kinds of projects that are generally of low budget priority in local and county areas—such as historical preservation (houses, objects, and records)—could also be accomplished with such assistance.

Public Policy in a Global Age

We realize that not all students completing high school will go on to college, but we are concerned that the recent heavy focus on technical, computer, and business careers without commitment to philosophical considerations or public policy understanding is a trend that needs careful scrutiny. Recent reevaluations of undergraduate liberal arts studies may also miss the mark if commitment to public policy and community service is not considered an important goal. The same is true of teacher training programs, which should help future teachers develop community service commitment and experience in public policy analysis.

We suggest the following required public policy-focused courses for all undergraduate students:

Year 14: An in-depth focus on one social science (sociology, psychology, anthropology), including its methodologies and current status, and emphasizing its usefulness in forming public policy.

Year 15: A course in social ethics and logic, again with a focus on how public policy issues must also be founded on philosophical grounds. Focus on how any policy affects the people and the conditions it presumes to serve. In a world of environmental challenges, medical engineering, human suffering, resource scarcity, and technological breakthroughs, the ethical questions and need for commitment to civic responsibilities will continue to grow.

Year 16: An intellectual history of the United States with an emphasis on how great ideas have informed, shaped, and continue to influence personal and public policy. Ideas of the Puritans, Jefferson, Madison, Emerson, Lincoln, Sumner, and Dewey are but a few of the thinkers with which students should be acquainted.

Year 17: Students should be firmly grounded in the examination of a major global issue. A suggested paradigm might be that of Kenneth Boulding's *The World as a Total System* (1985), in which the student would be asked to look at the issue in relation to the biological, physical (geographic, ecological), political, social, economic, communicative, and evaluative systems that are constantly interacting.

Community-based public policy forums or discussion groups should be publically financed and promoted. The National Issues Forum and Foreign Policy Association program are examples of existing programs that could serve the wider community. Public and commercial television should increase public policy programming in the prime-time schedule. Corporate sponsorship of "inservice" courses or quality circles given over to policy issues would advance the public's awareness of the importance of their involvement in the affairs of state.

Summary of K-12 Program Design

The scope and sequence of courses for a social studies program K-12 has focused on the centrality of citizenship through the lens of personal and public policy. No other program in the schools has a greater responsibility for helping students to study and train to assume the role of citizen. Other programs concentrate on literature, art, music, science, and math—all of which can help make a more informed person. But social studies has the prime responsibility of nurturing the knowledge and wisdom that will help students make personal and public policies, as part of a nation and members of the larger world community. Only by helping students see how knowledge can serve the community, as well as themselves as individuals, can the schools justify programs in history and the social sciences. And only by helping students see how knowledge can serve the community can public schools justify themselves. Without a conception of the public good, public school makes no sense.

Knowledge for its own sake is interesting, but knowledge when put in the service of the creative individual can result in service to the community as well. People today no longer have the luxury of selfish introversion; the issues that confront the very existence of life require attention to public needs—needs now measured in global dimensions. Even the youngest children must be given help in developing democratic, analytic, and communication skills so they become better makers of policy.

Given the major purpose of social studies and the concept of discourse, we have proposed a sequence that addresses both disciplinary and interdisciplinary content in vertical and horizontal patterns.

The sequence pattern presents grades 3, 6, 9, and 12 as the integrative study years and the other grade levels as discipline study years. In the broadest sense, the discipline study years provide for the development of knowledge, skills, and attitudes needed for projects and lessons that are emphasized at the integrative study years.

Within the primary program, all areas of the social studies are covered, with particular emphasis on geography, anthropology (stories/literature and art from several cultures), and political science (civics/social contract). Students will begin to locate themselves in time and space and understand civility as a necessary condition of community living.

At the third grade level, the central focus is on community. All social studies subjects are integrated and used along with knowledge from science, mathematics, the language arts, and the fine arts to engage students in discourse about how people from all over the world and from different time periods develop, enjoy, reform, and destroy communities.

Grades 4 and 5 focus on analyzing the state and nation within a global setting. History (emphasis on social history), geography, and economics play major roles at this level and particular attention is given to the development of reasoning skills.

The concept of culture is the central focus of the sixth grade program. Specific cultures are studied through an integration of the social studies subjects, science, mathematics, the language arts, and the fine arts. Cross-cultural studies are encouraged with attention given to the study of people at different times and in different places. Of particular importance is the synthesis of ideas that address the creation, use, and misuse of cultural artifacts, from language and laws to tools and technologies.

Grades 7 and 8 present students with opportunities to study in greater depth history, geography, the behavioral sciences, and the analytic disciplines of economics and political science in national and global contexts.

Particular attention is given to regions of the world and their interrelatedness.

Personal and social policy making are emphasized at the ninth grade. Students study their personal roles in local and state settings focusing on the social sciences and the other academic disciplines to improve their decision-making abilities. Other topics may include local environmental issues, the business climate of the state, the role of education in the student's life, and the nature of the global economy and the individual's place within it. Again, students will apply their knowledge and skills to personal and social policy making.

The temporal and spatial study of the United States within a global context is the focus of the tenth and eleventh grades. The history of Western thought and the influence of other cultures on the uniqueness of the United States is addressed, taking special account of interrelationships among those factors which illuminate contemporary society for students.

The twelfth grade, as the pivotal year in the K-12 program, addresses selected questions about the quality of life and the relationships among and between people and institutions and might be treated as a culminating experience for all that has gone before.

This sequence, then, presents a balance between disciplinary (vertical) and interdisciplinary (horizontal) studies that will allow students the opportunity to engage in the creative and meaningful process of being enlightened citizens. However, this will happen only if we can go beyond the 1916 NEA commission's recommendations which still dominate the social studies sequence in the United States.

A Look to the Future

Certain dominant trends have implications for social studies programs. Demographic data point to items such as an increase in the number of elderly citizens in the United States, an increase in the proportion of minority students in our schools, and employment and migration patterns reflecting changing economic conditions. The national debt, balance of international trade, unemployment, and growing military development and sales are also adding to citizens' "need to know." It is estimated that information is doubling every 24 months and the half-life of most technical undergraduate degrees is four years. Attempts to keep pace with societal changes often demand "researched" answers, and research, in turn, helps drive social change. Caught up in this whirlwind of change, the learner and teacher are forced to ask, "What knowledge is of most worth? Is learning how to learn most important? How can I become a better policymaker?"

Answers to these questions must be grounded in the notion that knowledge is created through discourse—connections between and among the student, the teacher, and information. This knowledge, however, is not value free. It is locked into the contextual limitations of the cultural setting, the bureaucratic structure of the school, the ideologies of the classroom actors, and the information in the text.

Textbooks, other data sources, and the larger community are the significant information sources from which social studies content can be drawn, but what criteria can be used to select the most useful content? The answer to this question is political—a decision based on the authority of individuals and groups steeped in tradition and the conventional wisdom of the profession. However, educators need to go beyond the conventional wisdom and address the abilities of seeing connections, using different logics, creating new knowledge, communicating with others, and making policy decisions. They need to apply those decisions to program development and improvement.

Before educators can ask students to become better policymakers, *they* have to make better curricular and instructional policy decisions themselves. If all educators take this process of curricular policy making seriously, then we will have a chance to develop social studies programs that are more comprehensive, current, and correct in developing good citizens. Attending to the above abilities can also give our programs the opportunity of being self-correcting relative to the rights, welfare, and obligations of each individual student. This decision-making process is also consistent with effective schools research.

A historical scenario reported by Daniel Boorstin (1983) offers an analogy to social studies educators. In the 15th century, Prince Henry, the navigator of Portugal, was intent on exploring the economic possibilities of the west coast of Africa. From 1424 to 1434, the Prince sent 15 expeditions to penetrate further down the coast, but everyone returned with the same report: Cape Bojador was as far as a ship could go. Cape Bojador is a slight bulge on the coast, hardly perceptible on modern maps. The water had some tricky currents and desert sands came down to the coast, giving an ominous appearance to sailors at a time when people still thought the earth was flat. When the 16th captain got near the Cape, he turned west out to sea and passed the Cape without incident. Boorstin comments that Bojador was only "a barrier in the mind."

We must identify the Bojadors in contemporary social studies education and, like the 16th captain, sail past them.

References

Banks, James. *Multiethnic Education: Practices and Promises*. Bloomington, Ind.: Phi Delta Kappa, 1977.

Bellah, Robert, et al. *Habits of the Heart*. New York: Harper & Row, 1986.

Bettelheim, Bruno. *The Uses of Enchantment*. New York: Alfred A. Knopf, 1977.

Boorstin, Daniel. *The Discoverers*. New York: Random House, 1983.

Boulding, Kenneth E. *The World as a Total System*. Beverly Hills: Sage Publications, Inc., 1985.

Boyer, Ernest. *High School*. New York: Harper & Row, 1983.

Boyer, Ernest, and A. Levine. *A Question of Common Learning*. Princeton, N.J.: Carnegie Foundation for the Advancement of Teaching, 1981.

Bragaw, Donald. "Excellence: A Professional Responsibility." *Social Education* 50, 3 (March 1986).

Bragaw, Donald, ed. "Scope and Sequence: Alternatives for Social Studies." *Social Education* 50, 7 (November/December 1986).

Burns, James MacGregor. *The Vineyard of Liberty*. New York: Alfred A. Knopf, 1982.

Butts, R.F., and L. Cremin. *History of Education in American Culture*. New York: Hold, 1954.

Cleveland, Harlan. *The Knowledge Executive*. New York: Harper and Row, 1985.

Denham, Carolyn, and Ann Lieberman, eds. *Time to Learn*. Washington, D.C.: U.S. Department of Education, The National Institute of Education, May 1980.

Dewey, John. *Democracy and Education*. New York: Macmillan, 1916.

Dewey, John. *The Public and Its Problems*. New York: Hold, 1927.

Edmonds, Ronald. "Programs of School Improvement: An Overview." *Educational Leadership* (December 1982): 4.

Engle, Shirley. "Decision Making: The Heart of Social Studies Instruction." *Social Education* (November 1960).

Ferguson, Marilyn. *The Aquarian Conspiracy*. Los Angeles: J.R. Tarcher Co., 1976.

A Framework for Teaching the Basic Concepts. New York: Joint Council on Economic Education, 1985.

Giroux, Henry G. "Public Philosophy and the Crisis in Education." *Harvard Educational Review* 54 (1984).

Goodlad, John. *A Place Called School*. New York: MacGraw-Hill, 1984.

Hunt, M.P., and L.E. Metcalf. *Teaching High School Social Studies*. 2d ed. New York: Harper and Row, 1968.

Marshall, Thurgood. Speech, reported, *New York Times*, June 1987.

Matthews, David. "Civic Intelligence." *Social Education* 49, 8 (November/December 1985).

Naisbitt, John. *Megatrends*. New York: Warner, 1982.

Newman, F.M., and D. Oliver. *Clarifying Public Controversy*. Boston: Little, Brown and Company, 1970.

Newman, F., et al. *Education for Citizen Action: Challenge for Secondary Education*. Berkeley, Ca.: McCutchan, 1975.

Raskin, M.G., and Herbert J. Bernstein. *New Ways of Knowing: The Sciences, Society, and Reconstructive Knowledge*. Totowa, N.J.: Rowman and Littlefield, 1987.

"The U.S. Prepares for Its Future." Report of the Task Force for Global Education in the U.S., 1987.

Wronski, Stanley P., and Donald H. Bragaw, eds. *Social Studies and Social Sciences: A Fifty Year Perspective*. Washington, D.C.: National Council for the Social Studies, 1986.

3. Content and Process in the English Curriculum

Charles Suhor

EVERY FEW YEARS, ENGLISH SPECIALISTS ASK THEMSELVES "What is English?" The question is not frivolous, but a sign of continuing self-criticism and an acknowledgment of change. Questions of identity are common in all school subjects, from physical education to ecology (or is it from "movement science" to "environmental studies"?). In discussions of English, there is a great temptation to bypass questions of content and talk only about teaching methods or learning processes. I will begin and end this chapter with a discussion of connections between content and process, but the main focus will be on the "English" in "English instruction."

English as Content (Knowing) and as Process (Doing)

Advocates of process-based instruction might argue that the question "What is the content of English?" is loaded to begin with, and perhaps unanswerable as stated. They hold that English is not a content subject but a process subject. English is not primarily something students learn about, but something they do. The old model of English as a tripod—with mutually supporting and converging "legs" consisting of literature, composition, and grammar (Figure 3.1)—fails to make this process-content distinction.[1]

Literature and grammar are substantive content areas—relatively definable bodies of scholarly knowledge—but composition is predominantly a

An earlier version of this chapter was prepared with funding from the Office of Educational Research and Improvement, U. S. Office of Education, under contract no. 85-0008. Points of view do not necessarily represent those of the Office of Educational Research and Improvement.

[1]Charles Suhor, "The Curriculum Edifice: A Metaphor for Language Arts Instruction." *Elementary English* 48, 9 (December 1971): 915-921. All graphics in this chapter are intended as visual representations for purposes of discussion and analysis, not as models in the sense of depictions or cause-effect chains.

Figure 3.1. A Model of English as a Tripod

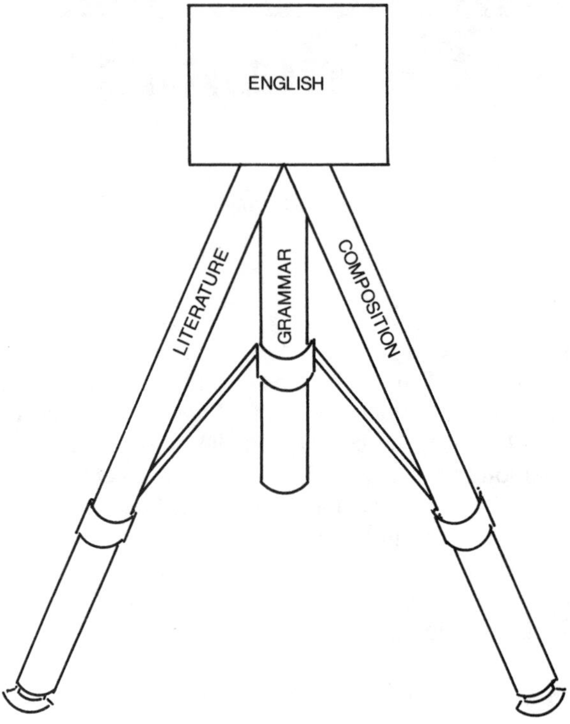

process. So the truer theoretical representation would be a "bipod" of two substantive legs with a composition component somehow nailed on (Figure 3.2).

Of course, that is a pretty shaky visual model. In fact, English curriculums that treat composition as an adjunct to the content areas of grammar and literature are not very serviceable. Overwhelmingly, research indicates that teaching grammar as a body of knowledge does not improve the writing performance of elementary and high school students. In 1969, John Mellon and Steve Sherwin did independent, intensive reviews of 20th century research on the teaching of grammar in relation to composition. Neither could find evidence that knowledge of grammar aids students' writing. George Hillocks' 1986 meta-analysis came to the same conclusion. Hillocks noted that grammar instruction might even be harmful.[2]

[2]George Hillocks, *Research on Written Composition* (Urbana, Ill.: ERIC Clearinghouse on Reading and Communication Skills and the National Conference on

Figure 3.2. Truer Model of English as a Bipod

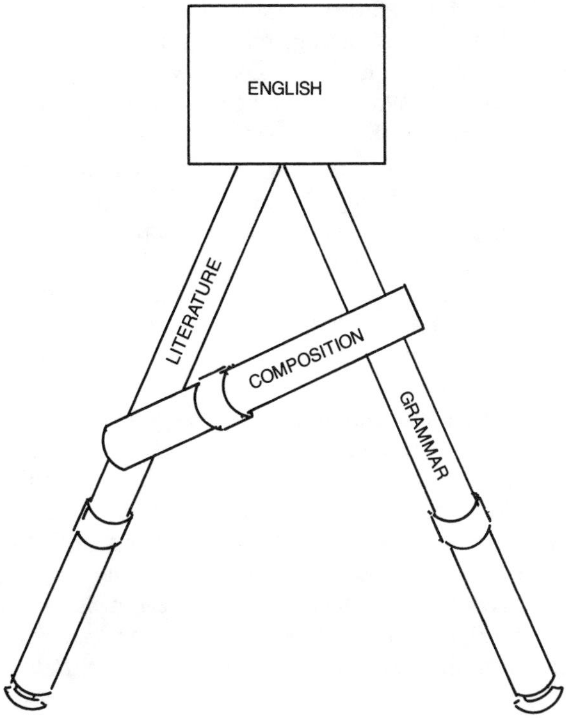

It does not help to substitute "language" for "grammar" on the tripod. The result then is that literature is the central content area, with language as part process (e.g., oral communication) and part content (e.g., grammar, history of language). Composition (again, a subset of language-as-process) must then be tagged on somehow.

Odd as such an approach sounds, literature-centered English programs are often imbalanced precisely in the direction of heavy analysis of literary structure, with speaking and writing focused almost wholly on *vicarious* experiences. The *personal* experiences of the students, and the potential of language for helping them organize and understand those experiences, are neglected. Arid formalism dominates. Concerns such as audience and an

---

Research in English, 1986); John Mellon, *Transformational Sentence-Combining*, Research Report No. 10 (Urbana, Ill.: National Council of Teachers of English, 1969); Stephen Sherwin, *Four Problems in Teaching English: A Critique of Research* (New York: International Textbook Co., 1969).

authentic expression in the student's own voice are downplayed.[3] The visual analog for such a program, terrible to contemplate, might be a literature "unipod," with splinters to represent the particular skills and information needed for improving oral and written language.

A view of English that favors process instruction is the idea of the four language arts—listening, speaking, reading, and writing. But this processed-based conception, in itself, provides few clues to content. What are the students listening to? What should they be speaking and writing about? And what in the world are they reading?

It is tempting to waffle on these questions by emphasizing process and saying that the content of English need not be specified as long as the processes are being nurtured—all the more tempting because our understanding of processes has become much more sophisticated in recent years. Instruction in writing processes has received greatest attention, moving from basic theory and research[4] to instructional models[5] to the educational marketplace, where even grammar-based texts often make bogus claims about teaching the writing processes.

However, process instruction in English and language arts ranges far more broadly than the teaching of writing. Its scholarly roots are in philosophy, cognitive psychology, psycholinguistics, and sociolinguistics.[6] An important instructional thrust is in reading and literature, areas in which schema theory and reader response theory have redefined the reader-text relationship. The reading process is seen not as a mere grasping of information and ideas contained in the text. Rather, reading is a meaning-making process in which the background knowledge and personal experience of the reader interact with the text. The content of *The Scarlet Letter*, then, is not

---

[3]Arthur Applebee, *Writing in the Secondary School*, Research Report no. 21, (Urbana, Ill.: National Council of Teachers of English, 1981; James Britton et al., *The Development of Writing Abilities (London: Macmillan Education, 1975);* Ken Macrorie, *Telling Writing*, 4th ed. (Upper Montclair, N.J.: Boynton/Cook, 1985).

[4]See, for example, Linda Flower and J.R. Hayes, "The Dynamics of Composing: Making Plans and Juggling Constraints" in Lee Gregg and Erwin Steinberg (eds.), *Cognitive Processes in Writing* (Hillsdale, N.J.: Erlbaum, 1980); Janet Emig, *The Composing Processes of 12th Graders*, Research Report No. 13 (Urbana, Ill.: National Council of Teachers of English, 1971).

[5]See, for example, Jackie Proett and Kent Gill, *The Writer in Action: A Handbook for Teachers* (Urbana, Ill.: National Council of Teachers of English, 1986); Charles Suhor, "Thinking Visually about Writing: Three Models for Teaching Composition, K-12" in C. Thaiss and C. Suhor (eds.), *Speaking and Writing, K-12: Classroom Strategies and the New Research* (Urbana, Ill.: National Council of Teachers of English, 1984).

[6]See Umberto Eco, *The Role of the Reader* (Bloomington, Ind.: Indiana University Press, 1979); Ulric Neisser, *Cognition and Reality* (San Francisco: W.H. Freeman, 1976); Frank Smith, *Psycholinguistics and Reading* (New York: Holt, Rinehart & Winston, 1973); M.A.K. Halliday, *Language as Social Semiotic* (Baltimore: University Park Press, 1978).

solely contained within the book's covers. In a real sense the content is created in the act and the process of reading.[7]

The process of oral communication, sometimes called oral discourse or dialoguing,[8] is perhaps even more complex and multidimensional. Everyday oral communication involves subtleties of body language, vocal inflections, variant subcultural vocabulary, syntax, usage, and a host of pragmatic elements like turn-taking and other tacit rules of conversation.[9] Small wonder that fascination with the complexities of processes in oral and written communication has drawn attention away from the question of what is being communicated.

But the question of content—of that-which-is-to-be-processed—persists, and traditionalists do not find the question hard to answer. There is an acknowledged core of great literature, they say, from works for children to adult classics. There are universal themes and fundamental issues and values that can be identified as central to the human condition.

Fancher, for example, holds that "every important literary work addresses important questions and makes claims about them. These claims are the source of much of the best knowledge that humanity possesses. Most often, 'classic' works are classics because of the depth and penetration of the visions of reality that they contain" (p. 55).[10] Such matters are certainly worthy subjects for listening, speaking, reading, and writing. We need only look to the best in our cultural heritage and then find appropriate places for this content in the English curriculum, K-12. Advocates of a classical curriculum believe that every normal child can succeed in a rigorous, more or less standardized curriculum if English teachers are knowledgeable in their disciplines and sufficiently willing to engage students in intellectual discourse.

Of course, there is more complexity in both the process and the traditional views of curriculum than I can describe here. Since my own approach to delineating content will be quite different, I recommend that readers interested in classical curriculums see works by Fancher, Adler, and

[7]Louise Rosenblatt, *The Reader, the Text, the Poem: The Transactional Theory of the Literary Work* (Carbondale, Ill.: Southern Illinois University Press, 1978); Wolfgang Iser, *The Act of Reading* (Baltimore: Johns Hopkins University Press, 1978).

[8]Robert Marzano et al., *Dimensions of Thinking* (Alexandria, Va.: Association for Supervision and Curriculum Development, 1988).

[9]Peter Farb, *Word Play* (New York: William Morrow, 1975); Walt Wolfram and Donna Christian, *Dialogue on Dialects* (Washington, D.C.: Center for Applied Linguistics, 1979); H.P. Grice, "Principles of Cooperation in Conversation," unpublished lecture notes, second lecture in *Logic and Conversation*, William James Lectures at Harvard University, 1967; Harvey Sacks et al., "A Simplest Systematics of the Organization of Turn-Taking for Conversation," *Language* 50, 4 (1974): 697-735.

[10]Robert Fancher, "English Teaching and Humane Culture" in Chester Finn et al. (eds.), *Against Mediocrity* (New York: Holmes and Meier, 1984).

Hirsch.[11] For an essentially process-based English and language arts program fleshed out in terms of sample content and appropriate methodology, see Moffett and Wagner.[12] A useful text by Mandel presents three curriculum models in English—heritage (traditional), process, and competency models, with variations thereon.[13]

Content of the Literature Program

Let me restate clearly the idea of content explored in the rest of this chapter, since my focus is probably less expansive than that of other chapters in this book. I will not discuss "content" in the broadest sense of "that which is taught in English" or "what we should teach at each grade level." As noted above, the debate over content instruction in English has been shaped by the emphasis on English as process, to the considerable neglect of the kinds of knowledge that are appropriate in the English curriculum. Admittedly, language processes and skills can be viewed as curriculum content in the broad sense; but these matters have been widely treated in the professional literature in the past decade.[14] This discussion will deal mainly with the "stuff" that is taught rather than the communication processes developed through English instruction.

Literature is a reasonable starting point for any discussion of content of the English curriculum, because it is the one area in which there is almost unanimous agreement on two points: it is a body of knowledge (a content area) and literature *as content* has a place in the English curriculum. Figure 3 represents all literature that I believe should be eligible for inclusion in the English language arts curriculum.

"Literature" is defined broadly here to include magazines as well as books, expository writings (e.g., formal essays, newspaper articles, certain technical documents) as well as poetry, the novel, drama, and the other genres usually called "creative." Some commonsense exclusions from the literature eligible for school programs are in order: expository writings such as corporation reports to stockholders (and most other technical documents written for adult specialists); pornography outright, in whatever literary medium. There is not sufficient space here to explore interesting questions such as the nature of literary genres or the boundaries of pornography.

[11]Robert Fancher, ibid.; Mortimer Adler, *The Paideia Proposal: An Educational Manifesto* (New York: Macmillan, 1982); E.D. Hirsch, Jr., "'Cultural Literacy' Doesn't Mean 'Core Curriculum'," *English Journal* 74, 6 (October 1985): 47-49.

[12]James Moffett and Betty Jane Wagner, *Student-Centered Language Arts and Reading, K-13* (Boston: Houghton Mifflin, 1983).

[13]Barrett Mandel, *Three Language-Arts Curriculum Models: Pre Kindergarten through College* (Urbana, Ill.: National Council of Teachers of English, 1980).

[14]The 1986-1987 NCTE *Catalog*, for example, contains 14 pages of books on composition, 5 pages on literature, and 3 on curriculum. While the profession has welcomed the coming of age of process instruction, an imbalance clearly exists, to the neglect of content.

Figure 3.3. The Range of Literature Eligible for Inclusion in the Curriculum

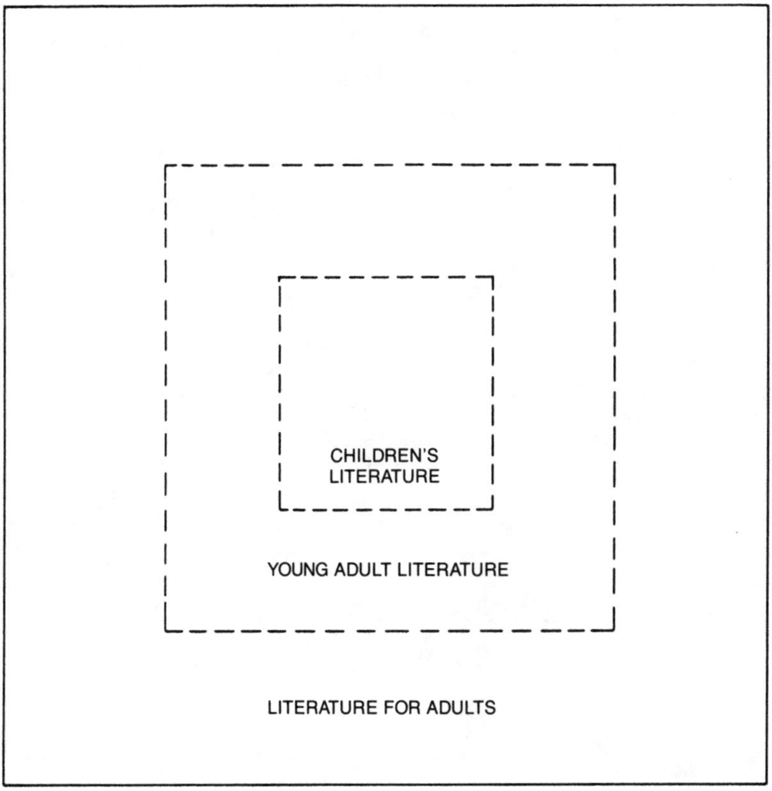

Suffice it to say that in outline, the universe of school literature should include a wide range of literature for children, young adults, and adults in a variety of print formats.

As the dotted lines in Figure 3.3 suggest, distinctions between the literatures are by no means absolute. For example, Robert Cormier's excellent story, "Guess What? I Almost Kissed My Father Last Night," can be read with interest by adults and teenagers alike. St.-Exupery's *The Little Prince* and Shel Silverstein's poetry cut across all age levels.

Few would quarrel with such an analysis. Questions of the *quality* of works eligible for inclusion in English curriculums are more difficult, however. Figure 3.4 deals with qualitative questions through an overlay that

Figure 3.4. The Range of Quality of Literature Eligible for Inclusion in the Curriculum

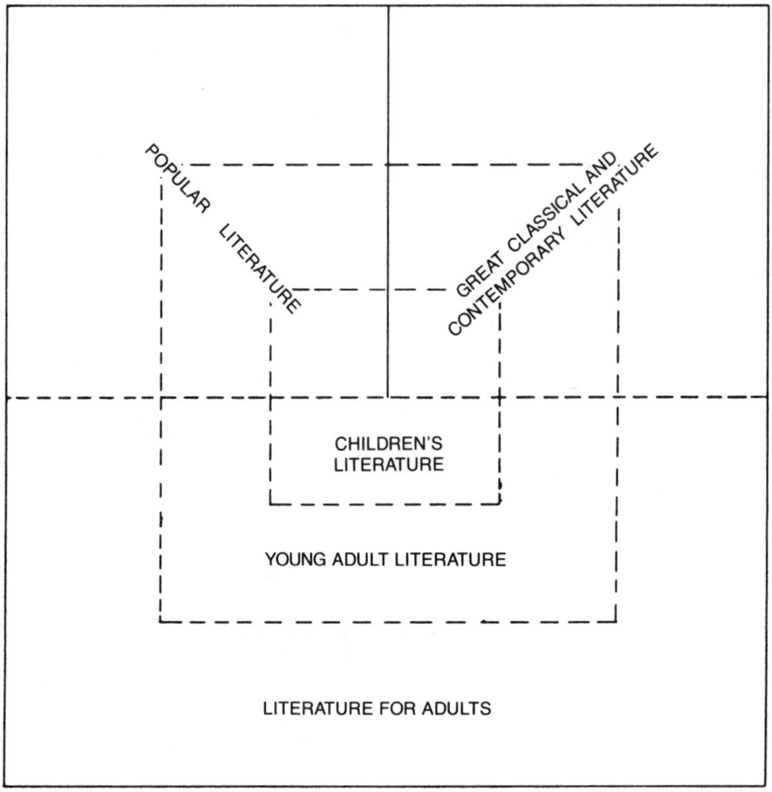

plicitly places popular literature (upper left quadrant) and great classical and contemporary literature (upper right quadrant) in the program. Good-quality literature, which comprises most of the works from which teachers and textbook writers might normally select materials for study, is represented in the remaining (bottom) half.

The division into segments in Figure 3.4 is *not* intended to represent recommended *proportions* of popular, average, and great literature in the English curriculum. The essential point is that materials representing a wide range of quality should be eligible for inclusion in literature programs and available to English teachers.

Neither specialists nor laypersons have trouble distinguishing between materials in the upper quadrants of the model, between the worst and the best. We instantly recognize differences between a pulp magazine love story and *Wuthering Heights*; hence, the solid line between popular literature and great classical and contemporary literature. Things are less clear, though, at the other borderlines of quality. Most Gothic romance series and popular astrology books are surely in the popular category, but a novelist like Irving Wallace or a playwright like Neil Simon will straddle the line between fluff and good literature. Similarly, the line between good and great literature is highly debatable. In my estimation, Hemingway's *A Farewell to Arms* is a great novel, but *For Whom the Bell Tolls* is merely excellent. Other English teachers would argue about all of these borderline categorizations, but that is the point. The lines of demarcation will be fuzzy in many judgments about quality.

Even after acknowledging such ambiguities, though, most teachers I have met agree that *some* great works drawn from children's, young adult, and adult literature should be part of every K-12 English curriculum. Most would also acknowledge the necessity of drawing from a wide pool of average-to-good literature. The real controversies are centered on two ideas: the belief that popular literature—from pop/rock lyrics to flimsy adolescent novels to gimmicky choose-your-own-plot adventure books—can play a useful role in school programs; and the notion that literature study should essentially be the study of great works. I will deal with these questions as problems of *cultivation* and *carryover*, and will suggest that a solution lies in connecting the world of the student with the world of ideas.

Popular literature was in greatest vogue in our schools during the neo-progressive movement of the late 1960s and early 1970s. The buzzword "relevancy" was often invoked uncritically to sweep vast amounts of bad popular literature into English classes. Critics of the movement complained, with some justification, that the reading of trivial materials was too common and that many English programs were catering to the undeveloped tastes of students.[15] The goal of cultivating students' responses to literature was frequently ignored.

At the other end of the scale, literature programs that draw predominantly on classics and other excellent works assure that students will have a certain amount of exposure to important works. But there is no evidence that classics programs succeed in making very many students into lifelong readers of fine literature. In fact, classics dominated the English curriculum for generations before the "relevancy" craze of the 1960s. Yet in the "good old days," Americans did not typically become avid adult readers of the classics or of anything else.[16] Most teachers will acknowledge that even when standard works like *Silas Marner*, *Julius Caesar*, and *David Copperfield* are

[15]For example, see Paul Copperman, *The Literacy Hoax* (New York: William Morrow, 1978); B. Crandall, "Decline in Reading of the Classics in Public School Causes Concern," *New York Times* (May 29, 1977): 1, 36.

[16]Although surveys of reading habits can be interpreted in a variety of ways, it is clear that we have become, overwhelmingly, a more literate society over the last

brilliantly taught, it is rare for high school students to go out and read, on their own, *The Mill on the Floss*, *King Lear*, and *Bleak House*. The essential element of *carryover* into personal reading simply has not been effected in the classics-based program.

What kind of literature program reckons with the need for cultivation and carryover? The term "cultivation" is relative, implying a nurturing process in which students' intellectual and emotional responses are advanced methodically, in accordance with their present state of growth. If cultivation is to go beyond mere exposure to culture, the teacher must find vital points of *connection* between the personal world of the student and the larger world of vicarious experience. For tens of thousands of reluctant readers, teen romances or adventure paperbacks are potentially the first point of personal engagement with printed-word narratives. Happily, many other students will enter the world of ideas through more richly organized works such as the poetry of Eve Merriam or the novels of Paul Zindel. A few come to school with the readiness to devour the great works that we wish everyone could read with relish. The literature program suggested in Figure 4 permits teachers to seek out, for each student, a door into the world of ideas that the student will willingly enter. It includes exposure to some great works—presumably, those most accessible to contemporary students—but provides a usable framework for connections and carryover.

Cultivation must be consciously pursued if the teacher is to avoid simply running in place with students' present reading habits. To carry the list of C's one step further, a "cut- above" strategy is necessary. That is, students who follow sports in newspapers and magazines can be led to read simple short stories and poems about athletes—materials that are a cut above their present tastes. From there, the connection can be made to biographies like Eleanor Gehrig's *My Luke and I* or autobiographies like those of Wilma Rudolph or Joe Garagiola. A knowledgeable teacher can then engineer the move to excellent works like Shaw's "The Eighty-Yard Run" or Malamud's *The Natural*. When the level of engagement is high, the chances of carryover into lifelong reading are much greater. Moreover, the teacher need not

two generations. See, for example (a) Book Industry Study Group, *The 1983 Consumer Research Study on Reading and Book Publishing*, prepared by Market Facts, Inc. (New York: Book Industry Study Group, 1983); (b) Gallup Organization, *Book Reading and Library Usage: A Study of Habits and Perceptions*, report of a survey for the American Library Association (Princeton, N.J.: Gallup Organization, 1978); (c) Thomas M. Sawyer, "Why Speech Will Not Totally Replace Writing," *College Composition and Communication* 28, 1 (February 1987): 43-48. Of course, calls for higher levels of literacy are clearly justified on two important bases: the remaining group of hard-core illiterates and the need for ever-higher literacy skills in contemporary society. See Irwin Kirsch and Ann Jungblut, *Literacy: Profiles of America's Young Adults* (Princeton, N.J.: National Association of Educational Progress, 1986); Sylvia Read Taber, "Current Definitions of Literacy," *Journal of Reading* 30, 5 (February 1987): 458-461; Richard Venezky et al., *The Subtle Danger: Reflections on the Literacy Abilities of Young Adults* (Princeton, N.J.: Educational Testing Service, 1987).

neglect the traditions of literary study during the nurturing process. Concepts such as setting, characterization, and plot development can be learned through the study of young adult literature as well as through classic works.[17]

Obviously, a developmental K-12 literature program based on the three C's will not include a forced march through a set canon of works which every student must read at any given grade level. The teacher must in fact be familiar with a wide range of literature, from classics to currently popular materials. Equally important, the teacher must have the freedom and the insight to apply that knowledge in connecting the student with appropriate works, in further cultivating the student's responses, and in encouraging carryover into lifelong reading habits by suggesting materials for leisure reading.[18]

I have already referred to literature as "vicarious experience"—that is, experience acquired not by direct interaction with the world but by imaginative entry into worlds created by others. Unfortunately, students today have their most frequent vicarious experiences through nonprint media—especially television, film, and popular song lyrics.

There is nothing inherently shabby in nonprint vicarious experiences. Some of the greatest expressions of the human spirit, from ancient times to the present, have been achieved through the nonprint medium of drama—and of course, drama is a long-established part of the English curriculum. Moreover, television sitcoms and feature films have some structural qualities that are found in drama, short stories, and novels. Popular songs have elements in common with folk ballads and lyric poetry. To some extent, there is overlap in the tools of analysis that can be applied to TV dramas, films, and narratives in print. But in America we are besieged and benumbed by television, and vicarious experiences of low quality are transmitted into our homes daily.

Nevertheless, I include both print and nonprint vicarious experiences in the content of the English curriculum (Figure 3.5). This is not to say that everything on television or every film is or should be an object of study. Again, the question is what should be *eligible* for inclusion. Nonprint media are included because the English teacher has an important stake in guiding students' understanding of the imaginative worlds presented in nonprint media.

---

[17]William Evans, "A Comparison of the Effects of a Superior Junior Novel and *Silas Marner* on the Ability of 10th Grade Students to Read the Novel," doctoral dissertation, Florida State University, 1961; Nathan Blount, "The Effect of Selected Junior Novels and Selected Adult Novels on Student Attitudes toward the 'Ideal' Novel," *Journal of Educational Research* 59 (December 1965): 179-182; Michael Angelotti, "A Comparison of Elements in the Written Free Responses of Eighth Graders to a Junior Novel and an Adult Novel," doctoral dissertation, Florida State University, 1972.

[18]Denny Wolfe and the NCTE Standing Committee on Teacher Preparation and Certification, *Guidelines for Preparation of Teachers of English and Language Arts* (Urbana, Ill.: National Council of Teachers of English, 1986).

Figure 3.5. The Range of Vicarious Experiences Eligible for Inclusion in the Curriculum

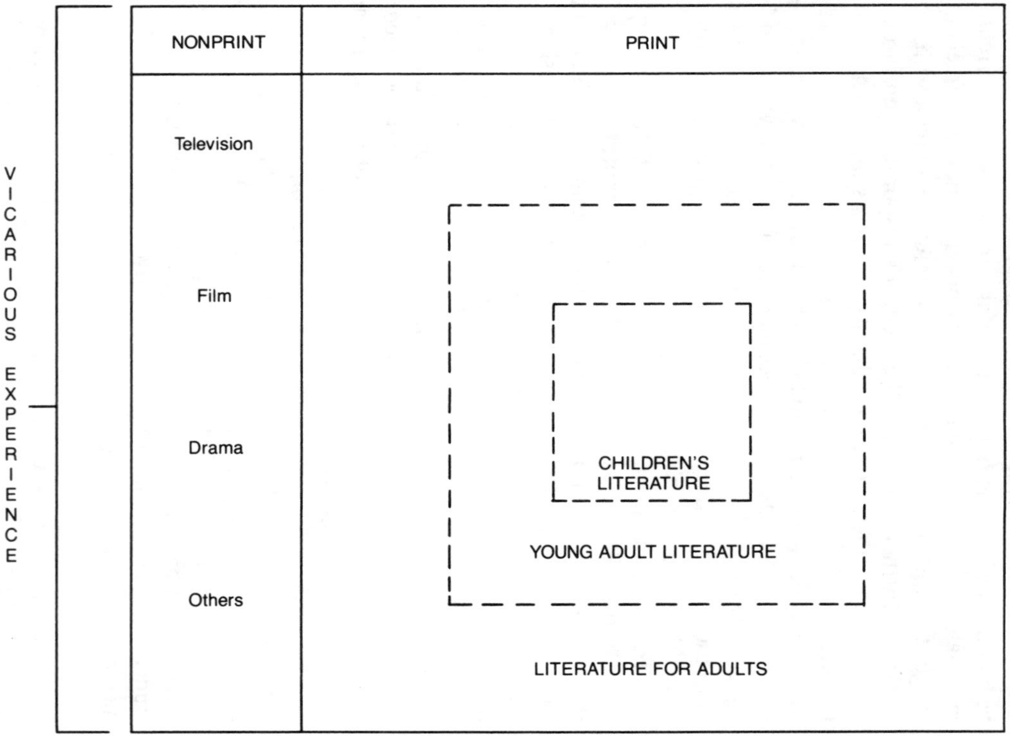

In complaining about the ill effects of TV on children, educators have largely ignored the potential for making positive use of its many flaws and few virtues. To begin with, reluctant readers are seldom reluctant viewers. A common experience exists for cultivation of taste through critical discussion and analysis of TV. Fran Lehr has summarized some of the complexities not usually recognized in discussions of the effects of television, noting that numerous possibilities for creative critiques of television have been insufficiently explored.[19] Teachers might conduct in-class critical comparisons and analyses of popular shows; provide advance preparation for high-quality TV dramas; link popular television shows with popular literature that is a cut above the TV experience; apply appropriate terms from literary analysis in discussing television; and teach about stereotypes, slanted observation and reporting, sound inference, and logical argumentation. The student who comes to realize that characterization and exploration of issues in *Cagney and Lacey* are often more subtle than those elements in stock TV detective shows is better prepared to discuss character and theme in short stories by Hemingway and O. Henry.[20] Facile discussions about the narcotic effects of television overlook the possibilities for development of a productive discussion of television within the English curriculum.

Personal Experience as Content

The *content* of the English curriculum was earlier described as *that which is to be processed*. Such a view of literary content differs from many traditional views in that it acknowledges a wide range of literary quality and includes nonprint media as part of the student's vicarious experiences. A point was also made about connecting literature with the student's personal experiences: if class discussion and writing focus wholly on vicarious experiences derived from literature, the links between literature and the student's life experiences are neglected. Equally important is the fact that the student's personal experiences can take on meaning through oral and written language in the classroom, even when those experiences are not linked with literature. It follows that much of the student's store of personal experience is part of "that which is to be processed"—part of the content of the English program.

To some extent, Figure 3.6 depicts processes as well as content. The dotted lines between personal and vicarious experiences suggest a constant interaction between reader and text, as noted in the earlier discussion of schema and reader response theory. "Identification" and "fantasy" are included because they are mental activities vitally linked with vicarious ex-

[19] Fran Lehr, "Television Viewing and Reading," ERIC/RCS Digest (Urbana, Ill.: ERIC Clearinghouse on Reading and Communication Skills, 1986).

[20] Howard Rosenberg, "A Rip-Roaring 'Cagney-Lacey'," *Los Angeles Times* (May 4, 1987), Sec. 4, pp. 1, 9.

Figure 3.6. The Interaction of Students' Personal and Vicarious Experiences

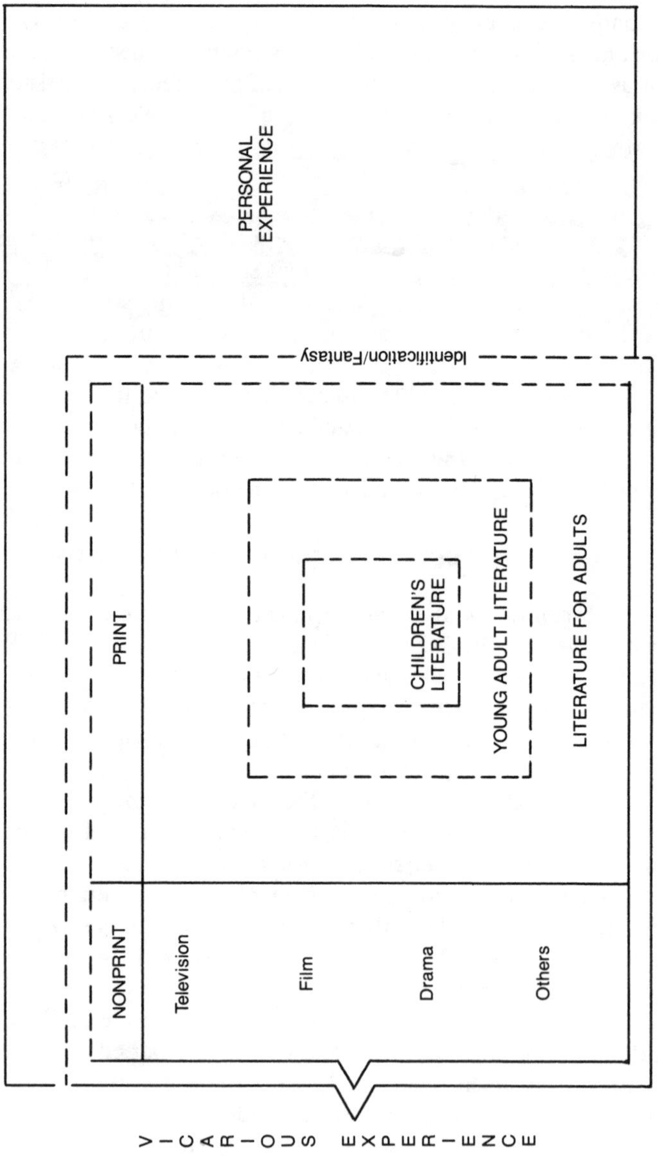

perience.[21] Through identification, we enter into print and nonprint vicarious experiences, connecting ourselves with the imagined people and events and with the ideas and feelings presented in stories, poems, films, and the like. Fantasy is a kind of internal vicarious event through which we imagine ourselves doing things we have not yet done, might do, or cannot do.

Figure 3.6 indicates, then, that vicarious experiences can be processed *not only as objects of formal study but also in relation to students' personal experiences*. Students enter imaginatively into the authors' worlds for purposes ranging from literary analysis to sheer entertainment to testing their own views of reality.

But Figure 3.6 advances a much broader point: students' personal experiences are themselves an important part of the content of English. Through the processes of speaking and writing in the classroom, students give clearer shape to the unexamined experiences in their own lives, and they assign significance to those experiences in the very act of processing them. The idea of "connecting" comes into play in a new sense here. Not only are students linked with the minds and emotions of authors, they are also put in touch with their own ideas and feelings, because the processing of personal experiences through language gives clearer form to their impressions of the world.

This is not to say that every cranny of the student's life and personal values should be drawn out in the classroom and made explicit through discussion and writing. Selectivity is obviously required, based on respect for the student's privacy and on pedagogical and practical considerations. Regarding the latter, all content areas correctly taught will call for verbalization of some aspects of the student's experience, because oral and written discourse are central processes that range across the curriculum.[22]

But English is clearly the subject area in which major responsibility is assigned for helping students to be effective users of language. In the English classroom, the student's exploration of thoughts and feelings through language is an end in itself. It must be practiced and modeled in large and small groups so students can become articulate in interpreting vicarious experience and in expressing their own experiences and inner states.

---

[21]For example, see S.I. Hayakawa, *Language in Thought and Action*, 2nd edition (New York: Harcourt Brace & World, 1964), 132-135, on identification in vicarious experiences. For a discussion of fantasy, see William Stockard and Frankie Eccles, "Unicorns and Dragons: Using Guided Imagery in the Classroom," paper presented at 14th Annual Meeting, California Reading Association, Nov. 6-8, 1980. ERIC Document 198 489.

[22]Christopher Thaiss, *Language Across the Curriculum in the Elementary Grades* (Urbana, Ill.: ERIC Clearinghouse on Reading and Communication Skills and the National Council of Teachers of English, 1986); "Composing" and "Oral Discourse," chapters in Robert Marzano et al., *Dimensions of Thinking*, op. cit.

Information as Content

English programs have greatly overemphasized information. School versions of organized bodies of knowledge—miniaturizations of grammatical systems or the history of literature—are built into innumerable textbooks and curriculum guides. The weight of tradition, not an attempt to match content with learners or to apply research knowledge, is the rationale for such programs. (Hawthorne once said, "The past lies on us like the body of a dead giant.")

The information presented is often fragmented and isolated from actual use. Definitions and terminologies—from diphthongs to absolute phrases to nonrestrictive clauses—abound in school grammar programs. Language textbooks, far from encouraging students to use language, are dominated by abstract definitions and follow-up drills that require identification of sentence parts or filling in blanks. In the literature program, students are expected to know (memorize) isolated information about authors' lives, particular works, literary movements, figures of speech, metric patterns, and the like. The textbook questions placed after literary selections rarely stress higher-order thinking skills or deal with students' responses to characters and plot.

Reactions against such programs have correctly resulted in recommendations for engaging students in the actual process of language-making. Yet it is clear that *some* information is essential, both in the study of literature as content and in the effective implementation of process-based instruction. Figure 3.7 suggests the place of information in English curriculums.

This final model suggests that students need information in order to discuss, and to gain deeper understanding of, their personal and vicarious experiences. I hasten to add that information can often be taught through inquiry methods rather than through assignment for memorization. Many literary concepts—narrative/lyric poetry, interior monologue, and point of view—are especially teachable through teacher-led inductive and deductive discussion. Certain concepts related to process instruction in oral and written language can be taught Socratically—transitional phrases, use of active/passive verbs, and methods for developing a point of argument. (Of course some information is taught most economically through direct methods. For example, the inductive teaching of metric patterns in poetry or a Socratic approach to studying the rules for quotation marks might be needlessly labored, and ultimately unrewarding for both teacher and student.)

In this model, information is primarily a tool rather than an end in itself. As an aspect of content, information is important insofar as it either helps teachers and students talk more readily about other aspects of content or makes discussion and implementation of processes easier and more fluid. In Figure 3.7, information "underlies" the English program and is not at the center of it. It is a relatively small yet essential support system for the exploration of personal and vicarious experiences through language.

Figure 3.7. The Place of Information in English Curriculums

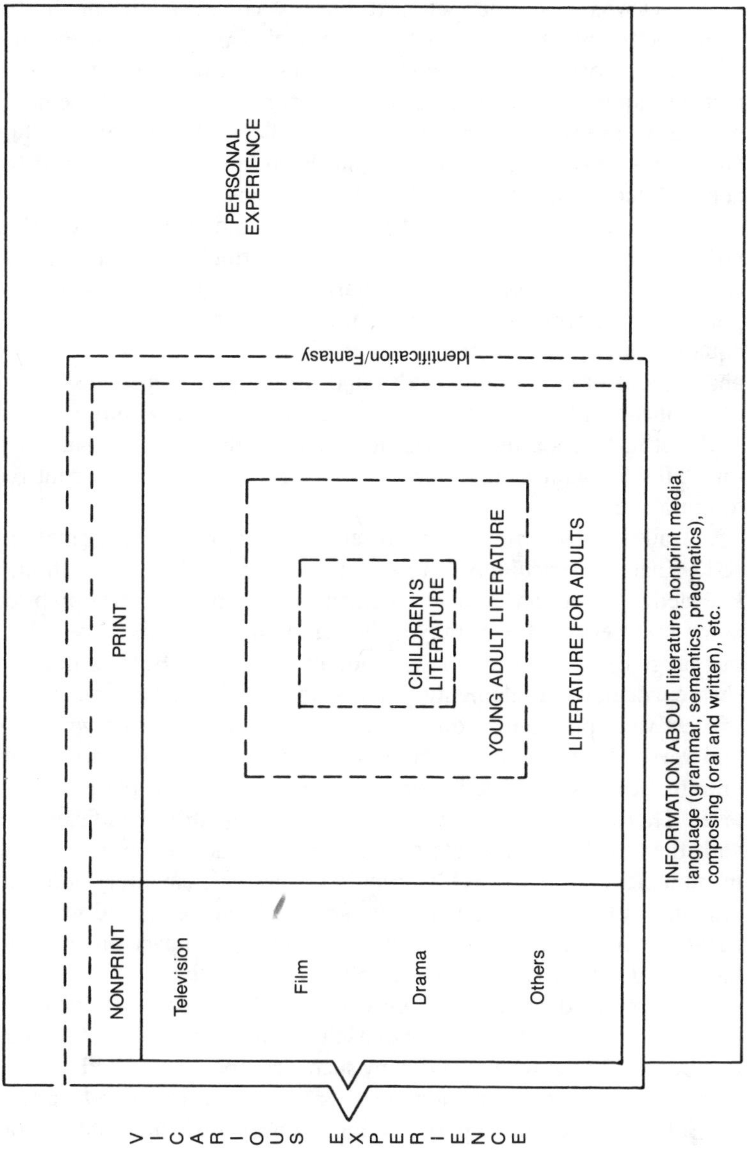

By "relatively small" I do not mean minuscule. The area of literature alone includes a substantial body of concepts that students must know in order to respond richly to their readings. In broad strokes, the process might look like this. In primary grades, students reading a short story are asked to predict what might happen next, guess what a character might do, speculate about why characters acted as they did, and draw conclusions about the most important ideas in a story. From such discussions, the concepts of plot development, character development, motivation, and theme are formalized in the upper elementary and middle grades. By grade 10 or 11, a large array of short story concepts has been introduced and used comfortably in Socratic and response-based discussions.

To be sure, it is important for teachers and curriculum developers to ponder appropriate points for formal and informal introduction of concepts of fiction such as plot, subplot, character, setting, theme, conflict, irony, point of view, symbol, allegory, genre, and myth, to name just a few. It is equally important to attend to the methods of instruction and to the form and content of curriculum guides and testing programs. Pressure for coverage of concepts can force dust-dry memorization of definitions and misuse of direct instruction techniques (for example, the Madeline Hunter model) that militate against higher-order thinking and authentic student response to literature.

Traditionalists frequently present the rationale for information-heavy K-12 English curriculums in terms of providing a liberal education, rich in knowledge that every educated person should possess. They point out that much knowledge—for example, the Latin and Germanic roots of much of our language—is worth knowing for its own sake. But, as noted earlier, such curriculums at elementary and secondary levels have been manifestly ineffective in producing adults who enjoy reading and who write with skill and verve. I believe survey courses in British literature and the study of grammatical systems and history of language have their place at the college level. There, larger numbers of students have matured sufficiently to deal with the sensibility of Keats or the intricate functions of absolute phrases in cumulative sentences. Our primary mission in elementary and secondary schools is to produce students who speak, listen, read, and write not only capably but with a joy that will have profound impact on their personal habits and will carry over to later phases of their lives.

The model of content in Figure 3.7, then, urges an essential information base that is culturally enriching in itself and utilitarian in relation to process instruction. Those who would deny such a component in the English curriculum take their positions ideologically; there is no research basis for doing so. But again, they are in part reacting against a sad history of factmongering in elementary and secondary English programs.

Teachers and curriculum developers should indeed guard against the persisting tendency to consider English as a conglomerate of facts about literature, grammar, and composition.

Further Implications for Practitioners

I have presented a view of the content of the English curriculum but must conclude with a reaffirmation of the process-content relationship. My view of content, especially the dimension of personal experience, does not make sense unless content is understood in relation to process. Again, the content of English represented in Figure 3.7 is "that which is to be processed."

English as a subject has identifiable content, but the goals of K-12 instruction require the *selection* of appropriate materials and the *processing* of those materials via oral and written language. Adapting the 1966 Dartmouth Conference idea, I see English as *the ordering of personal and vicarious experience through language.*[23] The central job of the English teacher is to elicit from students language that helps them to shape and give meaning to their individual experiences and the experiences of others—others whom they meet in the real world and in the imagined worlds of literature.

Information is an essential but limited aspect of the study of English. Within a far narrower range than was previously thought—a range that still lacks precise definition— there is a body of information that can illuminate the broader content of English and lubricate process instruction. By contrast, the range of usable content in the literature program is wider than was once specified, embracing study of some great works but emphasizing literary experiences that will engage students' interests, cultivate their responses, and promote lifelong habits of reading.

This view has many implications for curriculum developers, inservice leaders, and school principals. My inferences go beyond the models presented above, so I will combine candor with citations of references that support and amplify the six extrapolations that follow.

1. We should challenge the assumption that content need not be specified on one hand, and that complex processes cannot possibly be parceled out into charts, grade levels, and textbooks on the other. In the real world, scope and sequence charts, curriculum guides, and textbooks are part of the furniture of curriculum development and implementation. Granted, the best teachers can apply their knowledge of processes in the classroom without nudges and prescriptions from the district office or the adopted textbooks. But few teachers can work in this manner, and most benefit from good instructional materials and guidance from peers and other professionals in the district.[24]

2. Curriculum guides and scope and sequence charts can deal with English content and processes without overspecifying and oversimplifying,

[23]John Dixon, *Growth through English* (Reading, England: National Association for the Teaching of English, 1967).

[24]Joyce Bauchner et al., Models of Change, Vol. III, in D. Crandall (ed.), *People, Policies and Practices: Examining the Chain of School Improvement* (Andover, Mass.: The Network, 1982); M. Huberman and David Crandall, *Implications for Action,* Vol. IX, in D. Crandall (ed.), op. cit.

but few actually do so. In dealing with content, the simplistic tendency is to chop formal grammar concepts into segments and assign them to grade levels, and to list literary works by grade level and attach related concepts to those works. In dealing with processes, the tendency is to set grade level mastery standards for various oral and written forms. But mastery approaches, as Benjamin Bloom has noted, are inappropriate for teaching and learning complex processes like written and oral language. The erratic, developmental nature of such processes places them in a different category from declarative knowledge and skills that can be cultivated in a "building block" manner.[25]

A sound scope and sequence array for composition and oral language would take into account theoretical and research literature and practice on aspects of language such as students' sense of genre, awareness of audience, syntactic growth, dialects, communicative competence, spelling, and the like. Applying such knowledge, curriculum developers might appropriately set ballpark expectations that students will demonstrate growth in various aspects of oral and written language at various grade levels. But objectives such as mastery of the five-paragraph theme in grade 8 or elimination of dangling participles by grade 11 (besides being naive) breed a formalism that hinders genuine process instruction.

3. The content of K-12 English curriculums should not include extensive study of grammatical forms, traditional or otherwise. The study of grammar is at best a liberal arts pursuit, not unlike the study of musical forms. As such, it merits comparatively low priority in elementary and secondary programs. The main language goals of pre-college English are fundamentally the process goals of improving speaking, listening, reading, and writing.

Productive content instruction in grammar plugs into language process instruction. It is highly selective, focused on actual problems as revealed in students' speaking and writing, and it is frankly prescriptive in attacking and solving those problems. Moreover, the appropriate point for diagnosis of usage and mechanical problems in writing is at the late editing stage in the writing process.

Grammar instruction that bypasses the study of terminology in favor of sentence manipulation is also useful. A solid body of research has emerged dealing with sentence combining. Sentence manipulation materials, along with diagnosis and prescription, are among numerous accessible alternatives to an annual forced march through the parts of speech and other grammatical definitions and rules.[26]

---

[25]Benjamin Bloom, *Human Characteristics and School Learning* (New York: Teachers College Press, 1976), 51.

[26]William Strong, *Creative Approaches to Sentence Combining* (Urbana, Ill.: ERIC Clearinghouse on Reading and Communication Skills and the National Council of Teachers of English, 1986); Arthur Applebee et al., *Grammar, Punctuation, and Spelling*, Report No. 15-W-03 (Princeton, N.J.: Educational Testing Service, 1987).

4. Curriculums that define the content of literature in terms of lists of works to be studied by every student do not serve the goal of producing lifelong readers and learners. Lists can be helpful if presented as illustrations of types of materials usable with students at various levels. Such lists are particularly apt when teachers are charged with the responsibility to cultivate their students' intellectual growth and aesthetic standards as well as their pleasure in reading.

For example, a Brevard County, Florida, curriculum guide for American Literature presents "a sampler of ideas and activities," stressing "individual teacher freedom" and both process and content in the composition component of the program. A statewide California guide does not require particular works but provides criteria for evaluating instructional materials. The teacher is expected to build upon students' interests and strengths while developing their critical and analytical abilities.[27]

It follows that we should question curriculums that use terms like "rigor," "high standards," and "core curriculum" to mask lack of adequate attention to differences among students and the psychology of the learner. (The Paideia Proposal is one such program, I believe.) Worse, "cultural literacy" has emerged as a new wedge to assure that elementary and high school students are exposed to a list of surface meanings of elements in our cultural heritage, whether the students interiorize core values and understandings or not.[28]

5. To assure adequate process instruction in language, teachers at all levels should be encouraged, even mandated, to make extensive use of class discussion in large and small groups. This means that training in group techniques and in whole-class discussion beyond recitation and Socratic questioning will be needed by many teachers. Research has solidly demonstrated the value of classroom interaction of various kinds—inquiry teaching, scaffolding, reciprocal teaching, cooperative learning.[29] Yet many teachers are still uncomfortable in the role of discussion leader or orchestrator of classroom groups.

Whole-class discussion can be teacher-led but should not be formulaic or focused mainly on content. Routine "checking for comprehension," for example, generates an atmosphere of recitation rather than exchange of ideas. Students' understanding or misunderstanding of content in literature can be detected in responses to "thought questions" that encourage them

---

[27]Hope Ascher et al., *American Literature: Performance Objectives and Classroom Activities* (Cocoa, Fla.: Brevard County School Board, 1983); Theodore R. Smith (ed.), *Reading Framework for California Public Schools* (Sacramento, Calif.: California State Department of Education, 1980).

[28]E.D. Hirsch, Jr., "'Cultural Literacy' Doesn't Mean 'Core Curriculum'," *English Journal* 74, 6 (October 1985): 47-49; Stephen Tchudi, "Slogans Indeed: A Reply to Hirsch," *Educational Leadership* 45, 4 (December 1987): 72-74.

[29]Anne Di Pardo and Sarah W. Freedman, *Historical Overview: Groups in the Writing Classroom*, Technical Report No. 4, Center for the Study of Writing (Berkeley, Calif.: University of California, 1987); Marzano et al., op.cit.

to state ideas in their own language and to embed their knowledge of basic information in discussions of real issues.

The valuing of small-group discussion by curriculum leaders, school principals, and teachers implies that "noisy" classrooms must be perceived as a desirable outcome of English instruction and not as a sure indication of poor discipline. As a Virginia Department of Education guide for group learning notes, noise that reflects purposeful discussion of content is a sign of enthusiasm about the act of learning. More importantly, it is prima facie evidence of successful process instruction.[30]

6. Testing students' knowledge of content is important, but evaluation of student progress in English can never be reduced solely to content testing. Students "know" English when they "do" English well—stating significant ideas clearly in discussions, writing (and revising) with power and grace, reading with insight and enjoyment.

Regarding evaluation of language processes, external tests of writing that call for actual writing samples are useful in determining the abilities of groups of students; but an external test is never a legitimate measure of an individual student's language growth. Only teachers can truly monitor such growth as they provide multiple opportunities for speaking and writing and note each student's oral and written performance. Evaluation of language processes is partly impressionistic, partly quantifiable, and certainly based on patterns revealed through long-term observation rather than by a "final" examination, internal or external, of speaking and writing abilities.[31]

External testing programs that involve writing samples can spark composition instruction where it has been neglected. Testing tends to drive instruction, so tests of actual writing are clearly more beneficial than "language tests" in which students generate no language.[32] But many important aspects of language process instruction (e.g., students' discussion skills) beyond the capacity of external testing programs, so it is essential that administrators, supervisors, and inservice leaders support process instruction in other ways.

In the final analysis, students "do" English when they carry processes and content beyond the classroom and continue to grapple with more complex materials and ideas. The English curriculum is successful only when students read, speak, and write well in the worlds they inhabit after their K-12 educational experiences.

---

[30]Virginia Department of Education, *Helping Students Learn—Group Discussion. Concepts and Procedures* (Richmond, Va.: Virginia Department of Education, 1986).

[31]See, e.g., Brian Johnston, *Assessing English* (Sydney, Australia: St. Clair Press, 1983); Nancie Atwell, *In the Middle* (Upper Montclair, N.J.: Boynton/Cook, 1987).

[32]W. Doyle, "Academic Work," *Review of Educational Research* 53 (1983): 159-199; Charles Suhor, "Objective Tests and Writing Samples: How Do They Affect Instruction in Composition?" *Phi Delta Kappan* 66, 9 (May 1985): 635-639.

4. New Goals for School Mathematics

Patricia F. Campbell and James T. Fey

MATHEMATICS HAS A LONG AND IMPRESSIVE RECORD OF contributions to discovery and problem solving in science and technology, decision making in business and government, and creative expression in the arts. This record of achievement has earned mathematics a prominent place in school curriculums and in the spotlight of critical attention that is periodically focused on the schools.

Most recent analyses of school mathematics have concluded that students are not acquiring the skills and understandings they will need to participate effectively in the cultural, economic, political, and scientific environments of the future. Data from the National Assessment of Educational Progress (NAEP) and from college entrance testing programs reveal a discouraging pattern of mathematics achievement, particularly in important problem-solving and higher-order thinking skills. International studies show U.S. students lag far behind their counterparts in other highly developed countries—those countries we compete with in science, technology, and business (McKnight et al. 1987). We face this competition handicapped by a severe shortage of capable mathematics teachers and by curriculums that many experts judge to be in need of major reform.

There is no shortage of advice on new directions for the K-12 mathematics curriculum. The challenge of defining new curriculum priorities and new standards for teacher performance and student achievement has attracted attention from a broad range of groups interested in school mathematics. In 1980 the National Council of Teachers of Mathematics (NCTM) published *An Agenda for Action*, which included the following recommendations:

1. Problem solving must be the focus of school mathematics in the 1980s.

2. Basic skills in mathematics must be defined to encompass more than computational facility.

3. Mathematics programs must take full advantage of the power of calculators and computers at all grade levels.

4. The success of mathematics programs and student learning must be evaluated by a wider range of measures than conventional testing.

5. More mathematics study must be required for all students, and flexible curriculums with a greater range of options must be designed to accommodate the diverse needs of the student population.[1]

Challenges of Technology

Concerns about curriculums, teachers, and student achievement are familiar issues in educational policy debates. But the current situation includes new dimensions of challenge and opportunity. For over 20 years, prophets of the electronic age have argued that calculators and computers will dramatically alter the content and processes of mathematics education. Some have forecast the decline of traditional teaching modes and the emergence of computer-based tutorials. Others have predicted movement toward student-directed learning in which computer-based information resources and programming activities are used to develop broad conceptual understanding and high-level intellectual skills.

Calculators, computers, and videodisks do offer impressive opportunities to improve instruction, but technology will have an even more profound effect on the content and organization of the mathematics curriculum. As the report of a 1984 NCTM conference argued,

> The major influence of technology in mathematics education is its potential to shift the focus of instruction from an emphasis on manipulative skills to an emphasis on developing concepts, relationships, structures, and problem-solving skills (Corbitt 1985).

Technology will change *what* we teach as much as *how* we teach it.

Current elementary school mathematics programs emphasize paper-and-pencil procedures for operations with whole numbers, common fractions, and decimals. Since calculators are readily available to everyone who faces arithmetic problem-solving tasks, we can eliminate large portions of the curriculum now devoted to developing facility with the traditional algorithms. Because decimals, negative numbers, and scientific notation occur naturally in encounters with a calculator, we can and should alter the sequence and priorities of arithmetic topics in elementary curriculums to give these topics earlier and more prominent attention.

---

[1]These general principles were based on and have been elaborated by a variety of other reports from the NCTM Technology Advisory Committee (Corbitt 1985), the NCTM Committee to Implement the Agenda (NCTM 1985), NCTM yearbooks (Hansen 1984, Hirsch and Zweng 1985), the National Council of Supervisors of Mathematics (1978), the Conference Board of the Mathematical Sciences (1975, 1982, 1984), the Department of Education (NIE 1975, Romberg 1984), and the College Entrance Examination Board (1983).

Current secondary school curriculums emphasize paper-and-pencil procedures for manipulating symbolic expressions in algebra, trigonometry, and calculus. Since widely available scientific calculators and microcomputer software provide ready assistance with symbol manipulation and graphing tasks in those subjects, we can make significant changes in the content and organization of secondary school mathematics as well.

The National Science Foundation, the National Institute of Education, and several private foundations have provided major funding for research and development projects aimed at realizing these new goals. The content objectives and organization of the innovative curriculums that have resulted offer attractive alternatives to most current programs. Several states have already developed daring plans for new directions in school mathematics. A task force on professional standards appointed by the National Council of Teachers of Mathematics is formulating specific curriculum content guidelines for mathematics K-12, for release in 1989. The National Research Council's Mathematical Sciences Education Board has appointed a curriculum frameworks task force that is charting similar guidelines for a long-range, dramatic change in both the content and teaching of school mathematics. Given these developments, it is especially timely to reexamine the goals of school mathematics.

New Goals for Elementary Mathematics

Historically, the label for elementary school mathematics has been "arithmetic." Prior to 1955, mathematical topics in grades K-6 were generally limited to counting, the arithmetic operations with whole numbers, common fractions and decimals, and applications involving percent and measurement. In grades 7 and 8, emphasis was on maintenance of these skills, augmented by the study of measurement and interest formulas. Although the "modern math" reforms of the 1960s introduced new topics, the core of the curriculum remained arithmetic. Rather than emphasizing memorization of mechanical procedures, however, the focus was on generalizing the concepts underlying the algorithms, with an increased emphasis on student inquiry, mathematical rigor, and abstraction.

These curricular reform ideas were transformed into model instructional materials by well-funded development projects, and given formal approval by many administrators of mathematics and general school programs. However, most schools allocated only modest resources to inservice staff development, so the new content and instructional themes were not readily accepted by most elementary school teachers. Subsequent evaluations of "new math" curriculums were therefore more an assessment of teachers' support for their mathematics program and their skill in teaching it than a test of the curriculum itself (Brownell 1963, 1967, 1968). A more recent survey concluded that "it is probably wrong to say that it [modern mathematics] came and went. For most classrooms, it probably never came"

(Stake and Easley 1978, pp. 13-65). Despite this discouraging experience with reform, the goals and approaches of the elementary and middle school mathematics curriculum are once again being questioned.

The standard elementary mathematics program accentuates number and computational skills (including whole numbers, place value, fractions, and decimals) while providing periodic encounters with topics such as estimation, measurement, problem solving, geometry, graphs and descriptive statistics, ratio and proportion, and integer computation. The inclusion of geometry, graphs and descriptive statistics, metric measurement, and integer arithmetic is a consequence of the curriculum reform projects of the 1960s. Missing today, however, is the reform curriculum's emphasis on understanding mathematical ideas and procedures. Although this emphasis may not have been uniformly implemented in the classrooms of the 1960s and 1970s, it was part of the published curriculums. This is no longer the case. Today, the standard elementary mathematics program consists of three strands of disproportionate rank: computation, applications, and geometry. The intended and actual effect of each of these strands has been disparaged in nearly every recent critical analysis of elementary mathematics (Callahan 1985; Kennedy 1985; McKnight et al. 1987; Nicely, Fiber, and Bobango 1986; Trafton 1986).

Computation

Computation is a necessary component of the elementary mathematics curriculum. Without an understanding of number (whole numbers, fractions, and decimals) and the operations of addition, subtraction, multiplication, and division, a student's resources for self-sufficiency and potential for further learning of mathematics are severely limited. The problem is that computation, which dominates today's elementary school mathematics curriculum, is treated not as a vehicle for higher-order thinking—nor even as a subject that should be understood—but merely as a body of rules and procedures to be reiterated until students reach a state of habituated recall.

Elementary school mathematics must involve more than the development of computational skill and recall of facts; it must also be the study of concepts and principles. The goal must be to promote mathematical understanding of arithmetic operations, not simply to inculcate facility with symbolic manipulations.

For the less able student, memorizing isolated facts and meaningless symbolic procedures is a frustrating and nearly hopeless task. Nevertheless, teachers continue to offer symbolic demonstrations and to demand practice. For the able student, once he or she demonstrates computational facility with symbolic problems, the focus of instruction shifts—but not to the rationale behind the procedures, nor even to their application in realistic settings. Rather, the focus shifts to maintenance of the symbolic skills. A recent categorization of the pages in the textbooks of four major elementary mathematics series revealed that approximately 44 percent of the K-3 textbook pages and 34 percent of the textbook pages for grades 4-6 consisted of lessons whose sole objective was to provide practice with already-taught computational procedures (Campbell and Johnson 1983). Since, in mathematics, the textbook usually defines instruction, this means that over one-third of instructional time in elementary mathematics is being spent on practice.

Results of various assessments in elementary mathematics raise serious questions about the prevailing focus on practice of mechanical skills. Standardized achievement tests, National Assessment results in mathematics, and many mandatory state assessments of mathematics learning (generally restricted to only minimal functional literacy skills) indicate that students today can perform addition, subtraction, and multiplication computations with whole numbers. However, these assessments also reveal lower performance with whole-number division and with operations involving fractions and decimals. Most important, the assessments show consistently poor performance on items that require understanding of concepts underlying whole-number computation and on applications involving geometry, measurement, fractions, and decimals.

The development of computational skills, without understanding, commands an enormous amount of instructional time, energy, and persistence. One interpretation of results from the national evaluations is that the current curriculum produces stable mastery of each computational procedure for 85-95 percent of students, but only after three to five years of exposure in a variety of contexts (Bright 1978). These data suggest, for example, that with the current curriculum proficiency with long division should not be expected before ninth or tenth grade and mastery of straightforward application problems involving percent should not be anticipated prior to high school graduation. Critics charge that today's elementary mathematics curriculum is responsible for these results. They argue that good students eventually acquire some skill and a superficial understanding of mathematics, but less able students too often give up, convinced of their inability to learn this complex and confusing subject.

Research in teaching and learning of elementary mathematics has produced convincing evidence that computation and conceptual understanding must be viewed as mutually supporting domains within the elementary mathematics curriculum (Good, Grouws, and Ebmeier 1983; Hamrick and McKillip, 1978; Romberg and Carpenter 1986; Suydam and Weaver 1972). To appreciate the power of this approach, consider two illustrative examples.

Example 1: Place Value

A multi-digit numeral represents more than a sequence of digits. Each digit in a whole number or decimal signifies a multiple of a power of 10. This principle is illustrated by exercises of the following sort:

Write 364 in three different ways.

364 = 300 + ______ + 4

364 = ______hundreds + 6 tens + ______ones

364 = ______tens + 4 ones.

While the first two equations represent the rote or standard place-value intepretation of 364, the third equation demands a conceptualization of 364 as a quantity which may be expressed in differing symbolic forms by applying place-value generalizations. Since 1 hundred is the same as 10 tens, 3 hundreds are equal to 30 tens. 60 is equal to 6 tens. Therefore, 360 must be equal to 36 tens. Place value generalizes to decimal notation and provides the supportive reasoning behind algorithmic procedures for whole numbers and decimals.

Example 2: Division

Arithmetic operations are more than the source of drill exercises. They model relationships that repeatedly occur in the world, even in the world of an elementary school child. Sharing is a relationship which all children experience.

> $868 must be shared equally among 7 people. What is the maximum number of ten-dollar bills that one of the people could receive?

The mathematical structure of this problem is modeled by division. For the child with insight into division and place value numeration, however, the problem can be solved quickly without use of the traditional long-division algorithm. $868 can be viewed as 86 ten-dollar bills and 8 one-dollar bills. The solution to the problem is then obtained by dividing 86 (the maximum number of ten-dollar bills) by 7 (the number of people). Therefore, each person may receive at most 12 ten-dollar bills.

Following a mechanical approach to this problem, a student would commonly use the "sharing" cue to choose the appropriate operation (division) and then apply that operation to the given numbers (868 and 7). Without careful interpretation of the result, this approach leads students to the erroneous solution of 124 (i.e., 124 ten-dollar bills). Students with errant understanding of place value and division might recognize that 124 represents one total share of the money, but conclude that the tens digit 2 means 2 ten-dollar bills.

If children are to be prepared for further study of mathematics and for quantitative literacy in daily life, examples such as these must become the core of the curriculum's computational content. Only with a conceptualization of number and an understanding of the operations—the "why" behind the algorithmic procedures—can children ever apply arithmetic operations in a novel setting as a problem-solving tool.

The Role of Calculators

Critics have noted that the majority of time in today's elementary school mathematics programs is devoted to promoting skills that can be purchased for $7.95. With the advent of inexpensive handheld calculators, the high degree of computational proficiency that has traditionally been required for functional purposes is no longer necessary. Outside of school, applications involving multiplication problems with three-digit factors or division problems with three-digit divisors are routinely performed with calculators. Similarly, much time in the intermediate grades is devoted to algorithms supporting the addition and subtraction of seldom-used fractions with unlike denominators, although use of decimal equivalents is much more common in real applications. Endless practice of involved algorithmic procedures is drudgery which serves no practical purpose, given the existence of the inexpensive calculator.

A more important question raised by the readily available calculator is that of feasibility. The current emphasis on computational rigor denies the impact of technology on American society. Tomorrow's educated citizenry must be able to intepret events in terms of their mathematical structure, to identify appropriate solution procedures, to carry out those procedures, and to make judgments concerning the reasonableness of solutions. These competencies are not being fostered in the standard elementary mathematics program. The calculator provides an efficient means of carrying out procedures to obtain solutions and brings with it no adverse effect on computational skill involving basic facts (Suydam 1982, Wheatley et al. 1979). But development of the other computation-related competencies will require considerable instructional time across the entire elementary and middle school mathematics curriculum. That time may be garnered by eliminating redundant computational exercises and involved algorithmic procedures from the curriculum.

Further, integrating the calculator into the curriculum will require reordering the sequence of some traditional topics and reevaluating the priority accorded other topics. Decimals must be considered earlier, including the representation of very large and very small numbers. Estimation will take on new emphasis, both to predict and to confirm solutions generated by the calculator. Scientific notation, order of operations, exponents, and negative integers must be considered earlier and in greater depth.

Applications

In addition to number and arithmetic operations, the standard elementary and middle school mathematics curriculum includes intermittent consideration of problem solving, estimation, measurement, graphs and descriptive statistics, and ratio and proportion. In each of these areas, mathematical skills and concepts may be used in contexts separate from school-based mathematics. Consequently, these topics are generally referred to as "applications." The contexts for applications generally involve vocational or career settings, consumer decisions, or common events in daily life. Unfortunately, textbook presentations of applications within these contexts tend to be oversimplified, limiting the effectiveness of the instruction.

For example, problem-solving lessons are now incorporated throughout the units of elementary and middle school mathematics textbooks. Problem-solving instruction often entails the modeling of a step-by-step approach, leading to a solution. These approaches are applied to one-step word problems which present already mathematized situations to the student. Further, these lessons often follow presentations of a paper-and-pencil procedure (e.g., long division with remainder, formula for area of a circle, etc.) and serve as a setting for straightforward application of that procedure. Problem solving and applications are thus reduced to another form of computational exercise: you have to pick the operation or procedure, then you simply apply that operation or procedure to the numbers given in the problem.

What role should problem solving and applications involving measurement, estimation, probability, graphing, statistics, and ratio and proportion play in elementary and middle school mathematics? They should be a principal, not a parenthetical, component of the curriculum; they should not be limited to isolated, sterile exercises. The curriculum must continually involve students in the analysis of real events that will promote student interest; in the interpretation of those events as either mathematical structures or relationships; in the representation of those relationships or structures as arithmetic operations or procedures; and in the evaluation of their subsequent solutions. The stimulus problems should not simply apply the procedure which was last encountered; they must generate thought.

The potential of real applications in the mathematics classroom has been eloquently summarized by an exceptional sixth grade teacher:

> Bringing the real world into my mathematics classes has been at times dangerous or troublesome. Dangerous because it raises the expectations of the students (and myself), creates emotional as well as intellectual involvement, demands conceptual understanding while also demanding computational skill (although hand calculators can help bring the latter within reach), draws on mathematical skills not "in this unit," puts us on unsure ground, leads to murky waters, creates tangential interests, and *devours* time. Troublesome because it makes us ask for more, desire deeper understandings, see the world differently, ask increasingly more difficult questions about the world, and realize what a long way we've got to go to "get educated."
>
> So why try to deal with applications of mathematics within my classroom? Because it's exciting and invigorating; it develops mathematical power (and uncovers surprising personal weaknesses); it seems to create real intellectual growth; it has a high immediate impact on students and a long-term residual effect; it makes one want to understand and look for "why" as well as "how" (Ames 1980, p. 10).

Geometry

In the standard curriculum, geometry holds an unofficial status. In the elementary and middle school, geometry is informal, providing the intuitive background for logical reasoning about geometric figures in the secondary school. Topics generally include shape identification, categorization of angles, polygons, and curves, and informal comparison of figure size and shape. Typically, at each grade level elementary mathematics textbooks include geometry as a single chapter, although review items may occur periodically. Critics charge that, despite its firm place in elementary curriculum guides, geometry is often easily omitted from instruction because there is no assumption of learning from one grade to the next. All prerequisites for the study of geometric topics are reiterated from year to year (Usiskin 1985).

Geometry should be a vehicle that challenges elementary and middle school students to observe, describe, analyze, and test hypotheses regarding shapes and forms in the world around them. The curriculum must capitalize on geometry, not as a means of examining fixed line drawings for predetermined factual characteristics, but as a time to create figural models, to investigate properties, and to search for essential characteristics. Students should experiment with changes in the shape, size, and position of familiar figures to identify the fundamental properties of each.[2] The elementary and middle school mathematics curriculum must include a well-developed geometry strand, not as an enrichment topic but as an important field of inquiry to be expanded upon throughout each academic year.

Recommendations

The elementary and middle school mathematics curriculum gives students a foundation for further study of mathematics and a personal resource that is essential for quantitative literacy in adult life. This curriculum must prepare students for their future, not simply communicate skills generally required in the past. Any sound elementary and middle school curriculum must have the following characteristics.

Arithmetic Operations. All students must understand the meaning of basic arithmetic operations and ways that structures or relationships within real-world events can be interpreted by these operations. The study of number and operations must utilize concrete examples and models with accompanying verbal interpretations as a means of providing even young students with the experience of drawing generalizations and formulating

[2]The Turtle Graphics component of the Logo microcomputer programming language provides an environment for such geometric exploration.

abstractions. Symbolic representations should serve as a means of modeling situations already made meaningful. An increased emphasis on the conceptualization of number, place value, and the operations must be accompanied by a de-emphasis on practice of involved algorithmic procedures, particularly with numerals of three or more digits.

Understanding. Mathematical conceptualization and arithmetic operations must be presented as complementary—not competing—aspects of mathematical study. The traditional instructional style of teacher demonstration of a procedure ("show and tell") followed by student practice ("listen and do") must be replaced by a more active interaction between teachers and students. As often as possible, mathematical situations should be first represented and investigated with concrete models, in preparation for use of the powerful but more abstract symbolic forms and operations. Further, it is essential to emphasize that mathematics consists of richly interrelated topics, not a collection of isolated rules for rote operations on symbolic expressions.

Simply writing a new curriculum that focuses on meaning over practice will not foster student understanding; the curriculum must incorporate pedagogical approaches that are appropriate for the developmental level of the students. New goals for fostering student understanding cannot be attained without addressing the issue of teacher training. Too many teachers are ill-equipped to teach mathematics to elementary and middle school children in a meaningful way. Too many teachers believe that many children cannot understand mathematics and that most children need not understand it.

Applications. All students must become skilled in representing the structure of actual arithmetic events through manipulative, pictorial, or verbal models and in translating those models into mathematical expressions. Students must become adept at using the calculator as a problem-solving tool, searching for patterns, carrying out arithmetic operations, and evaluating solutions. Applications involving measurement should not simply require formula recall, but rather the interpretation of concepts, including defining and iterating a unit, partitioning space, and forming generalizations. The tools of graphing, descriptive statistics, and simple probability must be fully developed and applied in data gathering and interpretation, particularly in the middle grades.

Testing. Current standardized assessments, which cover a wide range of mathematical topics and emphasize skill development, are promoting exposure to procedures at the expense of understanding in the elementary and middle school. It is essential that testing be reorganized to admit use of the calculator and to parallel the new goals of the elementary curriculum: the development of mathematical understanding, the interpretation of mathematical events, and the application of mathematical procedures.

New Goals for Secondary Mathematics

Through elementary and middle school mathematics most students follow a common curriculum—a core of arithmetic and its applications, with informal introductions to geometry and statistics. Secondary school mathematics, however, offers students an array of curricular choices designed to match their achievement, ability, and interests. In traditional secondary school programs, the basic choice is whether to follow a college-preparatory or a general mathematics strand of courses. The core of the college-preparatory curriculum is two years of algebra and one year of geometry, with the most able students continuing to a fourth year of pre-calculus study and then on to calculus. The general mathematics option is essentially a continuation of the topics in elementary school mathematics, with an emphasis on applications to consumer problems and careers in business and vocational/technical fields. Recent criticisms have found fault with the goals and effects of both strands.

College-Preparatory Mathematics

The standard college-preparatory courses in algebra train students in a variety of procedures for manipulating symbolic expressions to solve equations and inequalities. Those procedures are applied to a collection of classic word problems. There are many indications that large numbers of college-bound students do not acquire adequate proficiency in the basic skills of algebra. Even those students who do become adept at the manipulative aspects of algebra often do so through rote memory. They then have great difficulty in subsequent mathematical study and in applying their skills to realistic problem-solving situations.

The standard college-preparatory geometry course develops properties of and relations among standard plane figures, in a style not fundamentally different from that proposed by Euclid over 2300 years ago. While this course is commonly justified as the vehicle by which students learn methods of logical and hypothetical reasoning, there is a long record of research evidence suggesting that most students fall far short of that goal. Further, the traditional course provides inadequate development of the spatial visualization that is critical in a variety of practical-life and career tasks and ignores coordinate, vector, and transformation methods that are increasingly important in contemporary applications of geometry.

For students heading toward collegiate study in a scientific or technical subject for which mathematics is fundamental, high school preparation beyond algebra II and geometry is critical. However, comparison of the syllabuses and student achievement in these advanced mathematics courses with counterparts in other countries suggests that we are offering and accomplishing far less than we might assume. The number of students reaching calculus in U.S. high schools is still rather small, and those students who do study advanced mathematics do not demonstrate sufficient skill and problem-solving ability.

Critics of college-preparatory mathematics curriculums have also noted that technology is creating a list of "new fundamentals" that merit space in secondary school programs. Since computers have made the analysis of complex data sets relatively easy, statistical methods in problem solving and decision making have greatly increased in importance. It is now unthinkable that students should leave secondary school without a substantial introduction to the ideas and methods of that subject.

Further, the growing use of computer information systems in a wide variety of home and work situations has made a case for the inclusion in secondary school curriculums of mathematical topics that are fundamental to the design and use of computer hardware and software. For example, the expert systems used in medical and mechanical diagnosis and the data bases used for legal research and business inventory/accounting depend on basic patterns of logical inference and the mathematics of graphs, networks, and matrices. These and other topics from discrete mathematics are being proposed for attention in college-preparatory curriculums.

Planners of college-preparatory mathematics curriculums face a formidable challenge. On one hand, we must find more effective ways to achieve objectives in the standard core curriculum. On the other, we must somehow find time to introduce a broad array of new topics—many of which current teachers are ill-prepared to teach. Suggested solutions to these problems come from many sources with frequently contradictory messages.[3]

The most straightforward approach to improving levels of achievement in basic skills of algebra and geometry is simply to raise our expectations for students. This strategy translates into actions to raise mathematics requirements for high school graduation, to increase the mathematics required for college admission, or to tighten grading standards. When this advice includes specific curriculum content recommendations, the proposals usually mention names of well-defined traditional courses and even details of particular mathematical topics or skills to be included in those courses.

In contrast to the essentially conservative suggestion that we simply make traditional courses more demanding, there are many suggestions for fundamental change in the goals of college-preparatory mathematics curriculums. These proposals frequently recommend sharp reduction in the traditional skill agendas of algebra, trigonometry, and calculus. They suggest that specific topics from statistics and discrete mathematics take the place

[3]Most of the current proposals for change in college-preparatory mathematics are presented and analyzed in the 1985 yearbook of the NCTM, *The Secondary School Mathematics Curriculum* (Hirsch and Zweng 1985).

of obsolete concepts and skills, frequently urging a rethinking of the curriculum that has for so long been designed to prepare all students for college mathematics at the level of calculus (Fey 1984).

One way to understand the spirit of debate over the future of high school mathematics is to reflect on examples that illustrate the nature and uses of some specific topics from algebra, geometry, or trigonometry—the core of secondary school mathematics. Three fairly typical settings for quantitative reasoning are described below. Each involves ideas and skills from traditional high school mathematics curriculums. The purpose of presenting these examples here, however, is to provide a backdrop for understanding the changes that technology will cause in those curriculums.

Example 1: Polynomials in Business

At the heart of secondary school algebra is the study of linear and quadratic equations and their uses. Such problems arise in a variety of quantitative reasoning tasks. For example:

> A company estimates that revenue (R in dollars) and costs (C in dollars) will be functions of unit sales (s) with rules
> $R = -.01s^2 + 12s$
> and $C = 3s + 100$.
>
> What will the revenues and costs be on sales of 250? What level of sales will lead to a break-even situation?

These questions call for evaluation of algebraic expressions and solution of an equation. The first requires substitution of 250 for s in the revenue and cost equations:

(1) Calculate $-.01(250)^2 + 12(250)$ and $3(250) + 100$.

The second requires finding a value of s that makes the revenue equal to cost. That is,

(2) Solve $-.01s^2 + 12s = 3s + 100$ for s.

Algebra provides a set of grammatical rules for expressing relations like these and procedures for transforming the given expressions or solving the equations. Furthermore, those grammatical and procedural rules can be applied to many other problems with similar underlying structure.

Example 2: Exponential Growth

One of the most fascinating applications of secondary mathematics is in the study of quantities that grow or decline exponentially.

> In 1985 the population of China was 1.1 billion and growing at a rate of 3% per year. If that rate of growth persists, what will the

> population be in 10 years? When will the population double? What change in the rate of population increase would slow the doubling time to 35 years?

The relation between population (P) and time (t in years after 1985) can be modeled well by the rule

$$P = 1.1*(1 + .03)^t$$

and the questions call for evaluation of an algebraic expression and solution of two equations.

> 1) Calculate $1.1*(1 + .03)^{10}$, to get the population 10 years from now.
>
> 2) Solve $2.2 = 1.1*(1 + .03)^t$ for t, to determine time when population has doubled to 2.2 billion.
>
> 3) Solve $2.2 = 1.1*(1 + x)^{35}$ for x, to determine the population growth rate that will cause doubling in 35 years.

These calculations and equations require a variety of principles and skills from the algebra of exponents and logarithms in second-year algebra. Those techniques can also be used effectively in the study of radioactive decay, compound interest, spread of disease, or speed of descent for a skydiver.

Example 3: Periodic Variation

Trigonometry is another core subject in college-preparatory secondary school mathematics. The subject has a rich variety of applications in scientific and technical problems. For example,

> If a city has 12 hours of sunlight on March 21 and 15 hours on June 21, how many hours of sunlight will it have on September 21? On December 21? When will it have 14 hours of sunlight?

The relation between hours of sunlight (S) and time in the year (d days) is modeled well by the rule

$$S = 3*\sin[.0172(80 - d)].$$

The questions posed again involve evaluating expressions and solving equations. Trigonometry provides the concepts and methods for modeling the relation and deducing new information. The same methods are very useful in similar problems involving waves of light, sound, or electricity.

What is the message in these illustrations of mathematics? What do they say about the nature of mathematics and, more specifically, about goals for college-preparatory mathematics? They underscore the fundamental role of mathematics as a source of descriptive and predictive models for real-life phenomena. The concepts and symbol systems of mathematics provide a very effective language for expressing relations among quantitative factors in a situation. The reasoning methods of mathematics provide powerful tools for deducing new information from those relations. While most mathematical ideas have their genesis in some specific problem situation, they typically evolve, through a process of abstraction and generalization, into abstract systems in which the concepts, symbols, and reasoning methods are of interest independent of particular applications. Those abstractions of specific experience have often proven invaluable as problem-solving tools in completely new situations.

This cycle of mathematical activity is summarized in a helpful way by the diagram in Figure 4.1.

The goals of mathematical education have always included development of student ability to represent ideas in appropriate formal language, to use inductive and deductive reasoning in derivation of new information, and to interpret the results of reasoning in applied settings. Nevertheless, traditional college-preparatory programs have nearly always concentrated on training students in the vast array of manipulative procedures and deductive reasoning methods required in the formal mathematics phase of that cycle. Even the most successful of such courses leaves students "all dressed up with no place to go"; they have some skill when presented with fully mathematized situations, but little ability to formulate or interpret mathematical models.

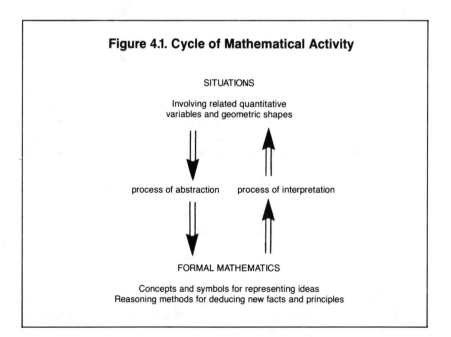

Figure 4.1. Cycle of Mathematical Activity

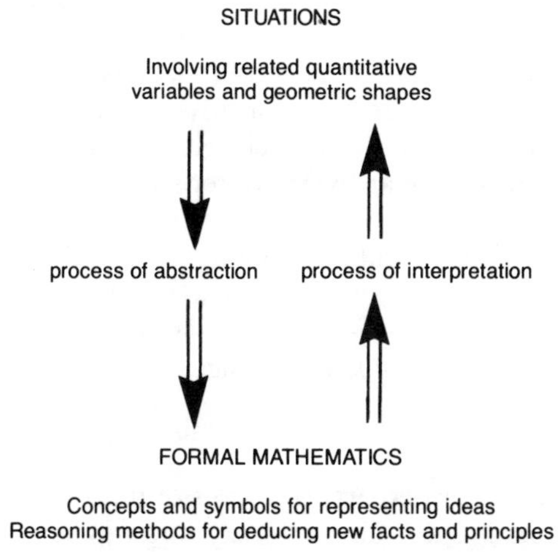

Recommendations

The power of calculators and computers for instruction and problem solving implies and demands new priorities. To prepare students for the future, a college-preparatory curriculum must treat the following major topic areas and themes:

Algebra. All students must become skilled in translating rules, physical principles, or collections of data into symbolic expressions relating variables. They must be able to answer questions about those relations—to solve equations and inequalities and to interpret the results of calculation in applied settings. However, top priority should be given to developing intelligent use of various technology-assisted methods such as graphing, numerical approximation, and computer symbol manipulation, with mental estimation providing a check on the use of electronic aids. For the most able and interested students, development of the traditional symbol manipulation procedures can come after the top-priority goal of ability to formulate algebraic models and to plan appropriate analysis.

Geometry. For all students it is essential that geometry instruction stress ability to visualize objects and relations in space, knowledge of the most important shapes and their properties and applications (not limited to the triangles, quadrilaterals, and circles of traditional courses), and ability to use the reasoning methods of coordinates, vectors, and transformations in studying shape, size, and position. While there is strong traditional support for making geometry the means for experience in axiomatic-deductive thinking, the lack of evidence that this approach succeeds—together with the urgency of other experiences—makes a strong case for reduced attention to deduction in geometry. Students should also gain familiarity with various computer-based tools for geometric exploration and problem solving.

Pre-calculus Mathematics. For students heading to technical careers in which calculus plays a prominent role, concepts and methods in trigonometry, analytic geometry, and elementary functions are essential. However, calculators and computers are having nearly the same effect on these topics as on arithmetic and algebra. In the long run it will become far less important for students to acquire an extensive repertoire of symbol manipulation skills—the skills required in pre-technology mathematics to "get answers." What will remain fundamental is the ability to interpret graphic, numerical, and symbolic information about the functions encountered and the ability to plan appropriate technology-aided analysis to answer questions about the functions. For example, a student who meets the rule

$$S = 3*\sin[.0172(80-d)]$$

will use computer-generated graphs, tables of function values, and symbol manipulation programs to evaluate the expression, solve equations, and find maximum/ minimum values for the number of sunlight hours as a function of number of days elapsed in the year.

Calculus. Without the burden of a long course in manipulative skill prerequisites, many more students should be able to reach at least an informal introduction to the ideas and methods of calculus. Since calculus is a fundamental tool in thinking about a wealth of scientific phenomena, this new opportunity should be an attractive boost to science courses.

Statistics. All college-bound students must develop the ability to gather, organize, interpret, and present data related to a problem or decision-making situation. They must develop an intuitive understanding of randomness and the type of reasoning to use when a probabilistic model is most appropriate. Already, application of that type of reasoning to data related to health, government, or product-quality decisions is almost essential for informed citizenship.

For mathematically able and interested students, an introduction to the more formal reasoning methods of statistics would be very appropriate, since probabilistic reasoning has become routine in computing, engineering, business, education, and science.

Discrete Mathematics. Today's college-bound students will almost certainly have many occasions to use computers for important information-processing tasks. Thus it is essential that they acquire mathematical skills and understandings needed for intelligent use of standard software tools (such as spreadsheets, data bases, and expert systems). More specifically, they should become familiar with the concepts, principles, and uses of logic, probability, graph and network theory, difference equations, combinatorics, matrices, and algorithmics. They must develop facility in thinking about problems in ways that lead to effective computational solutions. This requires careful structural analysis of solution procedures, preference (where appropriate) for procedures that are efficient and economical, and sensitivity to the special advantages and limitations of computer solutions.

The preceding list of topics and content themes prescribes a very ambitious definition of college-preparatory mathematics. It might seem foolish to aim higher when our success with a more pedestrian curriculum has been so limited. But the proposals outlined here, and endorsed by many of the recent advisory reports, do not simply add the burden of many new topics to an already overloaded curriculum; they recommend a major shift of emphasis from training in routine mechanical skills to conceptual understanding and problem solving. The revolutionary impact of computing on mathematics has made this shift both feasible and imperative.

Mathematics for All

In traditional high school mathematics programs, students who have no plans for post-secondary education are offered a curriculum that is very different from the college-preparatory courses. These students are generally assumed to have very little knowledge, ability, or interest in mathematics. They are offered courses designed to provide the skills judged necessary for "life survival," frequently packaged as courses in consumer or vocational/technical mathematics applications. This usually means some measurement geometry and a very heavy dose of remedial arithmetic—especially now that so many jurisdictions have instituted minimum competency tests for high school graduation.

The technology of calculators and computers has equally profound implications for the mathematics curriculum of students not bound for college as for their more academically ambitious classmates. While there is widespread emotional attachment to arithmetic skill as a minimum expectation in education, learning of detailed symbol manipulation skills is often the most difficult task for less able or uninterested students. Outside of school, everyone has access to calculators to perform complex arithmetic tasks. The tasks that remain are to identify problem structure, to choose appropriate operations, and to run informal estimates to confirm calculated results. To achieve these goals we need something quite different from the all-too-common sterile arithmetic. In 1978 the National Council of Supervisors of Mathematics proposed a list of 10 basic skills in mathematics. That list stands today as sound advice on curriculum for non-college-bound students.

1. Problem Solving: Students should be able to solve problems in situations that are new to them.
2. Applying Mathematics in Everyday Situations: Students should be able to use mathematics to deal with situations they face daily in an ever-changing world.
3. Alertness to the Reasonableness of Results: Students should learn to check to see that their answers to problems are "in the ball park."
4. Estimation and Approximation: Students should learn to estimate quantity, length, distance, weight, and so on.
5. Appropriate Computational Skills: Students should be able to use the four basic operations with whole numbers and decimals, and they should be able to do computations with simple fractions and percents.
6. Geometry: Students should know basic properties of simple geometric figures.
7. Measurement: Students should be able to measure in both the metric and customary systems.
8. Tables, Charts, and Graphs: Students should be able to read, make, and interpret simple tables, charts, and graphs.
9. Using Mathematics to Predict: Students should know how mathematics is used to find the likelihood of future events.
10. Computer Literacy: Students should know about the many uses of computers in society and should be aware of what computers can and cannot do.

If this list of topics recommended for all students looks similar to the mathematics prescribed for college-preparatory students, the similarity is not simply coincidental. We are now preparing students for a world where the benefits and responsibilities of full citizenship will require a substantial measure of skill and understanding in the mathematical foundations of science and technology. Some will obviously progress far deeper than others into the various facets of mathematics. But we can no longer settle for a secondary curriculum that provides many students only mindless training in mechanical skills. Calculators and computers must be available to all students for use when appropriate. This changed environment for mathematical study and application must be reflected in new goals for our curriculum.

* * * * * *

In the professional mathematics community, advisory reports and development projects are typical responses to a crisis in mathematics education. The persistent challenge is to find ways to implement recommended changes—to close the gap between the ideals of professional practice and the reality of mathematics education in schools and classrooms across the country. The goals for school mathematics outlined above are not simply a matter of style or approach; they constitute a fundamental change in the content of both the elementary and secondary mathematics curriculum. Implementation will require a detailed specification of appropriate instructional materials for classroom use, massive teacher training programs, and modification of assessment procedures. However, change can occur. The next ten years will see the retirement and replacement of much of the teaching staff in U.S. schools, particularly in secondary mathematics. The time to begin developing materials and upgrading standards for teachers is now.

Signs of change are already apparent at the national and state levels. The National Research Council has formed a Board for Mathematical Sciences Education with the charge to provide national leadership in curriculum, teacher education, and testing. Several state governments have supported major efforts to define new curriculum frameworks and achievement standards for all schools in their jurisdictions, and state legislatures have been increasingly willing to put the force of law behind those guidelines. While these efforts have not produced a firm consensus on details of a national mathematics curriculum for grades K-12, there is remarkable agreement that major changes are required if U.S. mathematics programs are to prepare students for the world in which they will live and work. We must direct those changes to achieve that goal; our responsibility as educators demands it.

References

Ames, P. "A Classroom Teacher Looks at Applications." In *A Sourcebook of Applications of School Mathematics*, edited by D. Bushaw, M. Bell, H. O. Pollak, M. Thompson, and Z. Usiskin. Reston, Va.: National Council of Teachers of Mathematics, 1980.

Bright, G. W. "Assessing the Development of Computational Skills." In *Developing Computational Skills* (1978 Yearbook), edited by M. N. Suydam, and R. E. Reys. Reston, Va.: National Council of Teachers of Mathematics, 1978.

Brownell, W. A. "Arithmetic Abstractions—Progress Toward Maturity of Concepts under Differing Programs of Instruction." *Arithmetic Teacher* 10 (1963): 322-329.

Brownell, W. A. *Arithmetic Abstractions: The Movement Toward Conceptual Maturity under Differing Systems of Instruction* (University of California Publications in Education No. 17). Berkeley: University of California Press, 1967.

Brownell, W. A. "Conceptual Maturity in Arithmetic under Differing Systems of Instruction." *Elementary School Journal* 69 (1968): 151-163.

Callahan, L. G. "Pressing Problems in Primary Mathematics Programs: Time, Texts and Tests." *Arithmetic Teacher* 33, 2 (1985): 2.

Campbell, P. F., and M. L. Johnson. "Computation Is Not Enough." *Principal* 63, 2 (1983): 38-43.

College Entrance Examination Board. *Academic Preparation for College: What Students Need to Know and Be Able to Do*. New York: Author, 1983.

Conference Board of the Mathematical Sciences. *Overview and Analysis of School Mathematics, Grades K-12*. Washington, D.C.: Author, 1975.

Conference Board of the Mathematical Sciences. *The Mathematical Sciences Curriculum K-12: What Is Still Fundamental and What Is Not*. Washington, D.C.: Author, 1982.

Conference Board of the Mathematical Sciences. *New Goals for Mathematical Sciences Education*. Washington, D.C.: Author, 1984.

Corbitt, M. K. "The Impact of Computing Technology on School Mathematics: Report of an NCTM Conference." *The Mathematics Teacher* 78 (1985): 243-250.

Fey, J. T., ed. *Computing and Mathematics: The Impact on Secondary School Curriculums*. Reston, Va.: National Council of Teachers of Mathematics, 1984.

Good, T. L., D. A. Grouws, and H. Ebmeier. *Active Mathematics Teaching*. New York: Longman, 1983.

Hamrick, K. B., and W. D. McKillip. "How Computational Skills Contribute to the Meaningful Learning of Arithmetic." In *Developing Computational Skills* (1978 Yearbook), edited by M. N. Suydam and R. E. Reys. Reston, Va.: National Council of Teachers of Mathematics, 1978.

Hansen, V. P., ed. *Computers in Mathematics Education* (1984 Yearbook). Reston, Va.: National Council of Teachers of Mathematics, 1984.

Hirsch, C., and M. J. Zweng, eds. *The Secondary School Mathematics Curriculum* (1985 Yearbook). Reston, Va.: National Council of Teachers of Mathematics, 1985.

Kennedy, L. M. "Geometry—More Than a Holiday Prelude." *Arithmetic Teacher* 33, 1 (1985): 2.

McKnight, C. C., F. J. Crosswhite, J. A. Dossey, E. Kifer, J. O. Swafford, K. J. Travers, and T. J. Cooney. *The Underachieving Curriculum: Assessing U.S. School Mathematics from an International Perspective*. Champaign, Ill.: Stipes Publishing Company, 1987.

National Council of Supervisors of Mathematics. "Position Paper on Basic Mathematical Skills." *The Mathematics Teacher* 71 (1978): 147-152.

National Council of Teachers of Mathematics. *An Agenda for Action: Recommendations for School Mathematics of the 1980s*. Reston, Va.: Author, 1980.

National Council of Teachers of Mathematics. *Alternative Courses for Secondary School Mathematics*. Reston, Va.: Author, 1985.

National Institute of Education. *The NIE Conference on Basic Mathematical Skills and Learning, Vols. 1 and 2*. Washington, D.C.: Author, 1975.

Nicely, R. F., Jr., H. R. Fiber, and J. C. Bobango. "The Cognitive Content of Elementary School Mathematics Textbooks." *Arithmetic Teacher* 34, 4 (1986): 60-61.

Romberg, T. A. *School Mathematics: Options for the 1990s*. Washington, D.C.: U.S. Department of Education, 1984.

Romberg, T. A., and T. P. Carpenter. "Research on Teaching and Learning Mathematics: Two Disciplines of Scientific Inquiry." In *Handbook of Research on Teaching*, 3d ed., edited by M. C. Wittrock. New York: Macmillan, 1986.

Stake, R. E., and J. A. Easley, Jr. *Case Studies in Science Education, Vol. 2: Design, Overview and General Findings* (NSF Publication SE 78-74). Washington, D.C.: U.S. Government Printing Office, 1978. (ERIC Document Reproduction Service No. 156513)

Suydam, M. N. *The Use of Calculators in Pre-college Education: Fifth Annual State of the Art Review*. Columbus, Ohio: Calculator Information Center, 1982. (ERIC Document Reproduction Service No. 220273)

Suydam, M. N., and J. F. Weaver. *Meaningful Instruction in Mathematics Education*. Columbus, Ohio: ERIC Information Analysis Center for Science, Mathematics, and Environmental Education, 1972. (ERIC Document Reproduction Service No. ED 068329)

Trafton, P. R. "Computation—It's Time for a Change." *Arithmetic Teacher* 34, 3 (1986): 2.

Usiskin, Z. "We Need Another Revolution in Secondary School Mathematics." In *The Secondary School Mathematics Curriculum* (1985 Yearbook), edited by C. R. Hirsch and M. J. Zweng. Reston, Va.: National Council of Teachers of Mathematics, 1985.

Wheatley, G. H., R. J. Shumway, T. G. Coburn, R. E. Reys, H. L. Schoen, C. L. Wheatley, A. L. White. "Calculators in Elementary Schools." *Arithmetic Teacher* 27, 1 (1979): 18-21.

5. Rethinking the Science Curriculum

F. James Rutherford and Andrew Ahlgren

FROM TIME TO TIME IT IS IMPORTANT TO REEXAMINE CURRICULUMS from the ground up. This requires asking what we want our students to have learned by the time they reach a designated age before we determine what should be taught at various grade levels and subject areas. It also calls for beginning somewhere other than with the accumulated body of content and practice that constitutes the current school curriculum.

In science, a complete rethinking of the curriculum ought to be undertaken about three or four times a century. Scientific knowledge—meaning significant discoveries and insights about the way the world works, not merely facts—grows at an enormous rate. In the process, some beliefs are shown to be misleading or wrong. Moreover, the stakes are high: Science, directly and through technology, greatly influences the lives of most people. The time comes when fine-tuning the science curriculum is no longer sufficient to ensure that it is either correct or relevant.

Oddly, there have been no major attempts in this century to conceptualize the entire science curriculum. *General Education in a Free Society*, published in 1946, presented an eloquent rationale for science education in secondary school and college. Since it assumed that the traditional sequence of courses in secondary school would continue, however, it essentially endorsed the current practices. There were course development projects in the 1960s, and many states and school districts have produced curriculum guidelines in science. But these have been either limited in scope (elementary only, middle grades only, or particular high school subjects) or corrective, rather than comprehensive and zero-based.

Project 2061: Education for a Changing Future[1] is an effort by the scientific community to completely rethink the learning outcomes of school

[1]Project 2061 was launched in July 1985 by the American Association for the Advancement of Science with funding from the Carnegie Corporation of New York and the Andrew W. Mellon Foundation.

science—and of mathematics and technology as well. The first task of the project is to answer the question: What science, mathematics, and technology should all students have learned by the time they complete their elementary and secondary education? What understandings of science and habits of mind would we like young adults to have gained from their school experience? Later phases of Project 2061 will take a fresh look at educational approaches necessary to achieve the learning goals and at strategies for implementing them. Project 2061 is not aimed at achieving a single curriculum but rather will try to engage educators and scientists in developing diverse approaches.

The recommendations of the first phase of Project 2061 are still being formulated as this paper is being written, but they should be available in the fall of 1988. While it is not appropriate to summarize here the entire set of recommendations, it is possible to discuss some of the key issues emerging from the project. We believe these are generic issues that apply to other subject areas and the work of other groups. These issues can be expressed as questions that need to be answered before the content of school science can be specified. If any group were to attempt reconstruction of the entire K-12 science curriculum for all students from scratch, we believe that it would have to address two central questions: Should we start by considering what should be taught, or how we would like students to turn out? Should all students have a common base of knowledge and skills?

Questions such as these would follow:

Strategy. How can the science curriculum for all students be specified in a way that will encourage building it from the ground up, rather than by a series of dilutions of university science? How can curriculum guidelines capture the importance of *how* science is taught as well as *what* science is taught? How can any new specification for science education avoid becoming simply a new set of headings under which all of the old content is reshuffled? What can be done to keep a new conception of the content of school science from just giving rise to a new list of items to be memorized?

Scope. Which sciences should "school science" comprise? Is mathematics part of science? What about the social and behavioral sciences, the computer and information sciences, or technology? Should the applied sciences—such as medicine, engineering, and agriculture—be included? What overlap, if any, should the science curriculum have with history, literature, and the arts and crafts?

Emphasis. Which aspects of science should the science curriculum concentrate on? The accumulated outcomes of science—its theories, concepts, laws, and facts? The history of how scientific ideas were developed? The cutting edge of science? The generalized methods of scientific inquiry? The scientific world view? Science as a social enterprise? The role of science in other human affairs? Should the emphasis be on the acquisition of knowledge of science, the development of science-related thinking skills, or the inculcation of attitudes?

Selection Criteria. What educational purposes should be used to guide the selection of the content of school science? The needs of citizens? The needs of the country? Preparation for work? Preparation for other courses, or for college admission? To improve student performance on science examinations? Should material be included because of its historical and cultural significance, even if of little practical use? What about the enrichment of childhood as a criterion? Are there exclusion principles that can be used to justify the deliberate omission of some content from the science curriculum?

Project 2061[2] wrestled with these and related issues, and in the process formulated a set of guiding principles, which we believe have wider applicability. These are presented below with some examples of how the project is responding to them. Before presenting the principles, however, it may be helpful to describe the likely format of the Project 2061 report, since we quote extensively from a working draft of it.

The report includes chapters that present recommendations related to understanding the world as seen through the eyes of science, technology, and mathematics. Other chapters focus on approaches to teaching, the nature of the scientific enterprise, and themes that cut across all of science, mathematics, and technology.

Strategies

Principle 1: To build an effective science curriculum, it is first necessary to identify what students should end up knowing.

This sounds self-evident, but apparently it is not. The usual starting place for reexamining the curriculum is "What should we teach in chemistry?" or "What should we cover in eighth grade general science" or "What should we do during 'science time' in the first grade?" or "What series of science readers should we adopt?" But there are several drawbacks to putting the teaching questions ahead of the learning ones. One is that it usually implicitly accepts the structural status quo, e.g., that there will be a distinct chemistry course. It also identifies the science curriculum as congruent with the courses and blocks of time labeled "science," and therefore pays no

[2]Project 2061 is an AAAS project engaging a large number of people. The major input of ideas comes from scientists, engineers, and mathematicians organized into five panels: the biological and health sciences; the physical sciences and engineering; the social and behavioral sciences; mathematics; and technology. The panels and the small project staff are assisted by many consultants and reviewers, including scientists, teachers and other educators, historians, philosophers, and others who participate in and reflect on science and its place in human affairs. Oversight and guidance is provided by the National Council on Science and Technology Education, a committee of distinguished scientists and educators. The Board of Directors of the AAAS will review all material before authorizing publication.

attention to what reading, history, or shop ought to contribute to science learning. It interferes with thinking in terms of how to provide for the gradual development and enrichment of scientific ideas throughout K-12.

This line of reasoning led Project 2061 to dedicate Phase I to the identification and articulation of knowledge and skills to be achieved by the end of elementary and secondary education. The Phase I report will not be a curriculum document. It will not talk about courses or scope and sequence by grade, nor even specify what comes before what, nor suggest how best to teach any particular concept. It will recommend what people should understand by the time they are 17 or 18, the residue of knowledge and skills that we would like them to carry through life and repeatedly build upon and refresh.

For an example, we turn to a recommendation from the social and behavioral sciences that calls for all students to gain an understanding of the nature, value, use, and misuse of categories:

> In science, categories—mammals, dictatorships, social classes, races, personalities—are defined for particular purposes, the most important being to discriminate clearly among things and processes on the basis of selected similarities and differences. The value of categorization is in promoting the accurate exchange of information, the pooling of observations, and the clarification of issues. The risk is that categories will be taken too seriously, e.g., as inevitable, or as including more characteristics than those on which they are based.[3]

Notice that this does not say what the schools should do to ensure such a view of categories. Clearly, however, it incorporates ideas and insights that would have to develop over time and be encountered by students in many different contexts. The same can be said of the following, which is one of the statements that defines the recommendation that everyone should understand the concept of emergent systems in increasingly complex systems:

> As a system becomes more complex, description of its detailed behavior becomes increasingly difficult. From this complexity emerge new phenomena which, although not inconsistent with the principles that apply to the detailed interactions in the system, are not readily predictable from them. For example, chemical reactions are consistent with principles of atomic physics, and in that sense are "no more than" physics. But chemical reactions involve such complexity of physical interaction that they require additional principles for their description that can be used conveniently without explicit reference to the underlying physics (e.g., buffering). Similar relationships of emergent phenomena exist between biology and the underlying chemistry and physics, between psychology and the underlying biology, and between sociology and the underlying psychology.

[3]This and any other ideas or quotes from current Project 2061 draft material are unofficial and subject to change. Also, they may be misleading inasmuch as they are presented here out of context. They should be taken as being indicative of the thinking of the project in mid-1987 at the time this material was being written.

Principle 2: The learning goals for particular student populations (vocational, college preparatory, general) and for students of different interests and ability, should build on those set for all students.

We are speaking here of direction of development. Traditionally, graduate departments and professional schools influence the content of undergraduate science courses at research universities and, indirectly, those in non-research colleges and universities. High school science is typically a diluted version of college science; junior high and elementary schools water down the high school content. One result is the design of science curriculums in a given district is likely to serve only those students—if any—who will study science in college. Many students seem to recognize this and stop taking science at the first opportunity.

Project 2061 argues that curriculum development should proceed in the opposite direction—from the common core of knowledge to that for particular categories of students. Addition, in the world of science learning, works better than subtraction. We believe that the only effective way to get a strong, relevant science curriculum for ordinary students is to figure out what we want them to know and how to get them to know it. Having accomplished that, it is not difficult to move to whatever level of sophistication is desired or to add topics for particular students.

The following statement is one of several that bear on the recommendation that all students should become aware of the nature, extent, and value of biological diversity. It suggests the kind of understanding all students should have of biological classification. Note that although it does not call for learning the names and hierarchy of all of the biological categories—only the concepts of kingdom and species are introduced—it sets no limit on how far and in what contexts the subject can be pursued.

In classifying organisms, the most obvious division is according to how energy is obtained—those that get their energy directly from sunlight by photosynthesis (plants) and those that consume energy-rich foods (animals). More recently, organisms have been divided into two groups on the basis of cell structure—those made up of cells without nuclei (mainly bacteria and blue-green algae) and those whose cells contain nuclei (all others). The distinction between single-celled and multicelled organisms is also widely used. Modern techniques now make it possible to use chromosomal and biochemical properties to determine kinship relationships among organisms.

Principle 3: In order to reduce the tendency to redistribute all of the existing science curriculum content into new categories, learning goals should be expressed conceptually rather than as a list of topic headings.

In order to increase students' understanding of truly important scientific ideas, and if we are to have time to put more emphasis on how to acquire new scientific knowledge and habits of mind, then we need to reduce the amount of material heaped on students in science (at least in high school science). Meaningful learning requires more thorough study of fewer ideas.

But the continuing prevalence of gargantuan textbooks and curriculum guides that list nearly every possible topic suggests that it will not be easy to cut back.

It is not clear that the Project 2061 approach to this problem will work. It is to formulate recommendations in terms of what understandings individuals would retain after leaving school. Each recommendation consists of three to six paragraphs that express, in content and sophistication, all that the ordinary student needs to understand in order to satisfy the recommendation.

One of the recommendations, not surprisingly, is that everyone should understand the concept of biological evolution. But what does such an understanding entail? The Project 2061 answer is as follows:

> The evidence for evolution comes from such separate fields as geology, paleontology, comparative anatomy, embryology, genetics, molecular biology, and ecology. The general concept of evolution—the gradual development and diversification of living forms due to natural selection—is regarded in the science community as the fundamental explanation for the diversity and relatedness we find among species. The detailed mechanisms of evolution are not yet completely understood, however, and research and lively debate continue as part of the scientific way of increasing our understanding of how evolution actually happens.
>
> Evolution provides an explanation for three main sets of observable facts about life on earth: the incredible array of diverse life forms we see about us; the different degrees of anatomical and molecular likeness among these; and the fossil record showing a sequence over billions of years in the kinds of organisms on earth. At the heart of the theory of evolution is the concept of natural selection: most kinds of organisms produce more offspring in each generation than the environment can support, these offspring vary genetically owing to sexual recombination and mutations , and only those offspring that survive and reproduce pass their genetic characteristics on to the next generation. As a result, the genetic make-up of a population changes: the proportion of those members with characteristics that help them to survive and reproduce gradually increases while the proportion of other, less well adapted, members decreases.
>
> The time frame for the evolution of complex organisms is vastly longer than the life span of individual organisms, and thus usually cannot be directly observed. But the general story of evolving life on earth can be pieced together from the combined evidence of fossil remains found in successive layers of sedimentary rock and the similarities and differences in the molecules of species that survive today. Life has probably existed for about three billion years, whereas the earth itself is five or more billion years old. During the first two billion years of life, only microorganisms without nuclei existed. Of these, certain species of bacteria and blue-green algae appear to have survived to the present day. When microorganisms with nuclei appeared about a billion years ago, there was a great burst in the rate of evolution, with the emergence of increasingly varied and complex organisms. Mammals started appearing about a hundred million years ago, and humans, newcomers on the evolutionary scene, less than a hundred thousand years ago.
>
> Evolution is not a ladder in which the lower forms are all eventually replaced by higher forms, with humans emerging at the top as the most advanced species. Rather, it is like a bush, with many branches emerging long ago: many of those branches have died out; some have survived with little change over time; and some have repeatedly branched, giving rise to sequentially more varied (and usually more

complex) organisms. Evolution produces variety, not necessarily progress in a set direction, and it continues to apply to all biological species, from the most ancient and primitive to the newest and most complex.

The continuity and connectedness of life is now highlighted by the study of molecules and biochemical processes. All self-reproducing organisms contain DNA, a complex molecule that carries the genetic information that controls the manufacture in cells of proteins from amino acids. Although the basic genetic code is the same in all organisms, the precise sequence of segments that make up DNA is characteristic of a given species. The closeness or remoteness of the evolutionary relationship between organisms is a function of the number of their DNA sequences that are alike or different.

Principle 4: A statement of learning outcomes in science should be accompanied by comments on teaching practices that are especially important for realizing those outcomes.

Every Project 2061 panel emphasized that the how and the what of science teaching are closely coupled. Although the educational means for achieving its content recommendations will be the business of the next phase of Project 2061, the Phase I report will include some general recommendations on essential characteristics of the teaching of science. The report is doing this in two ways: commentary on the teaching of science, mathematics, and technology in general; and a few key teaching recommendations that bear more specifically on each subject domain.

Two examples of teaching recommendations are presented here. The first is general:

Sound teaching begins with questions and phenomena of interest to students, not with abstractions or phenomena outside their range of perception, understanding, or knowledge. Students need to get acquainted with things, to observe them, collect them, handle them, describe them, become puzzled by them, ask questions about them, and then to try to find answers to their questions about them. Technical vocabulary can follow as needed to understand and talk about things, but need not and ought not to be the starting point.

Increasingly, as children progress, their interest in phenomena should be directed to finding out how things work. They need to move from description to explanation. The keen observation and careful description of things and events found in nature, including people and things made by people, should be emphasized in teaching at every level, but effective teaching can help extend those skills into curiosity about why things are as they are and behave as they do.

The second example could apply as well to all science teaching, but it gains pointedness, we believe, by being presented in the context of the life sciences:

Biology teaching must avoid dogmatism. As in all science education, students should experience biology as a way of investigating, thinking, and knowing—not as unalterable truth. This is particularly important when it comes to a topic such as evolution. An authoritarian, absolutist approach is not only unscientific, it is bound to be ineffective in the bargain. Evolution is central to understanding the biological world, as our recommendations emphasize, but it should be presented as a powerful set of concepts consistent with the results from many different lines of inquiry, not as an inevitable truth to be learned without question. Biology education should familiarize students with the kinds of evidence and arguments that support evolution and show the usefulness of the theory in making sense out of both the diversity and the relatedness of life forms and in leading to new research.

Scope

Principle 5: The content of the school science curriculum should be relevant to (but not necessarily exhaustively representative of) the full spectrum of the sciences.

If one takes a look at the world of science, the array is dazzling. In addition to the old favorites of chemistry and psychology, there are the hybrids, such as neuropsychology and materials science, that have become distinct sciences in their own right. Offshoots of established science, such as particle physics, have become independent, and whole new sciences, for example computer science, have appeared.

Project 2061 was designed to encourage input from all of the sciences. To that end five panels were established to conduct the study. In order to make it feasible for the panel members to meet often and engage in lively debate, each panel was small and its members were located in the same geographical region. To insure a wide input from fields other than their own, the panels called upon many consultants to attend their meetings. On top of that, extensive reviewing of draft documents is being used to see that significant input from any field of science is not being overlooked.

The intent of the representativeness was not, however, to ensure comprehensive coverage or to make sure that everyone understands the nature of each discipline. Rather, it was to encourage the identification from across the full spectrum of sciences of a limited set of ideas that are especially important for understanding the world and what goes on in it. Many of the most important ideas in science cut across disciplinary boundaries, and we regard it as more important that most people come to understand these than that they are informed about each particular science.

Principle 6: School science learning goals should incorporate mathematics content when mathematics is conceptually or historically linked to the recommended science concepts, but mathematizing science should be avoided when, as is often the case, it makes learning the science substantially more difficult.

Science and mathematics have had a long and successful relationship. On the one hand, science continually provides mathematics with challenges, calling for mathematical techniques suitable for analyzing scientific problems. On the other hand, pure mathematics—mathematics that was developed by mathematicians for the advancement of mathematics itself with no applications in mind—has often turned out to be crucial to the advancement of science. The science curriculum—and the mathematics curriculum, also—should help students become aware of this productive relationship.

Mathematics plays a featured role in Project 2061. As noted above, one of the Phase I panels was on mathematics. Its charge was to identify the mathematics all students should end up knowing as a consequence of their total school experience, not simply from math classes. In order to foster this wider vision of mathematics education, each of the other panels had a mathematician who was also a member of the mathematics panel. Three examples of the Project 2061 treatment of mathematics follow. From the general chapter on the nature of science:

> Mathematics is the language of patterns and relationships, and so it often is the preferred syntax of science. It provides the means for analyzing quantitative data, a symbolic language for expressing relationships, and the logic that connects theory to observation. Mathematical formulations that were developed mostly for their own sake frequently turn out to be useful for expressing physical reality, and even, sometimes, for suggesting new investigations in science. On the other hand, much of the growth of mathematics has come from attempts to deal with theoretical problems in science.

From the mathematics recommendations:

> Everyone should understand the basics of dimensional scaling, that is, that area varies as the square, and volume as the cube, of linear dimensions. More generally, they should understand that both form and scale can have important consequences for the performance of systems. Triangular connections, for example, maximize rigidity, while streamlining minimizes turbulence, smooth shapes optimize flow over surfaces, and sharp points facilitate piercing. Branching and looped patterns are used to optimize transport systems (air routes, blood vessels) and communication systems (nerves, sales routes). In addition, scale has enormous effects on the ratio of surface to volume and therefore on factors such as ability to retain heat. For a mouse, with its much greater surface to volume ratio, heat loss is much more of a problem than for a bear.

From the life sciences recommendations:

> The circumstances of the human population now and in the past are revealed in census data, population statistics, and demographic studies. Understanding population-related issues—disease prevention, resource distribution, environmental hazards, boundary setting, taxation, transportation systems, education, and many more—depends in some measure on the ability to read graphs and tables, to follow quantitative argument, and to discriminate between evidence and claims.

Principle 7: The science curriculum should include content relating to technology.

Science and technology are different enterprises, but they are becoming increasingly interdependent. Understanding both the differences between them and the nature of their dependence, in the view of Project 2061, ought to be among the learning goals of the science curriculum. The Phase I report will deal with this in a chapter devoted to technology, and aspects of it in the other chapters as well.

The example that follows is from the general chapter on the nature of science, in which it is recommended that everyone become aware of the science-technology connections.

Science and technology are fundamentally different undertakings. Science is concerned primarily with understanding how the world works, technology with figuring out how to arrange things to happen in the way we want. In an idealized sense, scientists are interested in phenomena and their relationships without regard to what use can be made of them, while engineers care about controlling what happens. Technology consists of the tools and processes used for manipulating materials, energy, and information in the service of individual and social purposes. Technologies can be developed and used without understanding exactly how they work, but increasingly they draw on the knowledge, logic, and methods of science.

Technology provides the eyes and ears of science, and some of the muscle, too. Sometimes new instruments and techniques are developed—radio telescopes or super-computers, for instance—to enable a line of investigation to proceed. At other times, technologies developed for commercial or other purposes—rockets or submarines, say—suggest and make possible whole new research thrusts. In either case, technology is essential to science for purposes of measurement, data and sample collection, treatment of sample material, computation, transportation to research sites (antarctic, moon, ocean floor), protection from hazardous research materials, communication, and more.

Science stimulates the invention of new technologies which then turn out to be useful in commerce and elsewhere. Genetic engineering provides a recent example of this. And as technologies become more and more sophisticated, their links to science become stronger. In some fields, such as solid state physics, science and technology are so interdependent that they can scarcely be separated.

Principle 8: Science education goals should be defined in a way that encourages frequent curricular crossover between the sciences and the humanities.

Project 2061 has tried to accomplish this by frequent references to historical, aesthetic, and practical aspects of science. This is to signal that it is appropriate to deal with such matters in science courses. Moreover, the philosophy of the project is to state the learning goals of the new science curriculum without reference to courses, disciplines, fields, or other academic territories. It is up to the school, in this conception, to decide what different subjects—including history, literature, shop, art, music, and government—can contribute to the science curriculum, and vice versa.

Three illustrations of this follow. The first is from the teaching recommendations in the life sciences:

History should be used in the teaching of biology. It is important for students to gain an accurate picture of how science progresses. This includes such matters as the key roles of some of the greatest biologists (Darwin, Mendel, Pasteur, Watson, and Crick), the dependence of even the greatest biologists on the work of others, the convergence of different lines of research, the false starts and mistaken notions that most scientists experience at one time or another, and the overturning on occasion of widely held beliefs. Such insights can only result if students have the opportunity to follow from time to time the development of new theories and the rejection of others.

The second example is one of the supporting statements for a recommendation that students learn how science and technology affect the complex system of agriculture:

Advances in agriculture came as people began to control lifeforms. At first they could control breeding only by choosing which of their animals and plants would reproduce. Combinations of the natural variety or characteristics could thus be attempted in order to improve the hardiness and productivity of plant and animal species. More recently, modern genetics has helped us to increase the natural variability within plant species by using radiation to induce mutations, so that we have more choice for selective breeding. Scientists are now learning how to design new organisms. As we learn more about how the genetic code works (virtually the same for all life), it is becoming possible to move genes from one organism to another. With maps of what code sequences control what functions, the possibility exists of giving a plant or animal new characteristics directly, and the new characteristics would thereafter be passed on from generation to generation.

The third example is taken from the teaching recommendations relating to technology:

As the earliest records show, technology has been a major force in the shaping of the history of the world. This is not evident, however, in most history courses and books. We believe that in studying both American and world history some of the ties between technological change and political, economic, and military history ought to be examined. The thread of geography in the curriculum should be designed to help students gain an understanding of the connection between technology and the worldwide migration of human populations, and an understanding of the use of scientific instruments and of transportation and communications technologies in charting the earth's surface.

Similarly, the social studies curriculum in general should include a study of current issues—resource distribution, health delivery, environmental quality, energy production, warfare, and the like—that implicate technology as part of the problem and part of the solution. The disparate use of technology in developed and undeveloped countries is also important for developing cultural perspective.

Emphasis

Principle 9: The science curriculum should deal with science in all of its aspects.

For the most part, school science concentrates on the findings of science: the facts, laws, principles, and theories that are the end result of the scientific endeavor. To a degree this is justifiable, but not at the price of excluding all other aspects of science. The Project 2061 recommendations treat science as a body of developing ideas, a way of thinking and conducting inquiry, an outlook on the universe, and a complex social and cultural enterprise. Some examples follow for each of these topics from the general chapter on the nature of science. Concerning the scientific world view:

The world of phenomena is not capricious. The things and events that make up the world behave in consistent ways. Belief in such a world makes it sensible to search for regularities and causal relationships.

The world is understandable. Through the use of intellect, and aided by instruments that extend the senses, humans are able to discover regularities in nature. Because some phenomena are extremely complex—for example weather and human behavior—scientific methods of inquiry may never produce more than approximate and incomplete understandings of them. Nevertheless, while our understanding of the world will never be total, it grows steadily as wrong ideas are eliminated and others are progressively corrected.

The universe is, as its name implies, a vast single system in which all of the parts are physically related to each other. Knowledge gained from studying one part of the universe—atoms, bacteria, stars, bridges—can often be applied to other parts: genes, forests, computers, weather, distant galaxies.

The world is manipulable. The ability to make accurate predictions and to improve technology is perhaps the most convincing evidence that we really are coming to understand some things about how the world works. By inventing more and more successful ideas about how natural phenomena occur, we increase our ability to arrange for predictable and useful occurrences. Knowledge makes it possible to use natural laws to advantage—but not, of course, to violate them.

The world is interesting. Not only is the universe understandable, it is worth understanding for the fun of it. Natural phenomena are generally captivating in their own right, but they invariably become even more so when we find out what is behind them.

Concerning the nature of scientific inquiry:

Science is evidence-oriented. When faced with a claim that something is true, the scientific response is to ask about what data support it. When presented with evidence, scientists may question its validity and determine to their own satisfaction whether the data offered are representative, relevant to the claim, and not fatally biased. Bias (of the investigator, the sample, the method, or instrument) may not be avoidable, and may not be so great as to invalidate a proposition, but scientists like to know what the possible sources of bias are and which way they are likely to influence evidence.

Science is speculative. Hypotheses—carefully crafted statements about the way something might be—are widely used in science as tools for deciding what data to pay attention to and for suggesting what additional data to seek. A hypothesis is a statement that may or may not be true, even in the opinion of the person who proposes it, but to be useful it must make clear just which evidence would support it and which refute it. Questions and statements that cannot in principle be put to the test of evidence may be interesting, but they are not scientific.

Science is creative. Most scientific advances involve a leap of imagination. The use of logic and the close examination of evidence is necessary but not usually sufficient for making significant scientific discoveries. There is no series of steps that can lead unerringly to scientific truth.

Concerning the scientific enterprise:

Science goes on in many different settings simultaneously. Thus scientific workers may be found almost everywhere: working alone, as part of a small group, or as a member of a large research team; in offices, laboratories, observatories, and classrooms; in every country; and employed by universities, business and industry, government, independent research organizations, or scientific associations.

Science is done by people who collaborate with little regard for time or place. Scientists use each others' theories and data even though they may never have met or corresponded. Findings and ideas that are published at one time are used at another, perhaps years or decades later. To make this feasible, publication in sources available to everyone has become crucial to progress in science.

At any time, however, the scientific consensus does not extend to all matters, particularly those that are currently being vigorously studied by many investigators. Disagreement may persist for years, since scientific issues cannot be settled by vote or proclamation. In practice, some scientists are more highly regarded than others, but none have the authority—beyond the quality of their evidence and the logic of their argument—to declare scientific truth.

Principle 10: The science curriculum should include content that deals with the role of science in other human affairs.

Science is interesting for its own sake and because it has so much to do with our lives. Sometimes it causes us to change our notions about who we are and where we are in the scheme of things. Besides having its own value system and code of ethics, science influences those of the greater society. Through technology, science continues to make an enormous impact (with both good and bad effects) on agriculture, medicine, transportation, communications, and other central aspects of the modern world. And science, through its knowledge and techniques, has a major role to play in helping to find solutions for most of the social issues of the day—population growth, environmental pollution, acid rain, waste disposal, energy production, and birth control.

Project 2061 has operated on the principle that these social concerns ought to receive attention in science education. This is not to say that the science classroom is to be turned into a social studies experience, or that it should promote certain social views. Rather, it takes the position that the school, as part of its science responsibility, needs to find ways to help students recognize the connection of science to these issues and to understand the science necessary to deal with them intelligently. The following illustrations come from different parts of the draft report.

From the general chapter on the nature of science:

Scientific knowledge is often surprising and can be disquieting. Sometimes science discovers that we or our world are not as we perceive it or would like it to be. This can be so wrenching that it may take generations to come to terms with the new knowledge. Witness the difficulty society had in accepting the idea that the earth was not at the center of the universe, and the continuing resistance to the concept of the evolution of species. But there may be no way out: part of the price we pay for obtaining the knowledge we want from science is knowledge that makes us uncomfortable, at least initially.

From the social and behavioral sciences:

In addition to rules and regulations that help control behavior within groups, group affiliation usually brings with it ideas or attitudes that influence how people think and behave toward other people and groups. These group attitudes help to ensure cohesion within the group but can lead to hostility between groups. Attitudes toward other groups usually are based on the characteristics of the group as a whole, rather than on the characteristics of individual group members and are often simplistic and biased.

Criteria

Principle 11: The selection of the content of school science should be based on explicitly stated educational criteria.

The purpose of this principle is to foster thoughtful debate on what ought to be part of the science curriculum for all students. It matters less that the stated criteria afford precise standards for making decisions about proposed content than that they raise basic questions about the purposes of the science curriculum (existing or proposed), that they offer alternatives to authority and tradition, and that they provide a basis for eliminating some traditional topics from the curriculum.

Project 2061 identified five criteria for judging what all students ought to learn. Only those topics for which a strong case can be made in terms of one or more of the criteria will be included in the project recommendations. By implication, other criteria—the demands of college admission and advanced placement examinations, what is currently taught, or the structure of a particular science discipline—are not relevant. The Project 2061 criteria are:

Education for knowledge. Knowledge of the world around us—knowledge for its own sake, not for its utilitarian value—still remains a major purpose of general education. There are simply some things about the world, including ourselves and our works, that educated people ought to know. We may not be able to agree always on just what this fundamental knowledge is in every detail, and, to be sure, claims for absolute and immutable knowledge are no longer coin of the realm. Yet not all knowledge is of equal importance, and some, at any particular time, would seem to be so significant that no other justifications, "practical" or otherwise, would be necessary to set it out as part of the common core of education.

Such knowledge may be, by its nature, historical, political, aesthetic, mathematical or whatever. In this project the focus is on scientific and technological knowledge. "Scientific knowledge" is here taken in its fullest sense and meant to include some understanding of the *modus operandi*, impact, limitations, values and history of science, as well as of its conclusions about the nature of the world. Similarly, "technological knowledge" includes knowledge of the process of technological development, of how technologies do what they do, and of their expected and unexpected impacts.

Education for human meaning. Throughout recorded history, if not longer, certain enduring questions of human existence have persisted. Each new generation has had to confront anew the main questions of life and death, of who we are, where we are, and where we are headed. These questions and the themes and dilemmas of everyday living—perception and reality, freedom and responsibility, individual and community, and the like—are found, in one form or another, in every culture in every age.

During the last three centuries, the contexts in which these questions and themes have presented themselves have changed, often radically and rapidly, due largely to the impact of science and technology. Thus it may be possible to justify certain science and technology knowledge as part of the essential content of general education on the grounds of its relevance to questions of meaning and human curiosity.

Education for work and productivity. As a practical matter, the schools are also expected to prepare students for a changing and elusive job market, and for making useful contributions to the greater economic and security needs of our nation in a competitive world.

In this context, the questions become: which specific elements of science education—knowledge of key scientific laws and principles, a sense of how nature works, inquiry skills, quantitative thinking skills, an ability to learn new technical material, attitude toward knowledge, a regard for precision, or whatever—contribute most to an enhancement of the high school graduate's value to the economy and of his or her long-term employment prospects? Which technological skills, attitudes toward the use of new technologies, and knowledge of the fundamentals of technological processes are needed by all future workers? What can science teach us that would help develop a sense of having control over our occupational and economic futures?

Education for social responsibility. Whatever else it does, education should also prepare students for informed participation in a democratic society, enabling them to act responsibly in the light of the values and demands implicit in freedom. Creating a social fabric that is at once both open to change and stable is becoming increasingly difficult in every part of the world and, for the United States at least, is something that demands more than the attention of a small educated elite.

More and more the issues confronting our citizens—toxic waste disposal, the use of life-support systems, public opinion polling, and a hundred more—implicate science and technology as part of the problem and part of the solution. What knowledge, skills, and attitudes from the domains of science and technology are central to the preparation of tomorrow's citizens?

Education for childhood enrichment. Most children spend a dozen years of their lives in elementary and secondary schools. That is a substantial fraction of their lifespan, and a very special one at that. Childhood is a time of life that is important for its own sake, for the value of what happens then and there and not solely for what it may lead to later in life. Not all of childhood is preparation for adulthood; it is also for living.

Schooling should help young people learn how to gain deep and lasting satisfactions from their lives, and help them develop the insights and skills they need to deal effectively with their existing problems. Surely science—the right selection of science presented in the right way—can contribute both to an enrichment of childhood and adolescence and to the development of problem solving-skills that youngsters can use right away. The question then becomes, what science is most suitable for organizing around the interests and concerns of elementary and secondary students?

Toward the Future

The basic premise of Project 2061 is that the identification of science learning goals ought to come before the design of science curriculums. In undertaking such a task, we believe it is helpful to consider the issues of territory, purpose, and magnitude outlined in this paper. The set of recommendations does not purport to be the only possible set, but to be one that the scientific community and education community can support. Nor is it intended to lead to a single curriculum. Phase II of the project will enlist the collaboration of educators in several different settings, to explore various ways in which the basic recommendations can be implemented. The translation of Phase I recommendations into workable curriculums still requires extensive input by educators who know how children learn and what is possible in school settings.

6. Tomorrow's Emphasis in Foreign Language: Proficiency

Myriam Met

Mark Twain said he thought the French were pretty stupid because when he was in Paris, he never did succeed in making those idiots understand their own language. Not too many years later, H.L. Mencken noted that taking beginning French was a waste of time. He'd been to France and discovered that no one there speaks beginning French!

FOR THE FOREIGN LANGUAGE TEACHING PROFESSION, THE PAST 40 years have been a period marked by substantial evolution in research and practice. In fact, as a foreign language professional hardly past 40 myself, I'm experiencing the second major shift in my profession in 20 years. Dramatic changes are occurring in the content of the foreign language curriculum, just as they did when I first entered the profession some 20 years ago.

Today's foreign language curriculum focuses on meaningful language use and practice. The study of modern foreign languages* is oriented to helping students use language for meaningful purposes: to function effectively in both oral and written forms in the culture(s) where the language is spoken, whether here in the United States or abroad.

Foreign Language Instruction Yesterday

Ever since the Tower of Babel, humankind has tried to identify how people of different language groups and cultures can be taught to interact. Historically, languages, particularly classical languages, were taught using

*The focus of this paper is on modern foreign language instruction, which excludes languages such as Latin and classical Greek.

the grammar-translation method. Language study, it was believed, improved students' reasoning and analytical skills. Mastery of the language itself was only of secondary value; of primary importance was the contribution language study made to "disciplining the mind."

This philosophy was drastically altered, however, during World War II, which ended American isolationism. Many U.S. servicemen became aware that monolingualism prevented them from benefiting from the linguistic and cultural diversity they discovered while stationed abroad. Our role as a growing world power during and after the war required the government, as well as academic institutions, to develop new and effective means of enabling Americans to take their place in a changed world. That role required the ability to use foreign languages to communicate. Thus, for the first time in American education, the purpose of foreign language courses was thought to be development of oral skills. This change revolutionized the content and processes of foreign language instruction.

The next decade brought experimentation with new methods (such as the audio-lingual method) and content (the sequential grammar-based syllabus). Sputnik provided further impetus for support of foreign language study. Unlike previous foreign language curriculums, which prepared students to translate classical works into English, the "new key" instead emphasized speaking ability.

The audio-lingual method (ALM), in vogue from the late 1950s through the '60s, was based on Skinnerian psychology. It purported to develop foreign language facility by positive reinforcement of skills acquired through carefully sequenced and structured rote drill and practice. The content of this curriculum was a series of sequentially-determined grammatical rules, hierarchically arranged from the simple to the complex, as determined by structural linguists. The spoken language was viewed as rule-governed behavior, and, as such, was to be developed in the same manner as other habits. Since Skinnerian psychology was interpreted to mean that unobservable mental processes are irrelevant to learning, the instruction focused on overt student behavior. Little attention was paid to developing students' understanding of the system underlying the language.

Audio-lingual teachers drilled students endlessly on grammatical structures. We had repetition drills, substitution drills, transformation drills, chain drills, and drill drills. Repetition was such a predominant form of instruction that we seemed to be teaching parrots, not people. (In fact, the ALM method earned the nickname "planned parrothood.") Audio-lingualism's treatment of language as a habit formed through repetition, drill, and reinforcement resulted in students who could imitate but not speak, hear but not understand.

The cognitive code method evolved in reaction to the audio-lingual method. The cognitive code method was based on developing an understanding of the structure of the language (as defined by transformational grammarians) and then using that understanding to develop proficiency in the language. Both methods shared the goal of communication, and, thus, a similar content. Both methods also shared the assumption that mastery of the language's system of rules would result in ability to use the language for communication. That assumption was wrong.

Neither the ALM nor cognitive code method produced proficient users of language. At social gatherings, when we foreign language professionals identify ourselves, we are usually quickly told, "I took a foreign language for two years in high school and I can't speak a word of it." With both methods disappointing students and teachers, and with the diminished emphasis on the contribution of foreign language study to general mental development, small wonder that foreign language study in our schools declined.

The 1970s saw the emergence of a dichotomy between "linguistic" and "communicative" competence. Originally, these distinctions discriminated between knowledge about a language's phonology, lexicon, and grammar (linguistic competence) and the ability to "get the message across" (communicative competence). Advocates of communicative competence, concerned that knowledge of the linguistic system did not assure that learners could use language meaningfully, began to focus attention on the importance of meaning in foreign language instruction. At the extreme, communicative competence proponents and related theoreticians questioned the value of emphasizing overt grammar instruction and practice (Savignon 1972, Krashen 1982). The controversy over the role of direct grammar instruction continues in some quarters today, but most foreign language professionals agree that while instruction must be directed at enabling learners to use language purposefully, linguistic accuracy (developed, in part, through grammar instruction) contributes to effective communication.

Secondary School Foreign Language Instruction

Today, foreign language instruction is the beneficiary of two fortuitous trends. One is a growing recognition of the critical role of foreign language proficiency in addressing our nation's political, economic, and social agendas (*Strength through Wisdom* 1979). The other is the development of new processes and approaches to achieving proficiency in a foreign language. Both of these trends have direct impact on the content of the foreign language curriculum.

Nationally there has been a growing recognition that American monolingualism is an unfortunate but real contributor to the lack of American competitiveness in world markets. After all, it's hard to sell someone your product if you can't even describe it! In diplomacy, we are hindered by an inability to communicate openly and directly with those with whom we share critical interests. Indeed, diplomacy through translation has been likened to talking with a mouthful of feathers! Within the United States, there is a growing recognition that ethnic and linguistic diversity among our population will continue to increase for decades to come. Students may need second language skills whether they sell computers in Columbia or pizzas in Peoria; whether their neighbors are from Japan or Jacksonville. Indeed, second-language proficiency may well be a social and occupational survival skill in many American communities tomorrow for the students we are educating today.

The language skills required to meet the political, economic, and social language needs of our society are not those of the traditional language student. We must prepare students to function effectively both in oral and written form, in culturally appropriate ways, on a range of topics, within a range of social contexts, and with a degree of accuracy.

Research in sociolinguistics and psycholinguistics has affected the thinking of foreign language professionals. In particular, the burgeoning fields of discourse theory and communication theory have caused us to look beyond the grammar rules to understand a language's meaning. Neither the structural linguists, who were concerned with describing the constitutive elements of language, nor the transformational grammarians, who were concerned with the relationship between surface and deep structures of languages, were preoccupied with how language users get and convey meaning. Today we know that the surface form of a message may differ substantially from its intended meaning. For example, "You're standing on my toes" is more likely to be a request to "Please move now!" than a simple description.

Discourse theory has helped language educators focus more on language functions (what people do with language) than on how the language is put together (grammar rules and vocabulary). In Europe, English-as-a-foreign-language educators recognized that different learners had different objectives. Some students were learning English with a vocational goal, preparing to become engineers, salespersons, or receptionists; others just wanted to learn English to be travelers. The English for Special Purposes movement was instrumental in establishing differing curriculums for differing learner objectives. The Council of Europe established exemplary models of curriculums, based on language functions appropriate to learners' communicative purposes. For example, *Threshold Level English* specifies the language functions all learners need before specialization (Van Ek and Alexander 1975). Later, similar documents were developed for other languages.

In the United States, the European developments have had serious implications for the curriculum content. These developments, coupled with the growing demand within our country for a citizenry capable of communicating within and beyond its borders, have changed how we think about what we teach. The result is a new emphasis on communicative language teaching or teaching for proficiency.

Communicative Language Teaching/Teaching for Proficiency

Communicative ability is the goal of foreign language instruction today. Unlike previous goals of language instruction, proficiency-oriented instruction focuses on what the learner *can do with language* rather than what the learner *knows about language*.

Language proficiency is currently defined through the performance features of language function, communicative context, and level of accuracy. These variables are addressed in a proficiency-based curriculum. Language function refers to the purposes for which language is used, such as requesting, persuading, complaining, arguing, or inquiring. Each language interaction takes place within a communicative context. Thus, one might request a meal in a restaurant, a book in the library, a person's phone number, or assistance in changing a tire. Context also includes social register, determining the level of politeness, familiarity, or formality appropriate to the communicative interaction.

Language users vary in their degree of linguistic accuracy. The foreign language curriculum needs to specify the degree of accuracy with which students will be expected to produce language. In this model, accuracy is not simply defined by the number of mistakes made (or not made) but by the degree to which students can accurately interpret incoming messages and encode their own intents. Thus, in the receptive skills (listening and reading), accuracy refers to the degree to which the student can interpret with clarity, precision, and flexibility messages received. In production (speaking and writing), accuracy encompasses a measure of the appropriateness of the message with regard to the social and cultural context, the acceptability of the message to the listener, and to the precision and clarity with which the student can communicate intent (Galloway 1987).

The Content of the Proficiency-Based Curriculum

The content of the proficiency-based curriculum is defined by how language is to be used. The curriculum specifies the communicative purposes learners will be able to accomplish: what the learner will be able to talk about, read about, and write about; and how well. As such, function, context, and accuracy are specified in a proficiency-based curriculum. For example, the function of making requests may be set in the context of requesting information and food in a restaurant (What's on the menu? Is there a special today? Please bring me the . . .). The curriculum may note that at this level students may use a restricted number of verbs, requests will be made using simple grammatical structures, and the vocabulary will be limited to a certain number of food items.

The proficiency-based curriculum is spiraling and recursive. It would be impossible to teach at one time all the grammatical structures that exist just for making requests in a restaurant. (In English, for example, there are at least a dozen ways to request a menu item from the waiter.) There are also innumerable other contexts in which one makes requests. Thus, each of the language functions and contexts spirals back into the curriculum, and, with each re-visit, the functions and contexts are elaborated and expanded, along with the expectations for the degree of accuracy.

The content of a proficiency-based curriculum answers the question, "Proficient to do what?" Is the goal survival in another culture? Communication with the folks next door? Satisfaction of occupational needs? Curriculum developers determine the content of the foreign language curriculum by first generating a list of communicative purposes, and then relating these purposes to the settings in which the language learner will be expected to function.

The Content of the Curriculum: Vocabulary

Language functions and context have a direct bearing on the vocabulary to be taught. Because language functions are taught within the context of a given communicative setting, the vocabulary content of a proficiency-based curriculum is thematic: foods, clothing, the house. Topics for language functions at the earliest levels of instruction usually are based on survival skills. Typically, curriculums and texts provide units on the family, foods, personal health, clothing, and numbers.

In a proficiency-based curriculum, the content of early instructional units is heavily oriented to vocabulary development. At this level of instruction, at which simple communication is the objective, vocabulary carries most of the meaning load. It is possible to communicate meaningfully with a restricted grammar and an extensive vocabulary. For example, the traveler ordering a meal in a restaurant will be better served by a broad familiarity with food names in the foreign language than by knowing a dozen different ways to ask for something, each of which varies with appropriateness to politeness level or grammatical complexity.

Because the proficiency-based curriculum is tied to the learner's communicative purposes, the vocabulary content may be partially specified by the learner's needs and interests. This is particularly true at the lowest levels of instruction, which deal with immediate survival needs. Clearly, the learner should be enabled to develop an individualized vocabulary for personal needs and desires.

The Content of the Curriculum: Grammar

Until recently, it was believed that the goal of language instruction—communication—could best be achieved by mastery of the language's grammatical structures. Mastery of the pluperfect subjunctive, however, is no longer believed to be critical to one's success in communicating in a foreign language.

Grammar continues to play a role, however, in language teaching. The degree of accuracy required of language users increases with the sophistication of the language user's purposes and tasks. Certainly the traveler can afford to mix present and past tense. Perhaps the salesperson can do without all the subtleties of noun declensions; the diplomat cannot. As language learners progress, and the intended uses of the language become more elaborate and diverse, the need for precision and flexibility increases commensurately.

For accuracy to be achieved at the upper levels of instruction, attention must be given to grammar instruction at the earliest levels. However, grammar must be at the service of communication; it is not an end in itself. Further, the complexity and number of structures introduced in the lower levels of instruction may be dramatically reduced from those that have traditionally dominated the content of the foreign language curriculum. Indeed, despite a long tradition of the grammar-based syllabus, it is clear that what is taught is not always what is learned. Although as many as seven different tenses may be taught in the first two to three years of secondary school instruction, students typically use only one (and miraculously, sometimes two!) tenses in extemporaneous speech.

Determining the grammar content of the foreign language curriculum should be based less on tradition and more on the communicative purposes of the learner. Traditionally, the present tense has been introduced early in the curriculum, the past tense much later. Yet in real life communication, it may be necessary to be able to talk about past events right from the start. Criteria for determining the content of the grammar component of the curriculum are suggested by the following questions (Galloway 1984 as cited in Medley 1985, p. 33; also Galloway, personal communication, 1987):

- How frequently is this structure found in authentic language use?
- How simple/complex is the concept?
- How badly does the student need to master this in order to use the language effectively?
- How interested is the student in learning to use this structure?
- To what degree is the native speaker irritated by misuse of this structure?
- How versatile is this structure?
- How many real-life functions can be carried out with this structure?
- How much time is required for internalization?

An additional consideration in specifying the content of the grammar component is the nature of the student's developing language skills. Research on student errors and on students' developing language systems ("interlanguage") indicates that the nature of students' errors reveals substantial information about students' language growth (Corder 1967). Error analysis may be used as a means to determine structures which the student may have already mastered, be ready to learn, or need to refine.

Developing Foreign Language Skills

While the profession has interpreted commmunicative competence as the ability to use language meaningfully in both oral and written form, proficiency-based instruction has been misinterpreted by some as a focus on speaking. Yet function, context, and accuracy determine the content for the development of all four of the traditional language skills: listening, speaking, reading, and writing. Students learn to comprehend language related to given topics; they learn to speak, read, and write about them as well.

Research on the role of listening comprehension in language development has led to an increased emphasis on the development of listening skills (Winitz 1981, Krashen 1982, Met 1984). Studies have shown that receptive skills generally exceed and precede productive skills. Comprehension-based approaches to language instruction allow students ample opportunities to match sound with meaning before requiring students to produce language. If students are to function effectively in communicative settings, clearly they must learn to understand the answers as well as to ask the questions.

In both the receptive skill areas of listening and reading, the use of authentic materials has been emphasized—listening and reading materials which come directly from the target culture, not those created only to meet the linguistic needs of the syllabus. Students must be prepared to function in authentic, communicative settings, and preparation can best be achieved by structured and supported contact with authentic materials.

> If 'communicative competence,' not knowledge about language, is our aim, then language must be reconnected to its natural setting and purpose, and thereby regain its own naturalness and authenticity (Byrnes 1985, p. 101).

Thus, the materials used to deliver the curriculum content may be films, television or radio tapes, magazines, newspapers, original works of literature, and other print and non-print media directly from areas where the language is spoken.

While language functions dominate the curriculum for development of oral skills, they are also the basis of written communication. Schema theory suggests that the background knowledge and experience of the reader influence the interaction between the reader and text, resulting in text interpretation. The foreign language curriculum must assist learners to develop new, or to expand existing, schemata by providing the information, both cultural and experiential, required to construct accurate meaning from text. Further, the print media serve a variety of communicative purposes. Foreign language students must learn to apply a range of reading strategies—skimming, scanning, reading for literal or interpretive meaning—in order to interact appropriately with the communicative intents of different forms of written materials.

Written communication requires that the foreign language curriculum include opportunities to write for a variety of purposes and audiences. Real-life written communication does not usually involve extensive opportunities for expository writing such as compositions. Beyond expository writing, however, real-life writing also includes taking notes, making lists for personal reminders (grocery lists, lists of things to do), writing brief notes, and correspondence. Such forms of writing should be used for students to communicate their thoughts or experiences within the language functions and contexts that form the content of the curriculum. Using a process approach to writing instruction allows students to assess the effectiveness of their written product as a communicative device. The process approach also enhances classroom opportunities for students to use their oral language skills to engage in meaningful, purposeful dialogue through peer response groups.

Culture in the Foreign Language Curriculum

Language is an inextricable part of culture. As such, communicative language teaching must develop students' cultural knowledge and skills to apply it.

The foreign language curriculum includes instruction in the "culture" and "Culture" of the people who speak the target language. The "culture" of a language includes the lifestyles, customs, and traditions of its speakers, and their attitudes, values, and beliefs. The "Culture" of a language encompasses literary, artistic, and historical features. Knowledge of both "culture" and "Culture" should be the basis for further student growth leading to appreciation of cultural differences and to a heightened sensitivity to one's own culture.

Students should also be enabled to connect language and culture. For example, among the most obvious differences between English and many other languages is that English no longer distinguishes between formal and informal modes of address (thou and you) while many other languages do (tu/Usted; tu/vous; du/Sie). In those languages, the ability to make these distinctions in speech is critical to one's effectiveness as a communicator. Other distinctions, such as the subjunctive vs. the indicative or perfect vs. imperfect past tense forms, carry meanings for native speakers that reflect a different way of understanding and organizing the world. Communication is enhanced to the degree that students are sensitized to these differences and can operate within the cultural framework that determines the use of specific linguistic forms.

Culture underlies effective comprehension and production of a foreign language. What you say, how you say it, and to whom you may or may not say it determines the expression of language functions within a given cultural context. In effect, without the development of cultural understanding, it is difficult to develop any real communication skills in another language, because the very nature of the contexts in which the language functions are used varies from culture to culture. Clearly, culture must be an integral part of the foreign language curriculum and integrated with all other curriculum contents.

The ACTFL Proficiency Guidelines

In recent years the American Council on the Teaching of Foreign Languages (ACTFL) has produced descriptors of the proficiency of foreign language learners. The purpose of the guidelines is to provide a common metric for the assessment of foreign language proficiency in listening, speaking, reading, and writing. The guidelines, recently revised and disseminated in a more refined form, describe how learners function at various developmental levels (*ACTFL Proficiency Guidelines* 1986). The guidelines are based on function, context, and accuracy, describing what a learner can do, under what circumstances and how well, at proficiency levels ranging from novice low to superior. Of these, the most refined and most commonly used are the oral proficiency guidelines. Developed in cooperation with Educational Testing Service, the oral guidelines are an adaptation and expansion of the oral proficiency interview developed by the Foreign Service Institute. Here is an example from the proficiency guidelines for the intermediate-mid level in speaking:

> Able to handle successfully a variety of uncomplicated, basic and communicative tasks and social situations. Can talk simply about self and family members. Can ask and answer questions and participate in simple conversations on topics beyond the most immediate needs; e.g., personal history and leisure-time activities. Utterance length increases slightly, but speech may continue to be characterized by frequent long pauses, since the smooth incorporation of even basic conversational strategies is often hindered as the speaker struggles to create appropriate language forms. Pronunciation may continue to be strongly influenced by first language and fluency may still be strained. Although misunderstandings still arise, the Intermediate-Mid speaker can generally be understood by sympathetic interlocutors.

In contrast, here is an example from the superior level in speaking:

> Able to speak the language with sufficient accuracy to participate effectively in most formal and informal conversations on practical, social, professional, and abstract topics. Can discuss special fields of competence and interest with ease. Can support opinions and hypothesize, but may not be able to tailor language to audience or discuss in depth highly abstract or unfamiliar topics. The Superior-level speaker commands a wide variety of interactive strategies and shows good awareness of discourse strategies. The latter involves the ability to distinguish main ideas from supporting information through syntactic, lexical, and suprasegmental features (pitch, stress, intonation). Sporadic errors may occur, particularly in low-frequency structures and some complex high-frequency structures more common to formal writing, but no patterns of error are evident. Errors do not disturb the native speaker or interfere with communication.

The ACTFL guidelines make a critically needed contribution to foreign language instruction. However, they are not statements of instructional goals. They do not measure *achievement* in the sense of measuring curricular outcomes, and they do not measure small increments of learning. They are intended to be independent of curriculum. But, in effect, there has been a move to use the guidelines as an outcome-driven basis for curriculum development. Some authors advocate that proficiency-oriented curriculum be developed with reference to the skills delineated in the guidelines (Medley 1985, p. 17). In local school districts across the country this advice has been taken to heart, resulting in curriculum guides closely aligned to the ACTFL guidelines. Despite the fact that the ACTFL guidelines clearly state that proficiency levels are not to be equated with years of instruction, some school district curriculums even specify equivalencies between levels of instruction and levels of proficiency.

While the ACTFL guidelines are a promising direction for the measurement of an individual's language performance, they are still in the developmental stage. Studies are under way to evaluate the guidelines, but as yet there are no available hard data on their validity or reliability (Dandonoli 1987). Because the ACTFL guidelines are not intended to bear a clear and direct relationship with foreign language instruction, and until demonstrable evidence is available that proficiency assessments based on them are indeed both reliable and valid, school districts should move very cautiously in developing curriculums based on the ACTFL guidelines.

Elementary School Foreign Language Instruction

There has been a resurgence of programs of foreign language instruction in the elementary grades during the last decade. These programs are generally classified as FLEX, FLES, or immersion (Met et al. 1983).

Foreign Language Experience (FLEX)

FLEX refers to a program of language instruction in which students gain exposure to one or more foreign languages and cultures, learning basic words and phrases. FLEX classes generally meet for 15-20 minutes two to three times weekly and are most often found in the upper elementary grades.

The language content of the FLEX curriculum is limited; its goal is simple exposure and limited mastery of language skills. No serious attempt is made to enable students to use vocabulary in connected discourse or for extended communicative purposes.

The content of some FLEX curriculums is primarily cultural. Ideally, the FLEX curriculum can be designed to bear a strong relationship to the content of the social studies curriculum in the elementary school. For example, FLEX students can learn about patterns of family living, shelter, food, schooling, customs, and traditions related to the target culture. This FLEX content can be quite similar to many of the units in the primary social studies curriculum which focus on the ways family living patterns, communities, and regions are similar around the globe. For example, many first graders learn that families around the world are very much like theirs, and that the roles family members play may be the same or different from their own. Later, students compare their community or region with others, discovering that all communities have needs which are met by services and products available within the community. What the services and products are may vary with the priorities each community sets. In this social studies orientation, it is natural for the FLEX teacher to highlight the role of the French *concierge* or the Spanish *portero* as a service common to the target culture and rare in the United States.

Foreign Language in the Elementary School (FLES)

FLES is a program of language instruction begun in any grade K-6, offered up to 40 minutes from two to five times weekly. The objectives of FLES programs are to develop students' language skills within a limited range. Most FLES programs emphasize listening and speaking; some offer no instruction at all in reading and writing. All FLES programs include cultural objectives.

On the surface, the content of the FLES curriculum looks like a junior vocabulary version of the secondary foreign language curriculum. While the vocabulary content of most FLES curriculums parallels that of most first-year secondary courses, the grammar content does not. In FLES, thematic vocabulary units prevail, with minimal amounts of grammar included when necessary. (For example, few FLES students ever learn anything but the present tense.) Indeed, the major difference between FLES and its older sibling in the secondary school is the reduced role of grammar in the curriculum, and therefore in classroom activities. Traditionally, grammar has ruled the secondary curriculum but not that of the elementary grades—young children simply won't put up with explanations about double object pronouns, nor can you get them to practice grammar drills for very long without resulting chaos. As a result, FLES programs discovered long ago that successful programs are communicative programs. (Those programs that didn't discover this are now defunct.)

FLES teachers provide students with language activities that are meaningful and purposeful. The content of the curriculum itself is geared to things children *want* to talk about: themselves, their families, school (numbers, colors, days of the week) and social activities. The emphasis on communication skills may be gaining momentum at the secondary level, but successful elementary-level programs have been communicative all along.

Immersion

A more intensive and innovative form of elementary school foreign language instruction is immersion. In immersion, the regular school curriculum is taught in a foreign language. Formal language teaching is only a minimal part of the instructional program, since this program model uses many of the same processes that operate when children acquire their first language. In the United States, immersion programs usually begin in kindergarten or first grade; they may be total (the entire school day taught in the language) or partial (half the school day taught in the language). Students in total immersion programs learn to read and write in the foreign language before they learn to read and write in English; later, in grade 2 or 3, English language arts are introduced and, gradually, other subjects taught in English are integrated into the program. Of FLEX, FLES, and immersion, the latter is the most effective in developing language proficiency (Gray 1984). Indeed, of all in-school foreign language instructional models, no program has ever been shown to be more effective than total immersion.

Of all elementary programs, the content of the immersion approach is the most clearly defined: it is, quite simply, the content of the elementary school curriculum. In total immersion, students learn reading/language arts, mathematics, science, social studies, and sometimes art, music, and physical education, in the foreign language. Foreign language itself is not a separate subject; however, language skills are addressed in the language arts component of the curriculum using the same objectives as those of the English curriculum. In partial immersion, some of the subjects (usually mathematics, and/or science, and/or social studies) are taught in the foreign language, with the remainder of the curriculum taught in English. Foreign language instruction is included in a "foreign language arts" block. The content of immersion curriculums parallels that of the elementary curricular areas, but the activities, materials, and approaches to evaluation used by teachers must differ to account for students' linguistic limitations (Met and Lorenz in press).

Foreign Language Instruction Tomorrow

We've come a long way from the days when students, clutching their dictionaries, toiled laboriously over classic works of literature to render them sensible in English. Today's emphasis on communication promises to reap positive results. But change is slow, and many promising practices need to be cultivated.

First and foremost, the theoretical premises delineated for the proficiency-based curriculum have to be put into practice. While the leadership of the profession has moved forward in giant steps, classroom change has not kept pace. Curriculum development (or revision) is a time-consuming and costly process, and most school districts have not yet garnered the resources needed to begin. Many are only just starting to revise the content of their curriculums. Some, adjusting slowly to change, cannot bear to forsake the traditional grammar-based syllabus. They produce strange hybrids that, in attempting to bridge conflicting theoretical positions, wind up being neither fish nor fowl. A few others have moved forward more boldly and have attempted to make radical changes. For the moment, however, proficiency-based curriculums exist more in the professional literature than they do in classrooms.

Dramatic changes in curriculum content will have significant implications for the retooling of the professional staff, for the development of new professionals entering our field, for the instructional materials we use, and ultimately, for the way in which programs and teachers are evaluated.

In a field that has (unfortunately) traditionally been textbook driven, change in what we teach may be determined more by textbook publishers than by curriculums. For many teachers, the textbook becomes the curriculum. Until textbooks become proficiency-based, instead of discrete-grammar-based, the pace of change may be determined more by economic factors than by instructional ones.

The Role of Grammar, Drill, and Communication

Grammar has traditionally been the keystone of foreign language instruction. The grammar-based syllabus is so deeply ingrained in foreign language teachers that some cannot conceive of language instruction without grammar as the organizing principle. Clearly, the new foreign language curriculum must have *communication* as its organizing principle.

That is not to say the grammar will be gone and forgotten. Accurate communicators are more effective communicators. There will always be a place for grammar instruction, but its role will be different. First, we must provide students opportunities to apply grammar in real communicative activities. While rote drill may be required for initial mastery of forms and structures, rote drill must quickly lead to application activities. Teachers must insure that skill-getting activities are well balanced with skill-using activities.

Second, if we are to be true to our goal of putting meaning above all, then grammar must also be meaning-oriented. Too often, grammar rules are divorced from the role grammar plays in real life to distinguish meaning. Obviously, the *-ed* ending on verbs in English tells us something about when events take place. How foolish it would be to learn to conjugate all the verbs in the past tense without focusing extensively on the notion that when you hear (or say, or read, or write) *-ed* at the end of the verb, there's a meaningful message communicated by it. The bane of students' existence—the subjunctive—would be ever so much easier to teach if teachers first focused on the differences in meaning that the subjunctive conveys. Native speakers understand messages framed in the subjunctive to *mean* differently from those in the indicative; if our students were sensitized to the nuances conveyed, they would have far less difficulty in knowing when to put their own messages in either of those modes. Instruction in the distinctions between the perfect and imperfect past tenses, the partitive, and many other grammatical distinctions would be well served if our approach to grammar were to be meaning-based.

Implications of the Elementary School Curriculum

One of the most promising trends in elementary school language teaching (seen also in the field of teaching English to speakers of other languages) is experimentation with content-based language instruction. In content-based instruction, one or two academic content areas are taught exclusively in the foreign language. Obviously, immersion is the ultimate form of content-based language instruction. But programs in which language instruction is provided for only 30 minutes, two or five times a week, can use the techniques and strategies of immersion to teach academic content instead of language content. Thus, a FLES program might consist of 30 minutes daily of art or music or physical education instruction taught entirely in the foreign language, substituting for English language instruction in those subjects. For example, one program offers students the opportunity to learn Arabic, Chinese, Japanese, or Russian beginning in kindergarten taught through the content of art, music, and physical education (*Cincinnati Public Schools Alternative Programs* brochure 1987).

Content-enriched FLES programs do not substitute foreign language for English instruction in the content areas; rather, they supplement English language instruction of concepts in selected content areas with foreign language activities which provide concept enrichment and extension. For example, if fifth graders are studying weather patterns in science, a FLES teacher may have students chart rainfall, temperature, and daily weather in selected cities where the foreign language is spoken, conducting these activities entirely in the language. Cooperative planning between content teachers and language teachers is required to insure the best possible instructional program for children.

A new proposition in immersion is to tie the content of the foreign language arts curriculum with that of the elementary subject areas (Genesee, Met, and Snow in preparation). Rather than specify language skills objectives in isolation from the content areas, planners of immersion curriculum identify the language structures and vocabulary domains necessary to learn that particular content. Such language is content-obligatory—you just can't learn the content without it. For example, to teach an inquiry lesson to first graders on objects that float/sink, you need to develop the language of questioning, the language of hypothesizing, and the terms for float and sink.

Some language skills fit nicely with given content areas, but are not obligatory for concept development. These language skills are content-compatible. For example, if a foreign language arts objective is skill in the use of 'if-clauses,' an immersion fifth grade social studies lesson might include an activity in which students complete the sentence, "If Christopher Columbus had been from France. . . ."

Immersion instruction and other forms of content-based foreign language curriculum are the ultimate in communicative language teaching. Language is a tool for communicating; it is not an end in itself. It is for talking, reading, writing, and listening about things other than language. Traditionally, students have found it hard to sustain an interest in discussing the numbers, the days of the week, or the use of the subjunctive in if-clauses. Communicative language teaching remedies the tedium of discussing language and its structure by giving students something else to talk about, something the students themselves want to discuss.

If the language classroom is the place where you talk about things, why not talk about the content of the curriculum? In elementary schools content-based approaches can integrate other curriculum areas; in the secondary foreign language classroom the academic content can be the culture content of the curriculum. One university has experimented with teaching its culture course in the medium of a foreign language, substituting this course for a language course. The results were impressive: students learned language and culture simultaneously (Lafayette and Buscaglia 1985). Tomorrow's foreign language curriculum in the secondary school should expand the content of language class beyond the survival needs of the student to other contents as well. The new immersion distinctions of content-obligatory and content-compatible language can serve to define the language content of those courses. Such a novel approach would move us dramatically beyond simple social interaction in the direction of preparing our students to function effectively in a foreign language.

***

An ancient Chinese curse warns, "May you live in interesting times." Today's foreign language professional lives in the most interesting time this century. We have the attention of the public, the support of those with economic and political clout, and enthusiasm within our own field. We have a chance to make a real difference by changing what we teach so we can change how we teach. The future will be very interesting.

References

American Council on the Teaching of Foreign Languages. *ACTFL Proficiency Guidelines*. Hastings-on-Hudson, N.Y.: ACTFL, 1986.

Byrnes, Heidi. "Teaching Toward Proficiency: The Receptive Skills." In *Proficiency, Curriculum, Articulation: The Ties that Bind*, edited by Alica Omaggio (Northeast Conferences Reports). Middlebury, Vt.: Northeast Conference on the Teaching of Foreign Languages, 1985.

Corder, S. Pit. "The Significance of Learners' Errors." *International Review of Applied Linguistics* 5 (1967): 161-170.

Dandonoli, Patricia. "ACTFL's Current Research on Testing." In *Defining and Developing Proficiency Guidelines, Implementations and Concepts* (ACTFL Foreign Language Education Series) edited by Heidi Byrnes and Michael Canale. Lincolnwood, Ill.: National Textbook Company, 1987.

Galloway, Vicki. "From Defining to Developing Proficiency: A Look at the Decisions." In *Defining and Developing Proficiency Guidelines, Implementations and Concepts* (ACTFL Foreign Language Education Series), edited by Heidi Byrnes and Michael Canale. Lincolnwood, Ill.: National Textbook Company, 1987.

Gray, Tracy, C., et al. *Comparative Evaluation of Elementary School Foreign Language Programs. Final Report*. 1984. [ED 238 255]

Krashen, Stephen D. *Principles and Practice in Second Language Acquisition*. New York: Pergamon Press, 1982.

Lafayette, Robert C., and Michael Buscaglia. "Students Learn Language via a Civilization Course—A Comparison of Second Language Classroom Environments." *Studies in Second Language Acquisition* 18, 3 (October 1985): 323-342.

Medley, Frank W., Jr. "Designing the Proficiency-Based Curriculum." In *Proficiency, Curriculum, Articulation: The Ties that Bind* (Northeast Conference Reports), edited by Alice C. Omaggio. Middlebury, Vt.: Northeast Conference on the Teaching of Foreign Languages, 1985.

Met, Myriam. "Listening Comprehension and the Young Second Language Learner." *Foreign Language Annals* 17, 5 (October 1984): 519-523.

Met, Myriam, Helena Anderson, Evelyn Brega, and Nancy Rhodes. "Elementary School Language: Key Link in the Chain of Learning." In *Foreign Languages: Key Links in the Chain of Learning*. Middlebury, Vt.: Northeast Conference on the Teaching of Foreign Languages, 1983.

Savignon, Sandra J. *Communicative Competence: An Experiment in Foreign Language Teaching*. Philadelphia: Center for Curriculum Development, 1972.

Strength through Wisdom: A Critique of U.S. Capability. A Report to the President from the President's Commission on Foreign Language and International Studies. Washington, D.C.: U.S. Government Printing Office, 1979. [Reprinted in *Modern Language Journal* 64 (1980): 9-57.]

Van Ek, J.A., and L.G. Alexander. *Threshold Level English* (Council of Europe). New York: Pergamon Press, 1975.

For Further Reading

Academic Preparation for College. What Students Need to Know and Be Able to Do. New York: The College Board, 1983.

Academic Preparation in Foreign Language. Teaching for Transition from High School to College. New York: The College Board, 1986.

Allen, Wendy. "Toward Cultural Proficiency." In *Proficiency, Curriculum, Articulation: The Ties that Bind* (Northeast Conference Reports), edited by Alice Omaggio. Middlebury, Vt.: Northeast Conference on the Teaching of Foreign Languages, 1985.

Ariew, Robert. "The Textbook as Curriculum." In *Curriculum, Competence, and the Foreign Language Teacher* (ACTFL Foreign Language Education Series), edited by Theodore V. Higgs. Skokie, Ill.: National Textbook Company, 1982.

Blair, Robert W., ed. *Innovative Approaches to Language Teaching*. Rowley, Mass.: Newbury House, 1982.

Cates, G. Truett, and Janet King Swaffar. *Reading a Second Language*. Washington, D.C.: Center for Applied Linguistics, 1979. [ED 176 588]

Gaudiani, Claire. *Teaching Writing in the Foreign Language Curriculum*. Washington, D.C.: Center for Applied Linguistics, 1981. [ED 209 960]

Guntermann, Gail, and June K. Phillips. *Functional-Notional Concepts: Adapting the Foreign Language Textbook*. Washington, D.C.: Center for Applied Linguistics, 1982. [ED 217 698]

Heilenman, Laura K., and Isabelle Kaplan. "Proficiency in Practice: The Foreign Language Curriculum." In *Foreign Language Proficiency in the Classroom and Beyond* (ACTFL Foreign Language Education Series). Lincolnwood, Ill.: National Textbook Company, 1984.

James, Charles J., ed. *Foreign Language Proficiency in the Classroom and Beyond* (ACTFL Foreign Language Education Series). Lincolnwood, Ill.: National Textbook Company, 1984.

James, Charles J. "Learning from Proficiency: The Unifying Principle." In *Foreign Language Proficiency in the Classroom and Beyond* (ACTFL Foreign Language Education Series). Lincolnwood, Ill.: National Textbook Company, 1984.

Kramsch, Claire J. "Proficiency vs. Achievement: Reflections on the Proficiency Movement." *ADFL Bulletin* 18, i (1986): 22-24.

Krashen, Stephen D. "Applications of Psycholonguistic Research to the Classroom." In *Practical Applications of Research in Foreign Language Teaching* (ACTFL Foreign Language Education Series). Skokie, Ill.: National Textbook Company, 1983.

Larsen-Freeman, Diane. *Techniques and Principles in Language Teaching*. New York: Oxford University Press, 1986.

Liskin-Gasparro, Judith. "The ACTFL Proficiency Guidelines: A Historical Perspective." In *Teaching for Proficiency, the Organizing Principle* (ACTFL Foreign Language Education Series). Lincolnwood, Ill.: National Textbook Company, 1984.

Liskin-Gasparro, Judith. "The ACTFL Proficiency Guidelines: Gateway to Testing and Curriculum." *Foreign Language Annals* 17, v (1984): 475-489.

Magnan, Sally Sieloff. "Teaching and Testing Proficiency in Writing: Skills to Transcend the Second-Language Classroom." In *Proficiency, Curriculum, Articulation: The Ties that Bind* (Northeast Conference Reports). Middlebury, Vt.: Northeast Conference on the Teaching of Foreign Languages, 1985.

Omaggio, Alice C. *Teaching Language in Context: Proficiency-Oriented Instruction*. Boston, Mass.: Heinle and Heinle, 1986.

Savignon, Sandra J. *Communicative Competence: Theory and Practice*. Reading, Mass.: Addison-Wesley, 1983.

Savignon, Sandra J. "Evaluation of Cummunicative Competence: The ACTFL Provisional Proficiency Guidelines." *The Modern Language Journal* 69, ii (1985): 129-134.

Slager, William R. "Creating Contexts for Language Practice." In *Developing Communication Skills: General Considerations and Specific Techniques*, edited by Elizabeth Joiner and Patrick Westphal. Rowley, Mass.: Newbury House, 1978.

Valdman, Albert. "Communicative Use of Language and Syllabus Design." *Foreign Language Annals* 11, v (1978): 567-578.

7. What Students Should Learn in the Arts

Paul R. Lehman

EDUCATORS' DISAGREEMENTS OVER WHAT TO TEACH IN ENGlish, math, and science seem minor compared with the jumble of conflicting ideas, assumptions, and practices one finds in the arts. Sometimes the diversity of opinion seems even greater within each of the arts than among them. Yet more agreement than is apparent exists concerning what the goals of arts education should be and how they can best be achieved.

I review in this chapter what should be taught in each of the arts and try to summarize and synthesize the learnings contemporary arts educators consider fundamental. I make four assumptions that guide what I believe should be included in an arts program:

1. *The arts are an essential part of the curriculum and should be an important component in the educational program of every young person.* Every writer and thinker who has made a major contribution to Western educational thought since Plato has emphasized the importance of the arts in education. This is no less true of the major contributors to the current debate on educational reform.[1] Most of the public seems to believe that the arts belong among the basic subjects of the curriculum, though this broad general support cannot always be translated into specific support when it is needed.

2. *The arts require serious study*. They cannot be learned through random or casual experiences any more than math or biology can. They require regular, systematic programs of sequential study leading to clearly specified outcomes. There is, indeed, content in the arts beyond superficial liking, warm feelings, and a vague belief in their inherent goodness. That content consists of skills and knowledge; the arts are not merely fun and games.

[1]See, for example, Ernest Boyer, *High School* (New York: Harper & Row, 1983), 97-98; John Goodlad, *A Place Called School* (New York: McGraw-Hill, 1983), 134-136, 286-287; Mortimer Adler, *The Paideia Proposal* (New York: Macmillan, 1982), 22-24; The College Board, *Academic Preparation for College* (New York: The College Board, 1983), 16-18.

3. *The arts program should be directed to all students and not only to the talented*. Many professionals in the arts got their start in the schools, but preprofessional training is not the reason for offering an arts program. The arts belong in the schools because of the joy, enrichment, and fulfillment they can bring to every human being. They are an essential part of the cultural heritage of every American and the essence of civilization. They are not for an elite; they are for everyone.

4. *There is no such thing as "arts education" as a single entity*. Arts education is simply a convenient term for referring, collectively, to education in the disciplines of music, art, theatre, and dance. These disciplines have much in common, but each has its own content, language, and traditions that must be learned separately. Brief instruction in "the arts" can be useful in pointing out their commonalities, but no comprehensive program can be built on the notion that the arts represent a single field of study.

The State of the Arts

People often speak of the problems facing the arts in the schools as though the same problems affect all of the arts. In fact, however, the problems of theatre and dance in the schools are very different from those of music and art, because theatre and dance have a very different status than music and art.

Music and art are widely accepted as part of the curriculum, and almost every school system in the nation employs teachers of music and art. Although some music and art programs have suffered cutbacks in recent years, and fewer children are experiencing balanced, quality programs, a vast structure is still in place for teaching music and art in the schools. This structure does not exist for theatre and dance, for several reasons:

- There is an entrenched procedure for training music and art teachers for the schools, but far fewer programs to train teachers in theater and dance. As a result, there are far more music and art teachers than theatre and dance teachers.
- State laws provide for certification of music and art teachers, seldom for theatre and dance teachers.
- Many state and local curriculum guides specify curriculum in music and art. There are fewer in theatre and dance.
- Most important, music and art education have abundant model programs in every state, traditions of excellence in instruction in many communities, and clear expectations from the community. This is far rarer in theater and dance.

While music and art are confronted with many problems in today's schools, theater and dance face even more. Theatre is widely considered an adjunct of the speech program, or perhaps even of the English literature program. Dance, where it exists at all, is often considered a division of physical education. Neither of these perceptions reflects an understanding of the aesthetic nature or the educational potential of the two disciplines. Recognizing the distinction between the status of music and art and the status of theatre and dance is essential in any serious effort to improve the standing of the arts in the schools.

Who Determines What Is Taught?

How do we decide what is taught in the arts? Who makes that determination? There is no simple answer in any branch of learning. The complexity is even greater in the arts, and the nuances less well understood. Textbooks play a less important role in the arts than in other disciplines; for one thing, there are fewer of them. They are important only in elementary general music, and even there it is unclear whether they determine practice or reflect it.

Colleges and universities, through their teacher education programs, play a major role in determining the arts curriculum. Whatever consensus exists regarding the arts curriculum is due in part to the preservice and inservice functions of colleges and universities. But, again, it is unclear whether they are shaping the curriculum or reacting to it.

Professional associations in the arts also play an important role in determining what is taught, and that role is probably more critical in the arts than in other fields. Their influence extends well beyond their members; professional associations, at both the state and national levels, produce the publications that lay the groundwork for curriculum construction and provide implicit guidance for many key decisions. Even more important, the associations provide a forum for the dialogues that continually reshape the curriculum.

The public, too, plays a major role in content decisions. Public expectations are more important in determining the place of the arts in schools than that of, for instance, foreign languages or social studies. The other disciplines are far less dependent on short-term, superficial yet influential public support. Whether the high school will have a marching band and whether that band will perform in the local Halloween parade, or whether the elementary art classes will take part in the spring art fair exhibit sponsored by the local public library are decisions that depend heavily on public support.

And, of course, the arts are also heavily dependent on the cooperation and support of school administrators, who control funds, facilities, and scheduling.

Finally, what is taught in the arts depends on the whims and idiosyncrasies of individual teachers, which has contributed to the lack of a clearly defined common core of skills and knowledge of the kind taken for granted in other subjects. Almost without exception, arts programs are in urgent need of more structure and sequence. They need clearer statements of expectations at each grade level so that administrators and the public will know what outcomes to expect. A program with no clear expectations cannot be taken seriously.

The catalog of desired learnings presented here is based on lists of learnings developed and recommended by the national professional associations of arts educators and on the curriculum materials of various state departments of education, materials developed by professional arts educators. They represent the collective judgment of professionals who have spent their careers teaching music, art, theatre, and dance in the schools.

These learnings are ambitious, to be sure, but they can be achieved. In a single list they may seem overwhelming, but many are less formidable than they appear. Schools achieve each of these learnings every day, though it is unlikely that any one school achieves all of them to a significant extent. Still, they represent realistic and useful goals for any school system making a serious effort to establish a balanced curriculum. Schools can achieve them to a much higher level than at present if administrators provide at least minimal staff and time and if art teachers are committed to them.

Music

The purpose of teaching music in the schools is to develop as fully as possible students' abilities to perform, create, and understand music. The elementary and secondary program should be designed to produce individuals who:

- are able to make music, alone and with others,
- are able to improvise and create music,
- are able to use the vocabulary and notation of music,
- are able to respond to music aesthetically, intellectually, and emotionally,
- are acquainted with a wide variety of music, including diverse musical styles and genres,
- understand the role music has played and continues to play in people's lives,
- are able to make aesthetic judgments based on critical listening and analysis,
- have developed a commitment to music,
- support the musical life of the community and encourage others to do so,
- are able to continue their musical learning independently.[2]

These outcomes apply to students who receive only the required instruction. Students who take elective courses in music will develop specialized skills and greater knowledge. For example, students who play or sing

[2] *The School Music Program: Description and Standards*, 2nd ed. (Reston, Va.: Music Educators National Conference, 1986), 13-14.

in a performing group should be able to perform the standard literature for their instrument or voice, and should be able to play or sing with greater skill than the student who has not had this experience.

In the elementary and middle schools, musical learnings may be categorized as (1) performing and reading music, (2) creating music, and (3) listening to and describing music.

Grades K-3[3]

The early years are a time of growth, wonder, excitement, exploration, and discovery. These years are crucial as the child learns musical concepts, gains fundamental skills, and develops sensitivity to the beauty of musical sounds. All children need regular and continuous musical experiences that lead to satisfaction through success in producing musical sounds and using them enjoyably.

In grades K through 3, children should come to realize that music is an important part of everyday life. They should respect music and its performance and creation, display a sense of enjoyment when participating in music, and use music as a means of personal enjoyment.

By the end of grade 3, students should be able to sing in tune using a clear, free tone and appropriate musical expression. They should be able to sing from memory a repertoire of folk and composed songs, and they should know the basic symbols of music notation. Children in the early grades should also be able to respond to music by means of physical movement, and to play simple patterns on melodic and rhythm instruments.

Students should be able to improvise and create short pieces and accompaniments using their voices, classroom instruments, or nontraditional sound sources. They should be able to create "answers" to unfinished phrases and new stanzas to familiar melodies.

Attention to music-listening skills is particularly important in the early grades. Students should be able to recognize the differences between high and low pitches, long and short tones, repeated and contrasting phrases, slow and fast tempos, duple and triple meters, major and minor modes, and other contrasting sound patterns. They should recognize the timbre of basic wind, string, and percussion instruments, and should be able to describe stylistic characteristics in musical terms. They should also be able to identify the patterns of simple musical forms (e.g., AB, ABA).

Grades 4-6

The skills and understandings introduced in the first three grades should be continued in grades 4 through 6, while others are added. In these

---

[3]These recommendations are based on *The School Music Program: Description and Standards*.

grades the emphasis should be on greater accuracy, facility, and ease of learning. Students should show increased awareness of music as an important part of everyday life. They should sing, play instruments, and enjoy listening to various types of music. They should be able to discuss their personal responses to pieces of music and to describe the musical phenomena which evoke their responses.

By the end of grade 6, students should be able to sing accurately and independently and to play simple songs and accompaniments on guitar, recorder, keyboard, autoharp-type instruments, synthesizer, or other classroom instruments by ear or using notation. Students should be able to sing harmonizing parts in thirds and sixths, and to sing one part alone or in a small group while others sing contrasting parts. Conducting in 2-, 3-, and 4-beat meters should also be taught by grade 6. Growth in the ability to read music and use music notation should be evident.

By grade 6, students should be able to compose coherent works of music. They should improvise accompaniments and descants and create thoughtful variations of existing songs. They should demonstrate the use of changes in tempo, timbre, dynamics, and phrasing for expressive purposes, and should use diverse sound sources, including electronic ones, when improvising or composing.

In the upper grades, teachers should place considerable emphasis on listening skills. Students should notate pitch and rhythm patterns presented aurally, and they should use correct terminology in discussing the characteristics of a musical work. Students should be able to recognize a basic repertoire of orchestral and vocal compositions. They should also be able to identify most orchestral instruments and classifications of voices when they are heard; to recognize basic formal patterns such as AB, ABA, rondo, and theme and variations; and to describe salient features of musical examples, such as tempo, meter, dynamic level, and major and minor modes.

Middle School or Junior High School

Early adolescence is a time of individual growth, self-discovery, exploration, and challenge. The musical growth of middle and junior high school students is most effectively guided by providing diverse routes to greater learning. During the middle school years, students should continue to develop a sensitivity to the aesthetic qualities of music. They should achieve satisfaction and enjoyment in creating original musical ideas and in performing music in both formal and informal settings. Music should be required every year through grade 7.

By the end of the junior high or middle school years, students should be able to sing accurately, expressively, and confidently, with an acceptable tone quality, a variety of folk songs, art songs, and contemporary songs. Further, students should be able to play various classroom instruments, such as guitar, ukulele, or recorder, and should be able to perform vocally or on instruments as soloist or member of a small ensemble. There should be continued growth in reading music, and traditional and invented notational systems should be used to indicate pitch, rhythm, dynamics, and articulation.

Middle school students should be able to compose musical works that reflect understanding of the basic principles of composition. They should improvise rhythmic and harmonic accompaniments to original and existing music, and they should be able to use electronic instruments.

Middle school teachers should cultivate students' critical listening to their own performances and to those of others. Students should be able to listen attentively for relatively long periods of time and to analyze music with attention to its form, genre, performance medium, and salient features. Music heard or performed should be discussed in terms of the musical elements of pitch, rhythm, dynamics, texture, and form. Music from a variety of styles and periods should be analyzed, compared, and contrasted using an appropriate vocabulary of musical terms. Students should be able to identify by title and composer compositions in a variety of musical styles presented aurally.

Many students in the middle grades elect to participate in instrumental or choral groups. These students should achieve not only the outcomes expected of all students, but should show increased ability to use the expressive qualities of music, to perform a variety of music from the standard concert repertoire, and to provide knowledgeable critiques of individual and group performances. Instrumental students might also be expected, for example, to perform 8 to 10 major and minor scales and arpeggios, and to demonstrate improved knowledge and skill on their respective instruments (including attention to posture, breath support, embouchure, bowings, fingerings, tone quality, and articulation). Choral students might be expected to demonstrate increased skill and knowledge in using the voice (including attention to posture, breath support and control, vowel formation and placement, attack, intonation, diction, and blend), and to demonstrate independence through singing with various types of accompaniment.

High School

At the high school level it is especially important that alternative curricular offerings in music be available. These should include experiences that meet the needs of students who do not choose to participate in the select performing ensembles.

Every school system should require at least one course in music, art, theatre, or dance for graduation from high school. These courses may focus on any of the recognized fields of specialization.

Students who have completed a course in music literature, music history, or fine arts should demonstrate enjoyment in listening to and studying music, a respect for high-quality music and skilled performance, and an interest in musical performances in the community. These students should recognize various musical forms and genres; know the historical, musical, and cultural background of a representative sample of musical works; and be able to identify the musical styles of different historical periods. They should also be able to describe and discuss music using correct terminology, and should know compositions, composers, and performers of recognized quality.

Students who have completed an elective course in music theory or composition should enjoy listening to and studying music, and should respect quality compositions and skilled arrangements. They should be proficient in analyzing musical works, notating original musical ideas, arranging pieces of music for instruments or voices, creating musical compositions in a variety of media, and improvising simple accompaniments on the piano or other instruments. The arrangements and compositions written by members of the class should be performed whenever possible.

Students who have completed a course in band, orchestra, or chorus should enjoy performing and be committed to performing well. These students should also be able to produce a good tone and accurate pitch, demonstrate the techniques of good performance, respond sensitively to the gestures of a conductor, and show growth in musicianship and music-reading skills. High school students should become familiar with a varied repertoire of performance literature, and learn the historical and cultural background of the works performed. Students should also be able to analyze the elements of works they perform and describe their forms and structures, and be able to assess the quality of their own performance.

Students in performing groups in the middle school and high school often take the same course for more than one year. Band students, for example, typically enroll in band each year. These individuals are not simply repeating the same course several times. By studying unfamiliar works each year and by improving their skills continuously they (1) learn to perform more easily, more quickly, and more accurately, (2) gain greater independence in performance, (3) develop a better understanding of music and musical performance, and (4) gain a greater appreciation for the value of music as a means of expression.

Art

Every elementary and secondary school should require students to complete a sequential program of instruction in the visual arts that integrates the study of art production, aesthetics, art criticism, and art history. Students should learn

- to develop, express, and evaluate visual ideas
- to produce, read, and interpret visual images
- to recognize and understand the artistic achievements and expectations of civilized societies.

These basic skills in art develop the intellect and increase visual sensitivity. They enable students to identify and solve problems more effectively through the manipulation of visual as well as verbal and numeric symbols; to discriminate among the mass of conflicting visual messages in an increasingly visual society; and to make positive contributions to society by communicating effectively through visual images.[4]

In the early grades children should use art to tell stories, relate experiences, fantasize, convey messages, express feelings, and represent ideas in concrete form. At every level students should use art as a means to observe, recall, discover relationships, accept or reject alternatives, respond, value, and make decisions. Learnings in the visual arts may be categorized as (1) aesthetic perception, (2) creative expression, (3) historical and cultural information, and (4) analysis, interpretation, and judgment.

Grades K-2[5]

By the end of grade 2, children should be able to recognize the visual elements of line, color, value, shape, texture, and space. They should be able to describe the underlying principles of design structure (e.g., repetition, rhythm, balance) and to discuss their impressions of works of art. Teachers should encourage students to imagine how objects would appear under varying conditions of light, position, motion, and relative size, and should ask them to describe the visual and tactile qualities of objects and works of art.

Students should become skilled in depicting objects, ideas, and feelings through drawing, painting, printmaking, crafts (e.g., weaving, modeling, construction), and photography. Works created should illustrate the principles of balance, repetition, and dominance.

Teachers should acquaint students with a variety of visual art forms, including works from diverse cultures. Students should be able to describe the many ways that people within their communities are involved with the visual arts.

Children should learn to describe the ways works of art are organized. Similarities and differences in style or media should be apparent to them. They should know how various media (e.g., paint, clay, wood, metal, stone) can be used in creating works of art, and should analyze and describe artworks using the vocabulary of the visual arts media.

---

[4] *Quality Art Education: Goals for Schools* (Reston, Va.: National Art Education Association, 1986), 3-4.

[5] These recommendations are based on *Basic Art Skills*, developed by the state departments of education of California and South Carolina and distributed by the National Art Education Association, 1916 Association Drive, Reston, Virginia 22091.

Grades 3-5

By the end of grade 5, students should be able to recognize and discriminate among the visual elements of line, color, value, shape, texture, and space. They should be able to describe and categorize the specific details of design (e.g., repetition, rhythm, balance, variation on a theme) in works of art and to identify the effects resulting from changes in the positioning of objects. Students should be able to explain why the visual and tactile characteristics of works of art evoke responses.

By grade 5, students should show increased skill in using drawing and painting techniques to organize and depict objects, ideas, and feelings. They should be able to use variations in line, color, size, and texture to illustrate the principles of balance, dominance, and repetition. Their skills should include modeling, printmaking, weaving, and stitchery.

Students should be able to describe a variety of visual art forms. They should recognize artworks produced by individual artists, identify artworks of the same style, and perceive common themes in the artworks of different cultures. The stylistic traits of contemporary American art should be familiar to students. Children should be conscious of the pieces of public art in the community, and know the ways that people within the community—such as artists, patrons, curators, and gallery owners—are involved with the visual arts.

Students should be able to describe, using the terminology of the visual arts media, how the elements of design (e.g., line, color, value, shape, texture) and the principles of design (e.g., repetition, rhythm, balance, variations) are used in a given work of art to represent ideas, feelings, and moods. The specific media and processes should also be identified and described. Students should be able to compare two artworks of similar or different styles or media and identify their similarities and differences. They should be able to describe, in the vocabulary of the visual arts, the aesthetic and unaesthetic elements in a specific urban or rural environment.

Grades 6-9

By the end of grade 9, students should be able to make fine discriminations concerning surface treatments and patterns of light and shadow, and to explain the interrelationships among the design elements. They should be able to compare the three-dimensional compositional details of forms as seen from various viewpoints, identify the visual effects that result from changes in position, size, motion, or light, and predict conditions that would cause other changes. To break stereotyped images, teachers should encourage students to describe alternative ways of perceiving the environment. Students should compare the differences between general and aesthetic perceptions in viewing and describing everyday life.

Students should be increasingly able to use drawing and painting techniques (e.g., shading, brush drawing, dry and wet brush, mixed media) to organize and depict ideas, feelings, and moods. Students should design objects useful in everyday life, such as fabrics, wrapping paper, tools, furniture, and mechanical devices, and create signs, posters, or wall designs to communicate ideas, sell products, or produce decorative effects. Students should show skill in modeling shapes, carving, joining forms to make simple sculptures, and making reliefs or intaglios. An understanding of the principles of design should be evident in these creations. Similarly, students should demonstrate skill in the crafts of weaving, stitchery, batik, and jewelry, and in the creation of still photographs, film, television, or animation sequences to communicate ideas of realism, illusions of movement, or story content.

A knowledge of history and culture should enable students to describe the role of art in their communities and to outline the processes by which painters, sculptors, architects, designers, filmmakers, and craftspeople produce art. Students should understand how works of art reflect the culture of a people, including their values, beliefs, level of technology, and ways of perceiving the world. Students should compare and contrast artworks from various historical periods, as well as works from American ethnic groups and the major cultures of the world. Students should be able to identify uses of the visual arts in business and industry, including architectural and commercial design, advertising, television, and film, and describe the art careers associated with each of these art forms.

By grade 9, students should be able to make distinctions based on the elements of design in describing works of art, and to explain how the elements of design can be used to express concepts such as tension, conflict, relaxation, courage, power, and wisdom. Further, students should be able to describe how specific processes such as watercolor, clay, or weaving are used to produce works of art. Emphasis on analysis and comparison will enable students to compare and contrast two or more artworks and identify the qualities that make the works similar or different. Students should also be able to compare two environments and describe the qualities that make them aesthetically similar or different, and pleasant or unpleasant.

Grades 10-12

By the end of grade 12, students should be able to make refined and subtle discriminations in analyzing the interrelationships of the elements and principles of design. They should be able to speculate about how works of art, works of nature, and environmental objects would appear under other conditions. Also, they should be able to distinguish between aesthetic and general perceptions of the quality of everyday life.

Students should show creative skills in drawing and painting, modeling, carving, and printmaking. They should be able to produce craft objects with functional uses, graphic designs featuring lettering and illustration, and wall designs with spatial impact, and should be skilled in construction techniques including soldering, bending, molding, and welding. Students should also be able to use still photography, filmmaking, television, or animation sequences to communicate ideas of reality, fantasy, history, or contemporary issues. Teachers should foster the ability to use the elements and principles of design to solve environmental, industrial, and commercial problems in creative ways. Each student should prepare a portfolio of original artworks.

By grade 12, students should be able to identify artists who have achieved regional, national, or international recognition. They should be familiar with the general style and period of major works of art, and be able to discuss the social, political, and economic factors that have influenced art. They should also be able to analyze differences in the media used by various cultures and to explain the effect of media on the achievements and practices of those cultures. Students should know the major stylistic trends in contemporary American art, as well as the social, cultural, and technological developments upon which contemporary art is based. Students should know the variety of art forms used in business and industry and the roles and functions of the artists who create those forms.

Students should be able to describe the relationships among design elements and principles that give a work of art its unique qualities. They should be able to explain the meaning of a work of art, evaluate its aesthetic content, and support that evaluation on artistic and aesthetic grounds. The ability to compare and contrast individual works of art or categories of works should be well developed. Students should also be able to compare two environments and analyze in aesthetic terms the qualities that make one more appealing than the other.

Theatre

Theatre is a metaphoric representation of human behavior. Rooted in the universal need for expressive communication, theatre imitates and symbolizes human life. It enables us to explore our thoughts, feelings, and behavior. It permits us to transcend immediate reality and to acknowledge our kinship with the human family.

Theatre educators use the terms *drama* and *theatre* to represent two ends of a continuum. Drama is an informal dramatic enactment designed for the educational value of the experience. Theatre represents a more formal study of the discipline which culminates in dramatic interpretations by actors and technicians on a stage before an audience.

In elementary education, the term drama indicates an improvisational, nonexhibitional process in which students act out their perceptions of the world in order to understand it. They may also have experience in playgoing and play production, but the primary emphasis in the elementary school is on personal development and creative expression. It is at the secondary level that systematic study of theatre as an art form and academic discipline begins.

The learning expectations in drama/theatre may be categorized as (1) developing personal skills, (2) creating drama/theatre, (3) understanding drama/theatre.

Grades K-3[6]

By the end of grade 3, children should be able to express and recreate images through dramatic play and storytelling. They should be aware of the uses of movement, language, behavior patterns, and voice inflection to express emotions and characterizations. They should be experienced in recognizing and imitating voice inflections, gestures, emotions, and behavior patterns in dramatic activities. Teachers should emphasize clear articulation and correct pronunciation in conversation and dramatic activities.

Teachers should provide extensive opportunities for young children to interact with others in improvised dramatic activities. These improvisations may be based on home or school life, and should embrace a variety of feelings and roles. They may involve imitation of actions or characters from stories, television, or films. Students should learn to identify problems and resolutions in stories and situations. Teachers should emphasize the use of imagination in portraying roles and in devising various responses to conflicts. Students should be able to differentiate through sound and movement a variety of people, animals, and objects. The use of props, costumes, music, and sound effects to express ideas or create moods should be an important feature of these dramatic activities. Each student should accept both leader and follower roles.

Children should be able to recognize the central ideas of stories or plays, including stories from other cultures. They should learn to describe the appearances and actions of characters in theatrical performances, and should be aware of those aspects of a character's personality that are considered good or evil. Teachers should encourage comparisons between dramatic situations and real life, but the distinction between actor and role should always be clear to the child. Even young children should be encouraged to express their personal reactions to theatrical experiences and to explain the bases for those reactions.

Grades 4-6

By the end of grade 6, students should demonstrate imagination in playmaking. They should show significant growth in using movement, language, behavior patterns, and voice inflection to express thoughts, feelings, and emotions. Considerable emphasis should be placed on speaking clearly

[6]These recommendations are based on *A Model Drama/Theatre Curriculum*, Report of the National Theatre Education Project, 1983-86 (Austin, Tex.: Texas Education Agency, 1986), 11-13.

and expressively, with appropriate articulation, pronunciation, volume, and phrasing, and upon the use of variations in pitch, stress, and tempo to convey mood and characterization. Students should move easily from one role to another, interacting freely with others and accepting and using others' imagery. They should be able to draw inferences about characters from their language and speech habits, and to suggest various ways of resolving conflicts.

Substantial growth in participating imaginatively, cooperatively, and empathetically in improvised dramatic activities should be evident by grade 6. Students should improvise dialogue to portray various characters and situations, assume roles of leader and follower, reenact the same scene with changes in key elements, portray the attitudes or physical attributes of characters, and construct creative dramatizations based on stories or life experiences. Students should be able to predict the probable resolution of a plot and devise alternative resolutions. They should use available furniture, light sources, sound effects, fabrics, clothing, masks, and other materials to create scenery, props, and costumes for dramatic activities.

Students should be able to describe similarities and differences between theatre and life. They should be able to identify major dramatic questions in stories or plays and to suggest alternative endings. They should be familiar with differences and similarities among characters from different cultures and able to generalize about the common themes in dramas of various cultures and historical periods. Students should be able to draw inferences concerning motivation from characters' actions. They should be able to foresee the consequences of a character's behavior and suggest alternative behaviors. The uses of the technical elements of theatre, such as sets, props, lighting, costumes, and makeup, should be familiar to them. They should be able to compare the conventions of theatre, television, and film, and they should show growth in responding to live theatre.

Grades 7-8

By the end of grade 8, students should be able to lead and follow in dramatic improvisations. They should extemporize freely, contributing ideas, playing off others' ideas, reacting spontaneously to the unexpected, and modifying their behavior on the basis of constructive criticism. They should be able to use movement, voice, and language effectively to communicate the ages, attitudes, feelings, and physical condition of characters. Their improvisations should show an understanding of the dramatic concepts of space, time, and energy. They should be able to identify and imitate vocal qualities, mannerisms, patterns of misarticulation, and habitual inflection problems in character portrayals. They should be able to deliver lines, memorized or from a script, with proper clarity, enunciation, volume, and variety of inflection. Students should understand the distinction between actor and role, and should be able to evaluate dramatic activities based on stated criteria.

By grade 8, students should incorporate the physical, emotional, and social dimensions of characters in their dramatic portrayals. They should write scenes in playscript format based on problem-solving improvisations, and they should invent logical and believable alternative solutions to fictional or real-life problems. Students should dramatize diverse personal behaviors and attitudes through role-playing and role reversal, and should respond in character to imaginary environments and given situations. They should be able to convert narratives into dramatic form, to write and perform scenes for television using existing characters, and to use scenic elements, properties, lighting, sound effects, music, costumes, and makeup to enhance a dramatic situation.

Students should be able to identify similar themes in stories, plays, television programs, films, and real life, and to explain how plays, television, and films resemble and differ from life. They should identify the central ideas of stories or plays, analyze the objectives and motives of the characters, and recognize elements such as rising action, climax, conclusion, and denouement. Students should create character voices and illustrate character traits by means of dialogue and movement. They should represent in dramatic activities the commonality of characters, situations, and motives found in various cultures and historical periods. They should know the ways diverse drama/theatre activities enrich people's artistic, intellectual, social, and spiritual responses. They should develop criteria for evaluating theatre and analyze live performances.

Grades 9-12

By the end of grade 12, students should be skilled in imaginatively expressing thoughts, feelings, moods, and characters; in applying language, voice, gesture, facial expression, and body movement techniques to characterization in improvised and scripted activities; and in recognizing and reproducing the subtleties of language and voice inflection that convey emotion and meaning. They should be able to extemporize dialogue governed by setting, situation, and characters; to respond to imaginary stimuli with appropriate actions and voice inflection; and to react to audience response with subtle adjustments. Analyses of texts should provide a sufficient basis for selecting and demonstrating the physical attributes and movement qualities of characters. Students should speak clearly and expressively with appropriate articulation, pronunciation, volume, stress, rate, pitch, inflection, and intonation, both as individuals and as characters. They should be able to use their theatre heritage and experiences as a means to evaluate philosophical, ethical, and religious issues.

Students should write, perform, and evaluate scenes and short plays. They should be able to identify and resolve conflicts effectively, manage personal emotions as an individual and as a character, and improvise within a defined style. They should show analytical skills in creating characters for dramatic activities, comparing problems and resolutions in dramatic literature and life, and identifying the physical, social, and psychological dimensions of characters in texts. Students should write, perform, and evaluate plots for plays based on spinoffs from existing scripts, stories, myths, news events, historical incidents, and life. They should describe how the different conventions of theatre, film, and television are evidenced in their scripts, and they should understand the interrelationships among the roles of playwright, director, actors, designers, and technicians.

By grade 12, students should be able to relate theatrical motifs, symbols, and metaphors to personal experience. They should be aware of the universality of characters, situations, and motivation in theatre across cultures and across time. In play analysis they should know the phenomena of inciting incident, rising action, exposition, complication, climax, conclusion, and denouement. They should be able to draw inferences concerning theme, setting, time, and character from a text. They should know the ways other art forms are incorporated in theatre, the role of spectacle in the total production, and the ways symbols are used to develop metaphoric thought. Students should know the repertoire, history, and traditions of the theatre and should be able to evaluate theatrical performances using predetermined criteria.

Dance

Even before children learn to communicate through speech they can communicate through movement. Movement may be functional, like walking, or expressive, like gestures that convey meaning. Dance is expressive movement.

Dance in the primary years focuses on the exploration of the body as an expressive instrument and on movement as a mode of self-expression and communication. During the intermediate years the emphasis is on more refined uses of time, space, and energy. In the middle school and high school, technique is emphasized.

The objectives of the dance program are:

A. Assist students through movement-centered dance activities to
- experience patterns of movement
- experience satisfaction through control of body movements for their own pleasure, confidence, and self-esteem
- expand their repertoire of movements through exploration, invention, discovery, and imitation
- increase their aesthetic sensitivity
- develop their appreciation of dance as art
- relate their movement effectively to accompanying music and sound
- participate with others in recreational, folk, and ethnic dances
- create and perform dances for themselves and others

B. Assist students through audience-centered dance activities to
- understand the traditions of dance as art and ritual
- develop sensitivity to movement as a mode of communication
- appreciate the diverse forms of dance that have evolved in diverse cultures
- understand and appreciate the discipline and training necessary in skilled dancing
- enjoy dance as an art form[7]

In the elementary and middle schools, learnings in dance may be categorized as (1) movement skills and elements, (2) creating and performing, and (3) social, cultural, and historical dimensions.

Grades K-3[8]

Children's dance begins with the discovery of the body as an instrument for expression. Exploring ways of using time, space, and energy are basic to children's understanding of the world around them. Teachers should encourage young children to be free and imaginative in expressing their feelings and ideas, and should foster a sense of spontaneity and joy in the classroom. Dance should be cultivated as one of several acceptable means of expression.

By the end of grade 3, children should know the capabilities and limitations of the body. They should know that different body parts can move in different ways and that different parts can support the body. They should be able to make movements that are large or small, curved or angular, heavy or light, vibratory or swinging, fast or slow, and repetitious or patterned. They should know techniques to develop flexibility and strength. They should distinguish between up and down, high and low, forward and backward, open and closed space, even and uneven time, and sustained and percussive energy. Children should be able to change easily from one body movement to another and to change direction while moving in space. They should know the concepts of personal and general space, and should be able to make and combine locomotor and nonlocomotor movements.

Young children should understand the movement implications of words and musical sounds, and should be able to represent stories, poems, or concepts in movement. They should perform movement sequences to accompany music or sound, and combine them to create dances. Improvising and performing dances and dance movements should be regular experiences.

[7] *Children's Dance* (Reston, Va.: The American Alliance for Health, Physical Education, Recreation, and Dance, 1981), 6-7.

[8] These recommendations are based on materials developed by the state departments of education of North Carolina and Texas and made available by the National Dance Association, 1900 Association Drive, Reston, Virginia 22091.

Further, students should be able to refine their original dance compositions on the basis of evaluations by themselves and others.

By grade 3, students should have developed a positive attitude toward dance. They should be able to use the vocabulary of dance and to work cooperatively in dance activities. They should be able to compare dance performances on the basis of aesthetic qualities and to describe the meanings perceived in dance as well as the bases for those perceptions.

Grades 4-6

In the intermediate grades the emphasis on creativity is expanded as children are introduced to more sophisticated concepts of dance. Skills and vocabulary are expanded. Teachers introduce books, art works, videotapes, and other sources of information on dance and its history. Students develop an enriched understanding and appreciation of dance by studying specific peoples whose use of dance reflects their cultures.

By the end of grade 6, students should know ways to warm up the body before dance. They should recognize similarities and differences in movement. They should have a wide repertoire of movement skills, and should be able to make different body parts perform different movements. Students should be able to move in general space while maintaining stillness in personal space. They should be able to explain the importance of proper body carriage, body mechanics, and body maintenance.

All students should be able to perform folk dances and other dances of increasing complexity. They should be able to represent thoughts, ideas, and feelings creatively through dance improvisation, alone, with a partner, or with a group. These improvised dances may be composed of sequences of skilled movements. They should represent various uses and combinations of time, space, and energy. They should employ repetition and contrasts in tempo and style. They should incorporate locomotor and nonlocomotor movements separately and together. They should reflect cooperative efforts with other dancers.

By grade 6, students should possess a large vocabulary of words representing or suggesting various kinds of movement. They should have a positive attitude toward dance as an art form, and should be able to understand and criticize dance performances.

Grades 7-8

Cognitive knowledge about dance and awareness of dance technique become increasingly important in grades 7 and 8. Teachers should emphasize basic knowledge of anatomy and kinesiology to promote proper care of the body as the instrument for dance, and should provide experiences to build strength, flexibility, and endurance. The treatment of ideas, images, symbols, and feelings becomes more precise, and students learn to make the discriminating choices required in dance performance, choreography, and criticism. Students are exposed to dance through live performances, films, and other media.

By the end of grade 8, students should be able to move the various body parts independently and combine those movements in diverse ways. They should know warm-up exercises for the various body parts, and should possess an extensive vocabulary of movements. Quality of movement should be a familiar concept, and students' technique should be markedly improved. Students should know varied ways to define directions and pathways in space. They should be familiar with traditional dance steps, and should understand the importance of proper alignment and care of the body. They should be able to identify and describe increasingly subtle aspects of movement and how those subtleties contribute to the overall effect in dance.

Students should be able to create dances through improvisation. They should improvise alone, with a partner, or with a group. They should create sequences and combine them into larger and more varied dance compositions. Improved memory for movement should enable students to recall and perform an increasing number of dances with increasing skill. At this level students should be able to write instructions for performing dances. They should show heightened self-confidence and self-awareness in dance performance. They should be increasingly able to refine their own dance compositions on the basis of self-evaluation and the suggestions of others, and should show increased sophistication in making movement choices to produce desired effects.

Students should be able to observe, analyze, and criticize dance performances. They should explain the ways people from various cultures express themselves in dance, and should prepare research reports dealing with the costumes, customs, legends, significance, and meaning of various dances. They should also be able to teach dances to other students.

Grades 9-12

Courses at the high school level should enable students to devote a portion of their school day to the formal study of dance. Each course should provide strong emphasis on technique to develop strength, flexibility, and endurance. Teachers should continue to emphasize improvisation. Students should choreograph as well as dance. All should have the opportunity to present their work to audiences.

The following recommendations are based on four courses, described as Dance I, Dance II, Dance III, and Dance IV. Other, more specialized courses may be offered including, for example, Ballet I, Ballet II, Dance History, Dance Composition, and Choreography.

Students completing Dance I should possess a repertoire of dance movements and knowledge of the factors that influence movement. They should possess fundamental skills in at least one of the basic dance techniques, including ballet, modern, jazz, tap, folk, character, and ethnic. They should be able to represent feelings, emotions, stories, and narratives by means of improvised expressive movement. Their dance compositions should show imaginative use of the design factors of time, space, and energy, and should use tempo, meter, accent, and phrasing effectively. Students at this level should be self-confident in using the body as an expressive instrument. They should make and explain critical evaluations of dance performances, and they should appreciate dance as an art form.

Students completing Dance II should have an expanded repertoire of dance movements and increased knowledge of the factors that influence movement. They should possess intermediate skills in one or several of the basic dance techniques, including ballet, modern, jazz, tap, folk, character, and ethnic. They should be able to compose movement studies using qualities such as swinging, suspending, sustaining, collapsing, and vibrating. They should be sensitive to the nuances of tempo, meter, accent, and phrasing in dance improvisation and composition. They should be able to use floor patterns and spatial concepts in dance improvisation and composition, and to choreograph movements based on imaginary, literary, or other sources. Students should have increased self-confidence in using the body as an expressive instrument. Their memory for movement should help them identify and describe various styles of dance, and they should make knowledgeable evaluations of dance performances.

Students completing Dance III should have knowledge of traditional dance steps and an expanded repertoire of dance movements requiring body strength, flexibility, and precision. They should possess advanced skills in at least one dance technique selected from ballet, modern, jazz, tap, folk, character, and ethnic, and basic skills in at least two others. Students should possess a vocabulary of movements based on kinesthetic awareness and movement memory. They should develop and analyze movement ideas through dance improvisation and composition. They should be able to compose movement studies based on imaginary or literary sources or on musical or dance forms. They should have increased awareness of tempo, meter, accent, phrasing, time, space, and energy in dance improvisation and composition. They should be able to use specific spatial concepts and floor patterns in dance studies, and should be self-confident in using the body as an expressive instrument by performing in public. Dance III students should be able to analyze dance styles and performances by dancers. Their enjoyment of dance performances should be apparent. They should understand the underlying principles of other art forms as they relate to dance, and the contributions of the theatrical elements of dance, including costumes, lighting, and music.

Students completing Dance IV should possess a large vocabulary of dance movements requiring increased body strength, flexibility, and precision. They should have extensive knowledge of traditional dance steps as well as advanced skills in at least two dance techniques selected from ballet, modern, jazz, tap, folk, character, and ethnic, and intermediate skills in at least three others. Their movement repertoire should be based on kinesthetic awareness, muscle memory, and visual recall. They should be able to express either concrete or abstract ideas in movement. They should be able to manipulate rhythmic elements, floor patterns, and spatial concepts freely in compositional studies. Dance IV students should understand musical terminology as it applies to dance. They should be able to perform dance works in public, choreograph complete movements for public performance, and analyze and evaluate dance performances. They should understand the uses of the theatrical elements of costume, lighting, music, props, and sets to enhance the effect of dance performances, and they should know the history and traditions of dance, including the role of dance in popular culture.

Time to Teach

It's easy to construct elaborate lists of what should be taught in a subject. It's often much more difficult to teach those things in the time available. This problem is especially acute in the arts, where a serious imbalance often exists between the high aspirations of teachers and the less-than-adequate amount of time allocated.

It's not unreasonable to expect to teach elementary school children to read music, but it cannot be done in 15 minutes a week. The time and resources allotted must be consistent with the goals sought. Sometimes, when goals are not achieved, the reason is not that they were unreasonable but rather that not enough time or effort was devoted to them. We should not abandon our goals; we should devote more resources to their achievement.

Unfortunately, our program evaluation procedures are typically so inadequate that we fail to notice the inconsistency between our proclaimed aspirations and the resources we allocate for instruction. But those of us interested in curriculum and instruction should demand that this issue be addressed.

Classroom Teacher or Specialist?

One of the eternal debates in arts education is whether arts instruction should be provided by classroom teachers or by specialists. Nearly all professionals believe it can best be provided by specialists, though classroom teachers can greatly assist by creating an atmosphere favorable to the arts and by carrying on instruction in the arts between the specialist's visits.

Specialists can best teach the arts because the skills and knowledge they possess are essential in developing similar skills and knowledge in young people. Some classroom teachers have these abilities, of course, but many do not. The major contribution of the classroom teacher can be to make the arts a part of the students' daily lives. At the same time, it is obvious that in some states and some communities, it will be impossible to provide specialists in the near future. Until specialists can be made available, every school district should consider the ability to teach the arts to be a firm requirement for every classroom teacher employed.

The Mismatch with Reality

One difficulty some arts programs face is a mismatch between the rationale offered for arts education and the public's perception of what actually happens in the classroom. This mismatch is particularly troublesome when it exists in the perception of the school administrator. Decisions whether to support the arts in the schools are made on the basis of perceived reality rather than on the lofty claims and abstract rhetoric of arts educators and their friends.

If schools claim to teach the arts because the arts are important and worth knowing, then their curricular materials must be selected on that basis. Even though the arts as a whole are worth knowing, that is not true of everything that is taught in the name of the arts. If schools claim to teach the arts because they are among the most powerful, compelling, and glorious manifestations of our culture, then the exemplary artworks that teachers choose to teach must be the best that our culture has produced. If schools claim to teach the arts because they provide outlets for creativity and self-expression, then teachers must ensure that their classroom activities actually do so.

These things do not happen automatically, and sometimes they do not happen at all. The result is confusion and eventual erosion of support for arts education. The methods and the materials of arts educators must be compatible with their stated objectives. The relationship must be clear for all to see, especially for school administrators and parents.

Evaluation

How can we evaluate learning in the arts? In the same way we evaluate learning in any other discipline: (1) define the universe of skills and knowledge to be taught, (2) express those skills and knowledge in terms of tasks, and (3) sample randomly from that universe to determine the extent to which the students can perform those tasks.

In practice, of course, it isn't quite that simple. The universe of skills and knowledge is not easy to define. Some of the most desirable goals of arts educators are difficult to express as tasks. And sampling the tasks may be difficult because some reflect tastes that are slow to develop, insights that are highly individualized, or attitudes that are essentially nonbehavioral.

Even if it were impossible to evaluate instruction in the arts, every school should still provide a balanced, comprehensive, and sequential program of arts education because the arts constitute the very basis of civilization itself. But, fortunately, evaluation is possible in the arts, just as it is possible in other fields. The key lies in curriculum design. The curriculum must be designed to achieve clearly defined objectives based on skills and knowledge, not on vague feelings, emotions, or impressions. Nor should evaluation be based on irrelevant factors such as attendance and effort.

Education in the arts consists essentially of performance, creation, and study. Evaluation is possible in each of these domains. It happens every day, in the professional world and in the world of the amateur and student.

> Evaluation in the arts need not be based on multiple-choice questions. It need not even be based on paper-and-pencil tests. But no one should imagine that the arts possess some sort of magic that makes them exempt from the demands placed on other disciplines: that there be a clearly stated curriculum to be taught and that there be a systematic effort to determine whether that content has been learned. If instruction is effective, then sometime, somehow, the student will behave differently as a result. This is as true in the arts as in other disciplines. And if the student behaves differently, there exists the basis for evaluation. If there is no difference in the behavior of the student as a result of instruction, then how can the school claim to have been effective?[9]

Coda

What should be taught in the arts seems somehow more mysterious than what should be taught in math. Part of this mystery arises from the reluctance of arts educators to provide clear, straightforward answers to certain basic questions. This reluctance, which could once be tolerated as mere eccentricity, is no longer acceptable today. Arts educators should be expected to explain what is being taught just as directly, completely, and satisfactorily as other educators. If the arts are finally to be accepted on an equal footing with the other basic subjects, as they most certainly should be, nothing less is good enough.

[9]Paul Lehman, "Time To End 'Disarray' in Arts Evaluation," *Education Week* V, 19 (January 22, 1986): 28.

8. Curriculum for Critical Reflection in Physical Education

Linda L. Bain

PHYSICAL EDUCATORS HOLD DIVERSE OPINIONS REGARDING the definition of a quality program. At least seven different curriculum models can be found in the physical education literature (Jewett and Bain 1985). These models differ not only in their descriptions of goals and program structure, but in their basic definitions of content. This chapter discusses the content of the physical education curriculum in relation to what Maxine Greene (1978) calls "emancipatory education."

Emancipatory education is based on the belief that education is a dynamic process in which students are active agents in the creation of the social conditions of their lives. Within the constraints of culture, context, and biography, individuals have the power of choice. The actions they choose have the potential to modify the constraints. That is, people, individually or collectively, can reinterpret experience in order to change their circumstances and possibilities. The goal of education is to encourage critical reflection and self-awareness, thus empowering students to create a better, more just society.

The development of a curriculum that stimulates critical reflection has implications for both content and methodology. Knowledge must be presented as problematic and situated in a particular historical and social context, but must also be linked to the personal histories and experiences of students. This linkage requires that the instructional methods used foster dialogue and reflection and create possibilities for action. In addition, social relationships in the classroom must be both "democratized and humanized" (Giroux 1981, p. 83).

To plan such a curriculum requires a delineation of content, an analysis of the ways individuals can interpret or use that content, and an examination of the social circumstances that influence or limit individual action in relation to the content. The recognition that knowledge is contextual is central to this educational view. Therefore, this chapter begins with an examination of the social context of physical education.

Social Context of Physical Education

The Fitness Boom

Health and well-being are basic values in every society. Modern societies promote health through three avenues: (1) services designed to protect the health of individuals, such as purified water and immunizations; (2) care for those who suffer from disease or injury; and (3) education to inform individuals how to protect their health. In the United States, emphasis has historically been placed on health services and health care. Recently, however, health education and preventive medicine have received increased attention—as evidenced by changing public policy and the expansion of public and private programs to promote "wellness" (U.S. DHEW 1979). These health promotion programs are among the most rapidly growing educational enterprises in the country (Naisbitt 1982). A "fitness boom" has resulted from this growing emphasis on health promotion through preventive behaviors.

While most physical educators consider the fitness boom beneficial, it has raised some concerns. Health promotion programs may define health as a personal responsibility and ignore the social circumstances that contribute to health problems (Ingham 1985). Moreover, many health promotion programs are available only on a fee basis and thus do not effectively serve the poor. This is of particular concern given the evidence that risk factors such as overweight are more prevalent among poor and minority populations (Bain 1986). Commercial enterprises also tend to keep clients dependent on services rather than providing knowledge for personal decision making.

Another concern is the tendency of many fitness programs to reinforce a "cult of thinness" that creates rather than solves health problems. The health risks associated with some weight-loss programs and the phenomenal increase of eating disorders among young women are serious issues (Schwartz and others 1982). Fitness programs may contribute to these problems by using marketing techniques that emphasize women's appearance and sexual attractiveness rather than health. The cult of thinness also contributes to the discrimination suffered by obese people in the United States (Allon 1982). This discrimination persists despite recent evidence that genetic factors play an important role in the susceptibility to obesity (Stunkard and others 1986).

The current emphasis on health promotion is having a significant impact on school physical education programs. Concerns about children's lack of fitness have created pressure for physical education programs to increase their attention to this problem (National Children and Youth Fitness Study 1985).

If we are to achieve health benefits without reinforcing existing social problems, however, teachers and students must critically examine issues related to health and fitness. Educators should also examine how an emphasis on fitness might affect other aspects of the physical education program. For example, what are the ramifications of de-emphasizing skill development and playful movement in favor of "working out"? Will such a curricular shift change the way students view the legitimacy of intrinsically meaningful activity? Will it encourage a dualistic view of mind and body in which the body is considered an instrument to be disciplined and trained? Can fitness programs be developed in ways that support rather than detract from a holistic view of human beings? Physical educators' responses to these questions must be carefully considered.

Sport

Sport receives enormous attention in American society. Millions of Americans participate in or attend sporting events, watch sport on television, and read and talk about sport. Sport influences clothing styles, language, and concepts of the hero. The popular concept of sport is a fair contest in which contestants respect each other and the rules, and participate for the satisfaction and joy inherent in playing. The reality is that sport, from youth sport to the professional leagues, has become increasingly structured and bureaucratic, with an emphasis on providing entertainment for spectators (Eitzen and Sage 1986). This "professionalization" of sport has shifted the emphasis from play for its own sake to winning at all costs. In schools, the effect of this shift is increased emphasis on athletic programs for the highly skilled and neglect of skill development and sport participation for less skilled students.

The common perception of sport as a fair, meritocratic system tends to obscure racism and sexism in sport. Although black athletes have made significant advances in the past 30 years, blacks are still underrepresented in coaching and administrative roles (Eitzen and Sage 1986). The overrepresentation of blacks in certain sports (basketball, football) and underrepresentation in others (golf, tennis, swimming) are based on social influences rather than physical differences.

Examination of a newspaper sports section or of television programming readily reveals that, despite recent advances for women, sport is still a male preserve. Although Title IX has dramatically increased the number of females in sport, women still have fewer opportunities to participate, often have inferior facilities and financial support, and hold fewer coaching and administrative positions (Eitzen and Sage 1986).

The issue of sexism goes beyond equal access to sport, however. We must examine ways in which sport reinforces or challenges gender stereotypes. Traditional gender beliefs portray men as strong and aggressive and women as weak and passive. Although sports participation by women challenges these stereotypes, that challenge has been neutralized by trivializing women's sport performance. Media coverage of women athletes tends to focus on their femininity and appearance rather than on their performance (Bryant 1980, Hilliard 1984, Rintalla and Birrell 1984). Differences in sport performance between males and females are interpreted in ways that reinforce the perception that men are superior to women.

In contrast, dance is viewed in the United States (but not in many other countries) as a "feminine" activity. For this reason, emphasis is placed on grace and flexibility rather than on strength and power. Male dancers are considered effeminate, or their performance is justified by emphasizing its athletic qualities.

Clearly, fundamental definitions of sport and skillfulness must be reexamined. Paul Willis (1982, p. 20) states that a critical theorist "accepts differences in sport performance between men and women, accepts that cultural factors may well enlarge this gap, but is most interested in the manner in which this gap is understood and taken up in the popular consciousness of our society." He asks why some differences but not others are viewed as important. Why, for example, are differences in strength important while differences in flexibility are not?

Selection of sport, dance, and exercise activities for inclusion in a physical education program is not value-neutral. Physical education programs have the potential to reinforce or challenge racial, gender, and class stereotypes. Educators committed to creating a more just society will help their students examine the historical and social contexts of physical education content.

Content of Physical Education

The subject matter of physical education is human movement. This includes movement itself as well as the human and environmental factors that affect and are affected by movement (Brown 1967).

Peter Arnold (1979) has identified three ways in which movement can be educational. Education *about* movement involves cognitive study of movement phenomena. Education *through* movement is the use of movement as a means to achieve worthwhile objectives that may be extrinsic to the activity itself (e.g., health, social and moral values, etc.). Education *in* movement provides students the opportunity to engage in intrinsically valuable activities that are whole-bodied, culturally significant, and an important source of personal knowledge. Education in movement emphasizes the process of moving, yet relates to and draws from the other dimensions. It is the central focus of physical education and underlies decisions about the selection and structuring of content.

The content of physical education can be classified into three major categories: fitness, motor skills, and movement forms (see Figure 8.1). Within each of these categories, we can identify performance skills and conceptual knowledge. The conceptual knowledge includes both technical information about performance and cultural information which permits stu-

Figure 8.1. The Content of Physical Education

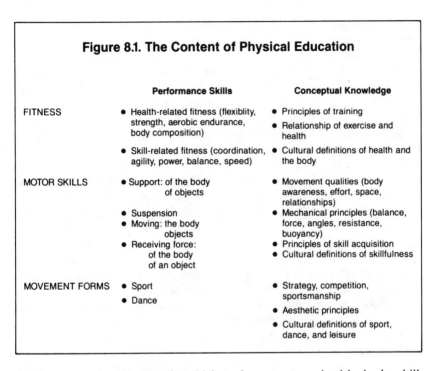

	Performance Skills	Conceptual Knowledge
FITNESS	• Health-related fitness (flexiblity, strength, aerobic endurance, body composition) • Skill-related fitness (coordination, agility, power, balance, speed)	• Principles of training • Relationship of exercise and health • Cultural definitions of health and the body
MOTOR SKILLS	• Support: of the body of objects • Suspension • Moving: the body objects • Receiving force: of the body of an object	• Movement qualities (body awareness, effort, space, relationships) • Mechanical principles (balance, force, angles, resistance, buoyancy) • Principles of skill acquisition • Cultural definitions of skillfulness
MOVEMENT FORMS	• Sport • Dance	• Strategy, competition, sportsmanship • Aesthetic principles • Cultural definitions of sport, dance, and leisure

dents to examine the ways in which such concepts as health, body, skill, leisure, and competition are socially constructed.

Fitness

Although fitness has been part of physical education since programs were first initiated in American schools, the definition of fitness and the emphasis placed upon it have varied. We have only recently differentiated between health-related and skill-related fitness (Updike and Johnson 1970). Health-related fitness components reduce the risk of cardiovascular disease, the incidence of low back pain, and the risk of injury (AAHPERD 1980; Pollock and others 1984). Skill-related fitness refers to factors underlying the efficient performance of motor tasks. The number of these skill-related factors needed depends upon the skill to be performed; one needs a different conditioning program to be a skilled performer in football than to excel in tennis or dance. In contrast, the basic components of health-related fitness are more generally applicable.

Many early physical education programs are more appropriately described as training than as education. Students were required to exercise and condition their bodies, but they were not taught the principles underlying such exercise programs. A notable feature of contemporary fitness programs is the effort to incorporate conceptual knowledge about fitness (Corbin and Lindsey 1983, Johnson and others 1975).

Considerable debate exists, however, about how much emphasis teachers should give to the performance and conceptual aspects of fitness. Maintaining health throughout one's lifetime requires a voluntary commitment to exercise. Unlike all other aspects of physical education content, fitness components are reversible. Once skills and knowledge are learned they are retained, but we maintain strength, endurance, and flexibility only as long as our exercise program is continued. This poses a difficult question: When and how should teachers shift responsibility for the maintenance of fitness from the program to the student?

Some physical educators consider knowledge a sufficient basis for good exercise habits. They argue that, while information about fitness should be included in physical education (or health education), students should develop the recommended fitness levels by building exercise into their daily lives. Others recommend that physical education programs incorporate fitness activities. These educators believe that students who have been required to achieve fitness are more likely to value it and to establish good habits that will persist. This debate is based in part on a practical concern about the time required to attain health-related fitness (20 minutes of aerobic exercise three times per week, plus stretching and strengthening exercises). Physical educators strongly committed to skill development may feel that they do not have time to provide both supervised fitness activities and skill instruction.

Despite disagreements about how to approach fitness, most physical educators agree that students must be able to make informed decisions about exercise and health. To do so, students need an understanding of cultural definitions of the body and health as well as technical information about fitness.

Motor Skills

The second category of physical education content is motor skills. Because of the vast movement potential of the human body, the number and variety of motor skills seems endless. Nevertheless, these skills can be classified into four categories based on the mechanical principles involved: supporting, suspending, moving, and receiving force (Broer and Zernicke 1979). Each category includes a wide range of skills, some relating to sports and dance and some having practical value. For example, the receiving force category includes learning how to catch a ball and how to absorb the force of the body in a landing or fall. By mastering a variety of skills in each category, students can develop a repertoire of movement patterns and learn the mechanical principles fundamental to efficient performance.

Skill instruction is often organized into units related to sports and dance, but teachers should try to include a broad base of skill development. One way to do so, especially in elementary school physical education, is to use a framework describing movement qualities to develop skill instruction within each unit. All motor skills can be described in terms of the qualities of the movement. Such descriptions usually rely on a system of movement analysis developed by Rudolf Laban and adapted for use in physical education programs (Logsdon and others 1984). As students learn skills, they examine the different elements of movement (body, space, effort, and relationships) and learn to use these elements to vary and refine their motor skills. For example, a student might examine ways to use spatial elements such as direction and level to improve performance in dribbling a ball. In this approach to skill instruction, students understand and create skillful movement rather than merely copying movement patterns demonstrated by others.

Because it is not feasible to include all motor skills in a physical education program, students must learn *how to learn* these skills. Instructors should teach concepts related to the principles of motor skill acquisition. Just as teaching study strategies has proved useful in cognitive learning, providing students with a practice strategy can help them learn motor skills more effectively (Singer and Suwanthada 1986).

The final area of conceptual information related to motor skills is an analysis of cultural definitions of skillfulness. Although many people treat "skill" as an objective, value-neutral term, definitions of skill are socially constructed and have important relationships to gender, race, and class. Students must reflect critically upon these meanings to take control of their own movement lives.

Movement Forms

Play is a fundamental human behavior. Aspects of early childhood play are institutionalized in the form of music, drama, art, dance, and sport (Siedentop 1980). These activities are part of every culture and are characterized by rules, rituals, traditions, and a complex set of skills and concepts. Because of this complexity, children must receive instruction before they can take part in these activities. The two forms of adult "play" most appropriate for inclusion in physical education programs are sport and dance.

To play a sport well, students must learn the skills, strategies, rituals, and traditions specific to that sport. This also allows them to be informed and appreciative spectators. Dance education includes performing, creating, and responding as well. Mastery of these activities requires both the development of skills and an understanding of aesthetic principles.

How do curriculum planners decide which sports and dance forms to include in the program? In large part, these decisions are based on practical factors (facilities, class size, teacher expertise) and on local traditions. While these factors are important, they may limit the choices available to students. An important means of helping students make critical, informed choices is an examination of cultural definitions of sport, dance, and leisure. Such an examination enables students to perceive how tradition and historical context can limit their movement choices, and helps them to discover new ways movement can enrich their lives.

Personal Meaning in Movement

Maxine Green (1978, p. 169) has said that curriculum "ought to be a means of providing opportunities for the seizing of a range of meanings by persons open to the world." The full development of human potential requires education in various forms of meaning. Human behavior and thought exist in both discursive symbols (linear forms such as language and mathematics) and in non-discursive symbols (direct, presentational forms such as music, visual arts, dance, and sport) (Langer 1951). Physical education provides experience that is both direct (non-discursive) and holistic. For that reason, it provides an important and unique opportunity for the discovery of personal meaning.

Individuals' motivations for participating in physical activity have received considerable attention. Ann Jewett and her colleagues have identified twenty-two purposes for moving that can be grouped in three clusters: fitness, performance, and transcendence (Jewett and Mullan 1977, Jewett 1980). (See Figure 8.2.)

Fitness

Fitness or well-being is a fundamental reason for participation in physical activity. Individuals may participate to improve their physical or mental health. The physical benefits of exercise are well established. Although documenting the mental health benefits is more difficult, most people report "feeling better" after exercise, and researchers have found exercise to be effective in alleviating depression and stress (Morgan 1984). There is some indication, however, that fitness is not a strong motivator for young children. Even among adults, who tend to be more health-conscious, other motives may be more important in sustaining participation in physical activity (Oldridge 1984).

Performance

The second cluster, performance, includes the development of competence in basic motor skills and in movement activities of importance in one's society. The development of competence in movement is very important to children, and their perceptions of personal ability have a strong influence on future participation (Roberts 1984). Teachers should therefore strive to enhance feelings of competence. Roberts has suggested that this requires de-emphasis on competitive achievement (Can I win?) and a focus on personal mastery of tasks (How can I improve?). There is some evidence that

Figure 8.2 Personal Meaning Value Clusters

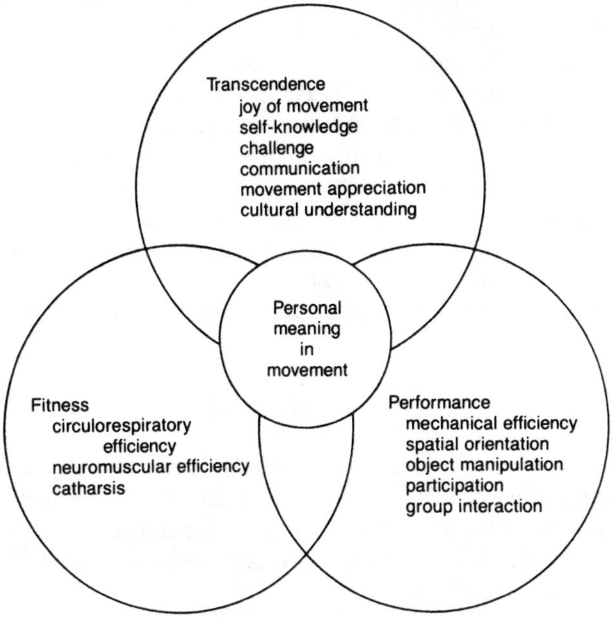

From Ann E. Jewett, "The Status of Physical Education Curriculum Theory," *Quest* 32 (1980): 163-173. Copyright 1980 Human Kinetics Publishers. Reprinted with permission.

people who adopt a mastery orientation are more likely to remain involved in movement activities.

Transcendence

The third cluster, transcendence, involves movement as a means of expression and communication and as a source of joy and understanding. Movement is an important aspect of what phenomenologists call "lived body experience." Peter Arnold (1979, p. 179) describes this potential as follows:

> The world of movement for the agent or the moving being is a world of promise towards self-actualization. It can expand his conscious horizons. It is a world in which the mover can come to understand an aspect of his socio-cultural world and in doing so discover more perfectly his self and his existential circumstances. To deny this world of bodily action and meaning because of prejudice or neglect is to deny the possibility of becoming more fully human.

In informal discussion, students (and teachers) often describe physical education class as "fun." Physical educators have been embarrassed by this commitment to enjoyment and have been reluctant to use it publicly as a justification of their programs. Due of the limitations of common vocabulary, however, students may use the term "fun" to describe transcendent experience. Personal expression, playfulness, and intrinsic satisfaction are important aspects of the movement experience.

To some extent, the clusters of personal meaning (well-being, competence, and transcendence) parallel the three categories of physical education content (fitness, motor skills, and movement forms). However, an individual may seek different types of meaning in any of the content categories. For example, a person might run for fitness (well-being) but also to improve her personal best time (competence) and to experience a "runner's high" (transcendence). The meanings will depend on the individual's characteristics and experience and on the historical and social context surrounding the activity.

Program Implications

The purpose of the physical education program is to provide students with movement experiences that foster critical reflection and self-awareness and that enable them to achieve well-being, competence, and transcendence. This philosophy has implications for curriculum design and for day-to-day program implementation.

The physical education program should have two basic commitments. First, it should focus on education in movement—that is, the inherent worth of the process of moving. Movement provides an essential form of direct knowledge that can be enhanced, but not replaced, by cognitive information. Second, it should make students increasingly reflective and responsible for their decisions and actions.

Donald Hellison (1973, 1978, 1985) has spent approximately fifteen years developing and field-testing a model of social development in physical education. His model is designed to help young people achieve a sense of control over their lives and contribute positively to the world in which they live. Hellison has identified five levels of social development and has proposed strategies for helping students move to higher levels (see Figure 8.3).

Hellison's model is helpful in two ways in developing a physical education program. First, students can be taught about the levels as a way to foster reflection on their own actions and circumstances. Hellison's students become adept at identifying levels of behavior and use this recognition to become more thoughtful and responsible. Second, the developmental sequence can be used as a rationale for selecting content for various age groups. Although considerable variation in social development occurs within age levels, students of similar ages share certain developmental needs that may serve as a basis for content selection.

Figure 8.3. Hellison's Five Levels of Social Development

LEVEL 0: IRRESPONSIBILITY
Unmotivated and undisciplined; makes excuses and blames others for behavior, denies personal responsibility, and may feel powerless to change one's life. Behavior includes discrediting others, verbally or physically abusing others.

LEVEL 1: SELF-CONTROL
Able to control own behavior; not involved but does not interfere with others' right to learn or teacher's right to teach.

LEVEL 2: INVOLVEMENT
Not only shows self-control but is involved in the subject matter under the teacher's direction.

LEVEL 3: SELF-RESPONSIBILITY
Self-responsible and self-motivated; able to work independently and to take responsibility for intentions and actions; can identify own needs and interests and plan and execute own program.

LEVEL 4: CARING
All of the above plus caring about others, responsible for others as well as self; cooperative, involved with others in a helping way; interested in collaborating on mutual goals, concerned with the well-being of others.

From Donald R. Hellison, *Goals and Strategies for Teaching Physical Education* (Champaign, Ill.: Human Kinetics Publishers, Inc., 1985). Reprinted with permission.

Elementary School

For most elementary school children, self-control and involvement are the primary developmental levels. Children learn not to interfere with others' rights and then progress to involvement in supervised motor activities. Because involvement depends heavily on feelings of competence, a major goal of the elementary school physical education program is to help children master a range of motor skills. These skills are usually related to games, dance, and gymnastics in order to increase student motivation and involvement. Inclusion of a wide range of experiences provides a foundation for students' subsequent choices and increases the probability that all children will find success in the program. The emphasis of the program, however, is on mastery of skills and concepts, not on competition and winning.

Fitness testing usually begins in upper elementary school. Students generally view such testing as a measure of competence rather than an indicator of health and well-being. Because health is not a strong motivator for this age group, fitness may best be handled by incorporating vigorous activity into skill instruction and game play, rather than by teaching fitness activities directly.

Critical reflection in the elementary school program focuses on how to attain self-control, and the factors that influence willingness to be involved in movement activities. Hellison notes that physical education includes a continuum of activities ranging from play to practice or work. The program should provide opportunities for children to see play as a legitimate, valued activity and to see work as worthwhile and chosen, rather than imposed.

Middle School

In the middle school, development of responsibility is a major concern. This level emphasizes students' need to take more responsibility for their choices and to make choices that contribute to their sense of identity. Students at this level learn to set attainable goals and to work and play independently.

The middle school physical education program includes several components intended to foster responsibility. One important component is the goal-setting process, which provides an assessment of students' interests, abilities, and fitness levels. Students examine and discuss influences upon their activity preferences, including personal experience and social influences such as gender stereotypes. Based on this reflection, students identify personal goals and develop strategies for attaining those goals.

At the middle school level, students' goals tend to relate to fitness and competence. Generally, all students are involved in fitness instruction but each student develops and carries out an individualized fitness program. The approach to the development of competence also allows for personal goal setting: students can choose which sport or dance activities they wish to learn. Rather than receiving introductory instruction in many activities, students select a few activities and receive the in-depth instruction needed to achieve mastery of them. During that instruction, students assume increasing responsibility for the achievement of personal goals. To assist them in this process, they are taught conceptual knowledge—such as the principles of skill acquisition—that helps them direct their own learning.

Secondary School

The secondary school physical education program continues to emphasize responsibility but adds an emphasis on caring—extending one's sense of responsibility beyond one's self to others. The full development of caring "requires that students develop a sense of purpose in life that extends beyond personal involvement and development to a commitment to bettering the world" (Hellison 1985, p. 132).

Critical reflection in the secondary program focuses not only on personal goals but on one's relationship to other students and to the larger society. While fitness and competence remain concerns, transcendence goals become more important. Expression, communication, and mutual understanding become important parts of the movement experience.

The program content continues to include personal goal setting, individualized fitness programs, and choices of sport and dance activities. Some modifications are made, however, to emphasize caring and social responsibility. Students establish shared goals as well as individual goals. Procedures such as peer teaching help them assume responsibility for each other's learning. Cooperative activities and student-created games can help students examine issues of competition and cooperation.

One way to emphasize mutual responsibility in the secondary school physical education program is to organize selective activity programs as "clubs." That is, a student enrolls for a semester in a gymnastics club, a tennis club, a dance club, etc. The club meets during class time and is run democratically, with the teacher serving as advisor and coach. Students establish personal and common goals, plan practices, and conduct competitions or performances. This approach fosters personal and social responsibility and provides an appropriate transition from required, supervised participation to voluntary, self-directed participation.

Summary

Physical education content, like all other forms of knowledge, is socially constructed; it derives from personal experience and historical and social context. Because movement experiences involve students immediately and totally, they provide a unique source of knowledge about self and the world. By teaching skills and concepts related to fitness, motor skills, and movement forms, the physical education program enables students to attain personal goals of well-being, competence, and transcendence. By helping students reflect on the personal and social meanings of movement, we empower them to attain new levels of personal integration and social commitment.

References

Allon, Natalie. "The Stigma of Overweight in Everyday Life." In *Psychological Aspects of Obesity,* edited by B. B. Wolman. New York: Van Nostrand, 1982.

American Alliance for Health, Physical Education, Recreation and Dance. *Health Related Physical Fitness.* Reston, Va.: AAHPERD, 1980.

Arnold, Peter J. *Meaning in Movement, Sport and Physical Education.* London: Heinemann, 1979.

Bain, Linda L. "Issues of Gender, Race, and Class in Health Promotion Programs." Paper presented at the 12th Conference on Research on Women and Education, Washington, D.C., November 1986.

Broer, M. R., and R. F. Zernicke. *Efficiency of Human Movement.* Philadelphia: W. B. Saunders, 1979.

Brown, Camille. "The Structure of Knowledge of Physical Education." *Quest* 9 (1967): 53-67.

Bryant, James. "A Two Year Selective Investigation of the Female in Sport as Reported in the Paper Media." *Arena Review* 4 (1980): 38.

Corbin, Charles B., and Ruth Lindsey. *Fitness for Life.* Glenview, Ill.: Scott, Foresman and Company, 1983.

Eitzen, D. Stanley, and George Sage. *Sociology of North American Sport.* Dubuque, Iowa: Wm. C. Brown, 1986.

Giroux, Henry A. *Ideology, Culture and the Process of Schooling.* Philadelphia: Temple University Press, 1981.

Greene, Maxine. *Landscapes of Learning*. New York: Teachers College Press, 1978.
Hellison, Donald. *Humanistic Physical Education*. Englewood Cliffs, N.J.: Prentice-Hall, 1973.
Hellison, Donald. *Beyond Balls and Bats*. Washington, D.C.: American Alliance for Health, Physical Education, Recreation and Dance, 1978.
Hellison, Donald. *Goals and Strategies for Teaching Physical Education*. Champaign, Ill.: Human Kinetics Publishers, 1985.
Hilliard, Dan C. "Media Images of Male and Female Professional Athletes: An Interpretive Analysis of Magazine Articles." *Sociology of Sport Journal* 1 (1984): 251-262.
Ingham, Alan G. "From Public Issue to Personal Trouble: Well-being and the Fiscal Crisis of the State." *Sociology of Sport Journal* 1 (1985): 43-55.
Jewett, Ann E. "The Status of Physical Education Curriculum Theory." *Quest* 32 (1980): 163-173.
Jewett, Ann E., and Linda L. Bain. *The Curriculum Process in Physical Education*. Dubuque, Iowa: Wm. C. Brown, 1985.
Jewett, Ann E., and Marie Mullan. *Curriculum Design: Purposes and Processes in Physical Education Teacher-Learning*. Washington, D.C.: American Alliance for Health, Physical Education and Recreation, 1977.
Johnson, P. B., W. S. Updike, M. Schaefer, D. C. Stoldberg. *Sport, Exercise and You*. New York: Holt, Rinehart & Winston, 1975.
Logsdon, B. J., K. R. Barrett, M. Ammons, M. R. Broer, L. E. Halverson, R. McGee, and M. A. Robertson. *Physical Education for Children*. Philadelphia: Lea & Febiger, 1984.
Morgan, William P. "Physical Activity and Mental Health." In *Exercise and Health*, edited by H. M. Eckert and H. J. Montoye. Champaign, Ill.: Human Kinetics Publishers, 1984.
Naisbitt, John. *Megatrends*. New York: Warner, 1982.
National Children and Youth Fitness Study. *Journal of Physical Education, Recreation and Dance* 56 (1985): 43-90.
Oldridge, N. B. "Adherence to Adult Exercise Fitness Programs." In *Behavioral Health*, edited by J. D. Matarazzo, S. M. Weiss, J. A. Herd, N. E. Miller, and S. A. Weiss. New York: John Wiley and Sons, 1984.
Pollock, M. L., J. H. Wilmore, and S. M. Fox III. *Exercise in Health and Disease*. Philadelphia: W. B. Saunders, 1984.
Rintalla, Jan, and Susan Birrell. "Fair Treatment of the Active Female: A Content Analysis of Young Athlete Magazine." *Sociology and Sport Journal* 1 (1984): 231-250.
Roberts, Glyn C. "Toward a New Theory of Motivation in Sport: The Role of Perceived Ability." In *Psychological Foundations of Sport*, edited by J. M. Silva III and R. S. Weinberg. Champaign, Ill.: Human Kinetics Publishers, 1984.
Schwartz, D. M., M. G. Thompson, and C. L. Johnson. "Anorexia Nervosa: The Socio-Cultural Context." *The International Journal of Eating Disorders* 1 (1982): 20-36.
Siedentop, Daryl. *Physical Education: Introductory Analysis*. Dubuque, Iowa: Wm. C. Brown, 1980.
Singer, Robert N., and Slipachal Suwanthada. "The Generalizability Effectiveness of a Learning Strategy on Achievement in Related Closed Motor Skills." *Research Quarterly for Exercise and Sport* 57 (1986): 205-214.
Stunkard, A. J., R. Sorenson, C. Hanis, T. W. Teasdale, R. Chakraborty, W. J. Schull, and F. Schulsinger. "An Adoption Study of Human Obesity." *The New England Journal of Medicine* (1986): 192-198.
Updike, Wynn, and Perry Johnson. *Principles of Modern Physical Education, Health and Recreation*. New York: Holt, Rinehart & Winston, 1970.

U.S. Department of Health, Education and Welfare. *Healthy People: The Surgeon General's Report on Health Promotion and Disease Prevention*. Washington, D.C.: Government Printing Office, 1979.

Willis, Paul. "Women in Sports in Ideology." In *Sport, Culture and Ideology*, edited by J. Hargreaves. London: Routledge & Kegan Paul, 1982.

9. School Health Education

Richard G. Schlaadt

SCHOOL HEALTH EDUCATION IS COMING OF AGE IN AMERICA. Our society is considerably more health conscious than at any other time in history, and we are asking more questions and looking at more ways to improve our health and create a quality lifestyle. Each day, the media reports on a multitude of health-related issues that profoundly affect our lives. Headlines announce, "Cocaine Overdose Kills Athlete," "Americans Consume Too Much Fat," "AIDS Epidemic Worsening," and "Teenage Driver Killed in Alcohol-Related Accident." Columns about physical, mental, and social health appear regularly in newspapers and magazines, and television and radio offer special programs on a variety of health issues.

As a result of this heightened sensitivity to health issues, state and local governments are paying more attention to the health needs of school children. Of the 43 states that include health education in the curriculum, 39 have made it a requirement. Many states are providing leadership in developing new health curriculum guides, increasing coverage of health topics, encouraging higher standards for health teacher certification, and offering inservice programs for teachers, curriculum directors, and supervisors.

At the federal level, the Bureau of Health Education, the National Center for Health Education, the Office of Comprehensive School Health, the Office of Disease Prevention and Health Promotion, and the National Institute of Health are all powerful units with impact on health education in schools.

Also at the federal level, the Surgeon General of the United States has developed several documents dealing with the health of Americans. Two of these have direct implications for schools. The first, *Healthy People*, lists general health goals to be achieved by 1990 for infants (from conception to one year), children (1-14), adolescents and young adults (15-24 years),

---

M. Patricia Fetter contributed to the final draft of this chapter. Fetter is Coordinator, Health Education Programs, Northeastern University, Boston, Massachusetts.

adults (24-64 years), and older adults (65 and over).[1] *Healthy People* emphasizes the theme that prevention is an idea whose time has come:

> . . . the health of the nation's citizens can be significantly improved through the actions individuals can take themselves, and through actions decision makers in public and private sectors can take to promote a safer and healthier environment for all Americans at home, at work, or at play.

The second document, *Promoting Health/Preventing Disease: Objectives of the Nation*, lists 15 priority areas, categorized as health promotion, health protection, or preventive health services. The priorities are related to 226 measurable objectives, 67 of which can be attained or strongly influenced by schools.[2] The Surgeon General believes that most of the objectives will be achieved by 1990, and he is planning now for a new set of goals and objectives targeted for the year 2000.

Not only do these reports offer a national blueprint for addressing health problems, they also provide clear direction for school health education programs: Schools *must* promote students' health and well-being.

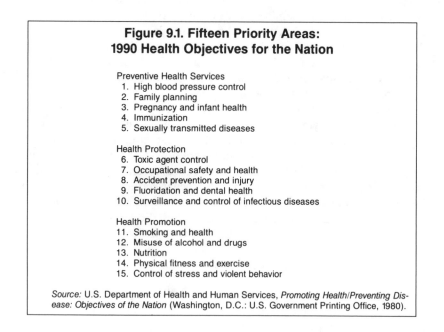

Figure 9.1. Fifteen Priority Areas: 1990 Health Objectives for the Nation

Preventive Health Services
1. High blood pressure control
2. Family planning
3. Pregnancy and infant health
4. Immunization
5. Sexually transmitted diseases

Health Protection
6. Toxic agent control
7. Occupational safety and health
8. Accident prevention and injury
9. Fluoridation and dental health
10. Surveillance and control of infectious diseases

Health Promotion
11. Smoking and health
12. Misuse of alcohol and drugs
13. Nutrition
14. Physical fitness and exercise
15. Control of stress and violent behavior

Source: U.S. Department of Health and Human Services, *Promoting Health/Preventing Disease: Objectives of the Nation* (Washington, D.C.: U.S. Government Printing Office, 1980).

---

[1] *Healthy People: The Surgeon General's Report on Health Promotion and Disease Prevention* (Washington, D.C.: U.S. Government Printing Office, 1979).

[2] D. C. Iverson and L.J. Kolbe, "Evolution of the National Disease Prevention and Health Promotion Strategy: Establishing a Role for Schools," *Journal of School Health* 53 (May 1983): 300-301.

Components of a Total School Health Program

The purpose of comprehensive school health education is to teach and reinforce the skills, attitudes, and practices necessary for a healthy lifestyle. School health education has three components: health services, a healthy environment, and health instruction.

1. *School health services.* To appraise, protect, and promote the health of students and school personnel, school health services are designed to aid in disease prevention, screening, and detection and to provide emergency care and follow-up referrals. These services are carried out by physicians, nurses, dentists, teachers, and others.

2. *A healthy environment.* A healthy school environment is clean, safe, and enhances learning. Schools must be constructed in adherence with building codes and well maintained to ensure good lighting, appropriate ventilation and heating, sanitary food services, clean water, and proper waste disposal.

3. *Health instruction.* While health instruction gives students factual information, it also encourages them to develop attitudes and behaviors that are conducive to developing and maintaining a healthy lifestyle.

The "wellness" approach, which focuses primarily on physical fitness, nutrition, and stress management, has gained some acceptance as a total health education curriculum. However, its narrow perspective does not address such crucial issues as substance abuse, disease prevention and control, environmental, community, and consumer health, and family life.

A well-planned, sequential health program does not overemphasize a few topics while giving short shrift to other equally important issues. Crisis issues appear and disappear over the years. The current AIDS crisis is an example. Many school systems in the nation do not have programs for sexuality education, and the need to talk about AIDS in the classroom becomes a panic situation. When students have not had appropriate sex education, it is difficult to teach them about AIDS. A well-developed program will approach all important issues and there will be no need for "knee-jerk" curriculum development.

Topics for Health Instruction

A balanced and comprehensive program of health instruction covers at least the following topics:[3]

1. *Accident prevention and safety.* Each year, more than 100,000 Amer-

[3]R. Kime, R.G. Schlaadt, and L. Tritsch, *Health Instruction: An Action Approach* (Englewood Cliffs, N.J.: Prentice Hall, 1978), 62-64; The National Professional School Organization, "Comprehensive School Health Education," *Health Education* 15 (October/November 1984): 6.

icans die in accidents, and accidents rank fourth as a leading cause of death. Accidental death ranks first for ages 1 through 38.[4]

Children are risk takers, and they must be aware of factors leading to accidents, ways to prevent them, and how to administer first aid. The National Safety Council focuses on four major categories of accidents: motor vehicle, work, home, and public.[5] These categories include situations such as falls, fires, drownings, and poisoning. Children need to learn safety in sports and play, traffic safety, bicycle safety, home safety, and protection from fire and other disasters. Natural disaster safety should also be taught.

2. *Community health.* The community can serve as a laboratory for schools and provide students with realistic, firsthand experience with health services. Students should know which government agencies provide services that protect, promote, and maintain personal health. They should know where to turn when they need help and should become familiar with groups such as the American Lung Association, the Heart Association, Planned Parenthood, the department of public health, hospitals, clinics, and HMOs.

3. *Consumer health.* We are all feeling greater pressure to take responsibility for our own health, but ignorant people, especially if they are ill, are easy prey to entrepreneurs and con artists intent on making a profit. The tremendous economic loss from purchasing fraudulent products is surpassed only by the potential harm to those who delay proper treatment. School health education programs should help students detect fraudulent practices, recognize false claims and appeals, identify consumer protection agencies, and evaluate alternative ways of financing medical care. Students should also have information about advertising techniques used to sell products to their age group as well as to adults.

4. *Environmental health.* Pollution, radiation, overpopulation, waste disposal, and other problems have forced us to take a closer look at our environment and how we can preserve it for future generations. Numerous local, state, national, and international measures are being taken to regain a better balance with the world we live in. In school health education, emphasis should be on teaching individuals to be responsible in maintaining and preserving the environment. This may range from not being a "litter bug" to participating in groups trying to eliminate the threat of nuclear war. Class discussion might focus on pollution issues such as attempts to clean the air (lead free gasoline, car pooling), renewing the water supply, landfills, or recycling.

5. *Family life education.* Investigation of the multiple roles and personal lifestyles individuals may choose is a social imperative. The classroom atmosphere should encourage students to freely question, discuss, and seek

---

[4]National Safety Council, *Accident Facts* (Chicago: National Safety Council, 1985), 8.

[5]Ibid, p. 3.

answers to issues about dating, human sexuality, marriage, parenting, divorce, birth control, abortion, and adoption.

Sex education should start in 1st grade with major emphasis on self-esteem and decision making. At each successive level, content will be more detailed, but at the same time sensitive to the psychosocial development of the child. Trained health educators should decide what should be taught and when, but it is advisable to consult an advisory committee made up of a cross section of the community so the program reflects local values.

6. *Mental and emotional health.* Although many Americans enjoy a high material standard of living, they pay a demanding psychological price. An estimated 50 percent of the patients visiting doctors are troubled by psychosomatic illnesses. Ten percent of all Americans will be mental patients at some point in their lives.

The impact of stress on the nation's physical and mental health is considerable. Some stress may be beneficial and lead to improved productivity. Unless suitably managed, however, stress can contribute to physiological and psychological dysfunctions such as depression, fatigue, obesity, coronary heart disease, and violence.

Suicide is a vital health issue. More than 20,000 Americans will commit suicide this year. Of particular concern are group suicides among students. Recently, such suicides have left behind classmates and friends who have no real understanding of why the situation occurred or whether it will happen again. Discussion in health education classes may help prevent further suicide attempts.

In health education programs, mental health can be treated as a separate topic or woven through all topics. In either case, students need to learn how to adapt to a variety of situations and respond to different kinds of problems. To maintain their own mental health, students should study and discuss how they deal with their feelings, how they make decisions to cope with everyday life, and how they can improve their communication skills.

7. *Nutrition.* Health education is incomplete without study of foods, weight control, and eating disorders. Anorexia nervosa, bulimia, excessive use of salt and sugar, cholesterol intake, and the relationship of diet to cancer are all areas of growing concern. Generally, poor nutrition is attributed to lack of knowledge, low income, and bad eating habits. An effective school health program should help students develop positive nutritional habits and attitudes.

8. *Personal health.* Personal health is the study of the structure and function of the body, including care of teeth and gums, eyes, ears, skin, and hair, and the need to balance rest with physical activity. Technology, automation, and affluence have contributed to the sedentary lifestyle of many Americans and such harmful conditions as obesity, lower-back problems, and high blood pressure. Students need to know about the positive mental

and physical side effects of exercise and to be encouraged to take up an activity they can pursue through life.

9. *Disease prevention and control.* Advances in preventing and controlling communicable and noncommunicable diseases have been remarkable in this century. These are the result, in large part, of the discovery of the microscope, immunizations, chlorinization of the public water supply, pasteurization of milk, improved sanitation, and antibiotics. Researchers are still challenged, of course, in their search for cures to numerous illnesses including the common cold, cancer, heart disease, diabetes, AIDS, and other sexually transmitted diseases.

With the continuing spread of AIDS, it is essential that education about the disease be increased. Surgeon General Koop recommends starting AIDS education in the 3rd grade. Obviously, program implementation must be preceded by inservice programs to prepare teachers for the task. Several good resources are available,[6] including "AIDS Prevention Program for Youth" from the American Red Cross. Many states have now developed their own curriculum guides that are available to school systems.

The top three killers in the United States are heart disease, cancer, and stroke. Students should learn that, according to the American Heart Association, people can guard against heart attack if they have regular medical examinations; exercise regularly; reduce consumption of saturated fat, cholesterol, and unnecessary calories; refrain from smoking; and control high blood pressure. Death from many kinds of cancer is avoidable; people need to know the cancer danger signals and have regular checkups. Effective school and public health education programs should provide information and encourage the kind of behavior that increases the quality and the length of life.

10. *Substance use and abuse.* There is a fine line between use and abuse, and individuals who are using a prescribed drug often don't realize that they are actually abusing the substance. Substance use—the taking of medically prescribed drugs according to the recommended dosage—has become an accepted part of the American lifestyle. Substance abuse is the escalation of use to the point that the drug interferes with one's economic, social, psychological, or physical well-being. Many familiar substances—including salt, sugar, and aspirin, as well as marijuana and cocaine—can be abused.

We are all aware of the problems associated with tobacco, alcohol, and heroin. A major concern today is the abuse of these substances by students. An effective program should include a K-12 curriculum and a substance abuse policy that addresses how to deal with emergency situations.

[6]See, for example, Peggy Brick, "AIDS Forces the Issue: Crisis Prevention or Education in Sexuality?" *ASCD Curriculum Update* (October 1987).

Curriculum Framework for a Comprehensive Health Program

While several curriculum models are available, the 1987 Wisconsin Curriculum Framework, developed under the leadership of a state health office, is exemplary.[7] This framework, illustrated in Figure 9.2, carefully identifies health topics that are appropriate for various grade levels, although these may need to be adjusted to your local school district. For additional information, contact your state department of education's health specialist, or college or university health teacher preparation departments. Another excellent resource on health curriculums is *The Compendium of Exemplary School Health Education Programs for Teaching and Learning Resources*, published by the Centers for Disease Control, 1600 Clifton Road N.E., Atlanta, GA 30033.

Developing and Implementing a Comprehensive K-12 Health Instruction Program

The School Health Education Evaluation provides documentation that school health education effectively improves student health knowledge, attitudes, and behavior. The evaluation was conducted under the auspices of the Centers for Disease Control and the Office of Disease Prevention.[8] It was a three-year study of four health instruction programs in 20 states. It involved teachers, parents, about 30,000 students, and others in more than 1,000 classrooms.[9]

Results showed that health education is most effective when implemented K-12 with administrative and pedagogic support for teacher training, integrated materials, and continuity across grades. The study supports the theory that youngsters can be taught to practice a healthful lifestyle, that educators can influence their students not to smoke; to restrict the amount of fat, sugar, and salt in their diet; to exercise; to have blood pressure checked; and to obey speed limits and use seat belts. With adequate time (a minimum of 40 periods per year), health education leads to significant gains in knowledge, attitudes, and behavior.[10]

---

[7]The National Professional School Organization, "School Health Education Evaluation," *Journal of School Health* 55 (October 1985): 291-355.

[8]The findings of the School Health Education Evaluation were published in L.W. Green, T. Cook, M.E. Doster, et. al., "Thoughts from the School Health Education Evaluation Advisory Panel," *Journal of School Health* 55 (October 1985): 300. Also see H.J. Walberg, et al., "Health Knowledge and Attitudes Change Before Behavior," *ASCD Curriculum Update* (June 1986).

[9]Ibid.

[10]D.B. Connell, R.R. Turner, and E.F. Mason, "Summary of Findings of the School Health Education Evaluation: Health Promotion Effectiveness, Implementation, and Costs," *Journal of School Health* 55 (October 1985): 316.

Figure 9.2. Curriculum Framework

A basic task for any local district curriculum committee is to determine how the curriculum will be structured. There are many ways to organize the curriculum in health education, such as by unit, by concept, by competency, by domain, by problem, or by a combination of these.

This guide identifies 10 major content areas as basic components of a comprehensive school health education program. They are taken from a 1981 report by a national health education task force and published in *Recommendations for School Health Education, A Handbook for State Policy-makers.* These 10 areas establish the overall framework for the body of knowledge to be included in a K-12 health education program. It is recommended that local districts develop their curriculums around instructional units consisting of specific lessons that are developmental and sequential from kindergarten through 12th grade.

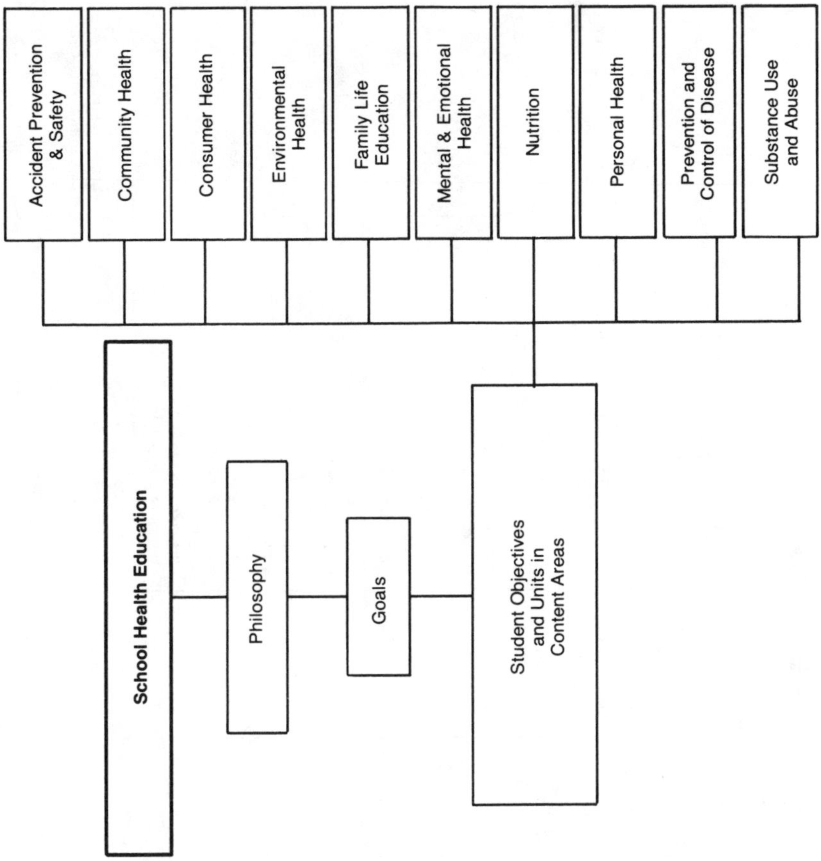

Continued next page.

Curriculum Progression Chart

This chart has been prepared to give a brief overview of the content to be covered to meet the student objectives identified in this curriculum guide. It is not all-inclusive, but provides an adequate review of the scope and sequence of a comprehensive K-12 health instruction program.

A specific *topical reference* has been placed in parentheses under the title of each of the ten content areas. Sample objectives, as written in the guide, which support that specific topical reference appear in the column below the content area at the various grade levels. This demonstrates the developmental nature of the curriculum and shows how a topic can be supported by objectives and instructional units throughout the grades, K-12.

The other items in each column identify additional topics for instruction which are covered under other objectives. Once again, these topics are not all-inclusive, but provide an overview of content recommended in this guide.

NOTE
All objectives (*) in this guide are prefaced by the words, "Students will . . ."

Major Content Area Topical References	**Accident Prevention and Safety** (Emergency Referral)	**Community Health** (Resources)
Grade Level K	*Recite the names of people who can help in case of an accident. —poison signs —protective behaviors —rules —life hazards	
1	*Dial the emergency phone number in case of an accident. —school safety —fire drills —bus and auto safety	
2	—water safety —electrical safety —basic first aid —fire escape plans —accident prevention	
3	—pedestrian safety —reflective clothing —home fires —safety patrols —safety laws	—characteristics of a healthy community —problem solving —assistance with health promotion

4	*Develop a list of telephone numbers for emergency contacts. —hiking safety —first aid for bleeding —bike safety —minor injuries	*Explain the role of community health agencies in protecting and promoting the health and safety of community members. —public health workers —disease prevention
5	—boating safety —water safety —choking symptoms	—health benefits —personal and family activities that promote health —community health issues —community health specialists
6	*Develop a babysitter's guide of accident prevention and safety procedures. —shock —heart attack —safety attitude	*Explain how the environmental health section of a health department serves the community. —community health planning —community action —volunteer health agencies
7-9	—first aid for drug overdose —artificial respiration —first aid for chocking victim	*Identify local health resources available to meet specific community health needs. —community help for the aged —health organizations —community health careers
10-12	—careers in safety —CPR —bandaging —splinting —safety in sports and leisure	*Demonstrate the skills for locating, evaluating, and using community health resources. —individual versus community rights —medical care trends —personal action plan

Curricular Progression Chart, continued

Major Content Area Topical References	**Consumer Health** (Health Advertising)	**Environmental Health** (Waste Disposal)	**Family Life Education** (Positive Relationships)
Grade Level K			*Describe qualities of friends. —promoting a healthy family —similarities and differences between people
1			—groups and their importance —kinds of families —responsibilities —trust
2			*Recognize and value caring adults who are significant in one's life. —growth differences —human needs —abuse prevention
3	*Identify the impact of advertising and other influences on the use of health products and services. —health products —TV ads and health	*Participate in a program aimed at reducing litter in school and within the community. —causes of air pollution —sources of environmental pollution	*Describe different kinds of friendships. *Identify trusted people who can help with personal and family problems. —families working together —life cycle —reproduction

4	—questionable health practices —family practices, values, and emotions in choosing health products	*Describe community facilities and procedures that ensure safe water supplies and sanitary trash and sewage disposal. —water pollution —parks —recreational sites	*Realize that learning to get along with others is a process unique to each individual. —the reproductive system —puberty changes
5	*Explain how information contained on a label can be used in selecting health products. —OTC drugs —prescription drugs —quackery versus legitimate health practice	*List sources of and methods to deal with solid waste. —land pollution —natural resources —population and land use	*List the characteristics that help maintain friendships and compare oneself to this list. —family impact on each member's development —death's or divorce's impact on the family
6	*Identify advertising techniques used in media promotion of food, tobacco, alcohol, and health-related products. —evaluation of product claims —why people select certain health products	—rodents and insects —environmental changes in the year 2000 —sanitation	*Discuss dating as one way of exploring friendships and learning new social skills. —peer pressures —family roles —decision making —dating behavior
7-9	—cost, quality, warranty, and availability of health products and services —criteria for selecting health products and services	—technology and the environment —agencies involved in environmental health —noise pollution —environmental carcinogens	*Develop the ability to resolve conflicts and formulate new friendships. *Identify the responsibilities and consequences inherent in sexual relationships. —a mother's effect on the unborn —communication with parents —the need for love and affection
10-12	*Analyze techniques used to promote health-related products and services, including insurance. —consumer rights —governmental agencies and their regulatory powers	*Evaluate the environmental impact of toxic waste disposal. —energy sources —environmental health careers —government regulation of the environment —environmental preservation	*Analyze the interrelationships of career and family roles, responsibilities, and family harmony. —teen pregnancy —birth defects —nutrition and development —sexual assault prevention —spouse selection

Curricular Progression Chart, continued

Major Content Area Topical References	**Mental and Emotional Health** (Stress)	**Nutrition** (Nutrients)	**Personal Health** (Fitness)
Grade Level K	—valuing self as unique and worthwhile —feelings and behavior —how to help others feel good about themselves —where to go for help	—breakfast —nutritious snacks —food versus non-food items —food advertisements	—personal grooming —cleanliness habits —tooth care —posture
1	—respect for others —how emotions affect the body —belonging —effort and its effect on skill development	—sensory characteristics of food —plant and animal sources of food —food forms —mealtime behavior —need to eat a variety of foods	*Recognize the relationship between physical activity and muscular development. —heart health —rest and relaxation —human senses
2	—emotions—pleasant and unpleasant —how the environment affects feelings —appreciate consequences of behavior choices —how people express feelings	*Compare varying amounts of nutrients and energy needed throughout the life cycle. —wide varieties of food choices —dental caries —sugar —ingredient order on labels	*Recognize that the heart is a muscle that is strengthened by exercise. *Value physical well-being by practicing fitness behaviors which contribute to health. —major body organs —quiet activities
3	*Define stress and cite examples of positive and negative stressors. *Identify positive ways of dealing with stress. —physical health and feelings —group membership —grief	*State that food supplies nutrients that are needed for growth, repair, and maintenance of cells. —food choices —sensory qualities of food —food chain —energy needs	*Cite ways to build physical activities into daily routine. —lifestyle choices —body and self-image —the senses and safety, learning, and play —handicapping conditions

4	—respect for others' feelings, rights, and property —factors that affect self-image —communication skills —personal health and esteem	*Define nutrient. *Identify the major classes of nutrients and their functions. —calories —ideal weight —reliable sources of nutrition information	—rewards for positive health behavior —"prioritizing" health activities —inherited characteristics —mechanics of the circulatory system
5	—group decision making —peer influence —interpersonal behaviors —desirable personal qualities —risk-taking behavior	*Identify major sources of key nutrients. *Classify foods into groups based on their major nutrient contribution. —portion size and servings —diet and blood pressure —fiber —sample menu evaluation	*Identify benefits of both aerobic and anaerobic exercise. —functions of body systems —interdependence of body systems —effects of puberty on development
6	*Identify situations that are stress producing. —expression of feelings —decision-making strategies —significant people —fairness	*Compare nutrient density of foods. —nutrient excess —nutrient deficiencies —food economics —dietary plan for a day's energy needs	*Recognize the importance of establishing an ongoing and effective exercise plan which accommodates personal requirements and limitations. —components of a healthy lifestyle
7-9	*Identify stress management techniques. —personal goals —suicide prevention —defense mechanisms —grief and coping with grief	*Identify factors affecting basic nutrient and energy requirements and compute caloric needs. —health impact of diets —nutrition and dietary careers	—adolescent health care practices —fad behaviors —skin problems and their care —interpretation of "wellness" inventories
10-12	*Demonstrate stress management techniques —effective communication skills —selection of a satisfying career —positive mental health plan —mental health careers	—construct a weekly diet —evaluate a diet in terms of sugar, sodium, fat, fiber, etc. —compare nutritional value of supplements and additives	*Design and implement a personal health plan adaptable to changing lifelong needs. —social forces affecting health practices —energy balance and body weight —personal health careers

Curricular Progression Chart, continued

Major Content Area Topical References	Prevention and Control of Disease (Communicable Disease)	Substance Use and Abuse (Resources)
Grade Level K	—comparison of wellness and illness —proper dress and disease prevention —personal hygiene habits	*Explain reasons for consulting a responsible adult before using medicines and chemical substances. —medicines at home —names of medicines used or abused
1	*Discuss the relationship between germs and disease. —"We are well most of the time." —medical personnel —public health efforts	—what a medicine is —how medicines are helpful or harmful —good risks versus bad risks —risks in using substances
2	*Describe how germs cause illness. *Explain communicable disease. —immunization —effect of exercise, diet, rest on disease prevention	—recognizing names given to medicines —rules for taking medicines —avoidance of certain drugs —drug effects
3	*Distinguish between infectious and noninfectious disease. —disease symptoms —early steps to combat illness —wellness lifestyle	*List people and places who can provide help with medicine and chemical substance use problems. —use versus abuse —effects on physical, social, and emotional well-being —caffeine —nicotine

4	—personal behavior and wellness —heredity and illness —illness and personal responsibility —family influences on health	—misuses or abuses of drugs —drug effects on body organs —misuse of OTC drugs —effects of smoking
5	*Explain the process of communicable disease transmission. —avoidance of disease —motivation and health behavior	—decision making about drugs —peer and adult influences —community impact of drug abuse —laws
6	—positive versus negative health behaviors —immune system —major killers	*Identify and utilize the names of people and organizations who can provide help concerning problems related to tobacco, alcohol, marijuana, and other drugs. —alcohol effects —confronting the pressure to use drugs
7-9	*Identify sources, symptoms, and treatment of sexually transmitted diseases. —past, present, and future health practices —factors that enhance health or cause illness	*Identify local resources, services, and support groups that are available for substance abuse treatment and control. —alternatives to drug use —negative consequences of drug abuse —careers in drug-related areas
10-12	*Identify agencies and referral procedures for communicable disease or chronic disorders. —disease prevention planning —disease prevention careers	*Describe how to utilize programs and facilities designed to help individuals and families with tobacco, alcohol, and other drug problems. —the right to say "no" —drugs and health status —drugs and vehicle operation —drugs and pregnancy

10. The Transition from Industrial Arts to Technology Education

M. James Bensen

THROUGHOUT THE COUNTRY, INDUSTRIAL ARTS PROGRAMS ARE undergoing major changes in content, organization, and delivery reflecting a new emphasis on technology. Technology education is "a comprehensive, action-based educational program concerned with technical means, their evolution, utilization and significance with industry, its organization, personnel, systems, techniques, resources and products, and their social and cultural impact" (ITEA 1986b).

First suggested 50 years ago (Warner et al. 1937), technology education was born during the curriculum reform movement of the 1960s, when leaders in the field became intensely interested in its possibilities. During this period, over 50 curriculum projects proposed alternatives to the traditional "wood, metal, and drawing" content of industrial arts. Prominent among these projects were the Industrial Arts Curriculum Project and the American Industry Project, developed at the Ohio State University and the University of Wisconsin-Stout respectively (Towers et al. 1966, Face and Flug 1966).

During the 1980s, the transition to technology education has been dramatic. State-level curriculum guides, local curriculums, equipment, and published materials have all changed to provide support for technology-based programs. Over 30 state industrial education associations have changed their names to include "Technology." The four affiliated councils of the International Technology Education Association—groups composed of teachers, teacher educators, supervisors, and state association officers—have changed their names as well.

Much remains to be done, however, at the classroom level. Teachers in the field have resisted making the necessary leap forward. This resistance can probably be attributed to lack of understanding, inadequate inservice programs, poorly developed change models, and fear of the unknown.

State and local school districts have also been reluctant to commit themselves fully to technology education. Many districts call their transitional programs "industrial technology." This hybrid term is considered less threatening, but unfortunately it emphasizes the industrial side of technology and downplays the personal side concerned with tasks of consumers and community decision makers.

A Rationale for Technology Education

Students need technology education because, as citizens and consumers, they need to understand our technological culture. As Johnson (1986) writes,

> Perhaps the ultimate question in this technical world is, "Who will develop and control the technologies so that they can best serve all citizens?" (p. 4).

As citizens, we must make community decisions: we must plan the future of our cities, decide when to build schools and how to dispose of waste. As consumers, we must know how to maintain our cars and homes; we must decide when to purchase services and when to do it ourselves. In order to make intelligent choices, we must be technologically literate.

Careers

Since technology provides the basis for work for a large segment of our society, many technology education programs provide career exploration. These programs examine the total spectrum of technical work from the semiskilled to the professional, from trades to engineering (see Figure 10.1). Students learn the requirements for entering, maintaining competence, and advancing in the technological workplace—requirements ranging from short-term trade training to postgraduate study.

Program Goals

The goals of a technology education program vary greatly from preschool to adult levels. Figure 10.2 shows the program goals for each level and the educational experiences designed to achieve those goals.

Preschool and Elementary School

The International Technology Education Association supports providing technology education at the preschool and elementary levels, even though most school systems do not presently do so. The goals for technology education at this level are to:

- Develop technological awareness.
- Familiarize students with the use of tools, materials, processes, and technological concepts.
- Reinforce and enrich concepts in science, mathematics, language arts, social studies, and other areas in the curriculum.

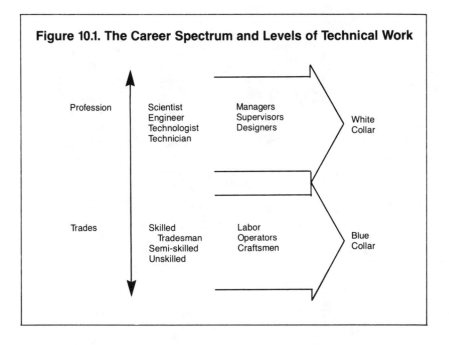

Figure 10.1. The Career Spectrum and Levels of Technical Work

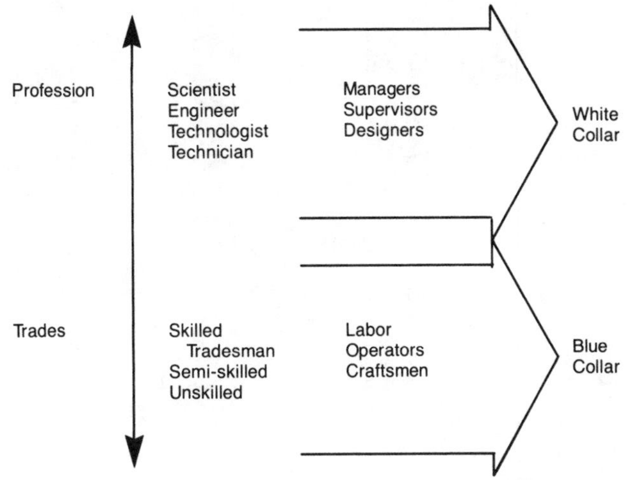

• Help students understand how people create and control their environment.

Schools can achieve these goals in two ways. The regular classroom teacher can integrate technology activities into the school day to give life to the concepts taught in math, science, and social studies. (For example, rather than just working triangulation problems on paper, teacher and students can make a simple transit and survey the school property.) A less common alternative to this integrative approach is to set up a technology lab in the school. Terry Thode, of Hemingway Elementary School in Ketchum, Idaho, teaches in such a lab. She has her elementary students work with lasers, optics, robots, and computers, giving them firsthand experiences with technology.

Middle/Junior High School

The program at the middle school level emphasizes exploration. The focus is on understanding general technology, with additional study of the special technologies of communications, construction, manufacturing, and transportation. A common thread running through these courses is problem solving: inventing, designing, and carrying solutions through to development. The program goals at this level are to enable students to:

• Appreciate the scope and impact of technology on the development of societies in the past, present, and future.

Figure 10.2. Level of Experiences and Goal Emphasis Preschool to Adult

	Level of Education				
	Preschool/ Elementary	Middle/Jr. High	Early Senior High	Advanced Senior High	Adult Education
Educational Experiences	Integrated into the Curriculum Careers Tools Machines Processes Problem Solving	General Technology Industrial Enterprise	Communication Systems Transportation Systems Production Systems	Advanced Enterprise Research & Experimentation Design & Development Engineering Trade & Industry Vocational preparation	Individualized courses to meet needs & interests
Goal Emphasis	Technology Awareness Industrial Awareness Career Awareness	Technology Orientation Indsustrial Insight Career Self Concept Development & Exploration	Technology Exploration Industrial Understanding Career Cluster Exploration	Technology Utilization Industrial Interpretation Career Development & Beginning Specialization	Technology Assessment & Transfer Industrial Applications Career Re-orientation & Leisure Pursuits

- Identify career opportunities in the field of technology.
- Understand what educational background is necessary for entering various levels of technological work.
- Use tools, machines, materials, and technological processes safely and creatively.
- Experience the organization and management systems of business and industry.
- Solve problems through the process of research, experimentation, design, development, construction, service, and evaluation.

Senior High School

Secondary programs are generally elective and offered as semester or yearlong courses. Often, at the advanced level, students pursue independent studies on a contract basis. The program goal at this level is in-depth application of technology. Teachers should provide students with experiences that promote adaptability and transfer skills, while preparing them for advanced education or entry into the workplace. The specific goals are to enable students to:

- Utilize tools, machines, materials, and processes safely, confidently, and with a measure of skill.
- Make decisions regarding careers, for entering into a vocation or profession.
- Gain an in-depth understanding and appreciation of technology in our society.
- Experience applications of math, science, economics, and transfer of know-how to everyday life situations.
- Solve problems involving advanced enterprises, robotics, lasers, fiber optics, computer-aided design, manufacturing, rocketry, mass transit, and synthetics.

Adult Programs

Offers for adult learners are are usually night classes designed to fit local needs. The goals of these programs are to:

- Provide personal and professional technical updating (e.g., computer applications, desktop publishing, inventions and patents).
- Enhance leisure activities (e.g., amateur radio, furniture refinishing, and model rocketry).
- Teach skills and develop a measure of technological literacy for meeting everyday challenges and making intelligent decisions (e.g., home repair, general auto mechanics).

Program Models

Program models for the study of technology are at varying stages of implementation in New York, Indiana, Illinois, Virginia, Iowa, Minnesota,

Figure 10.3. Wisconsin Secondary School Technology Education Program Model

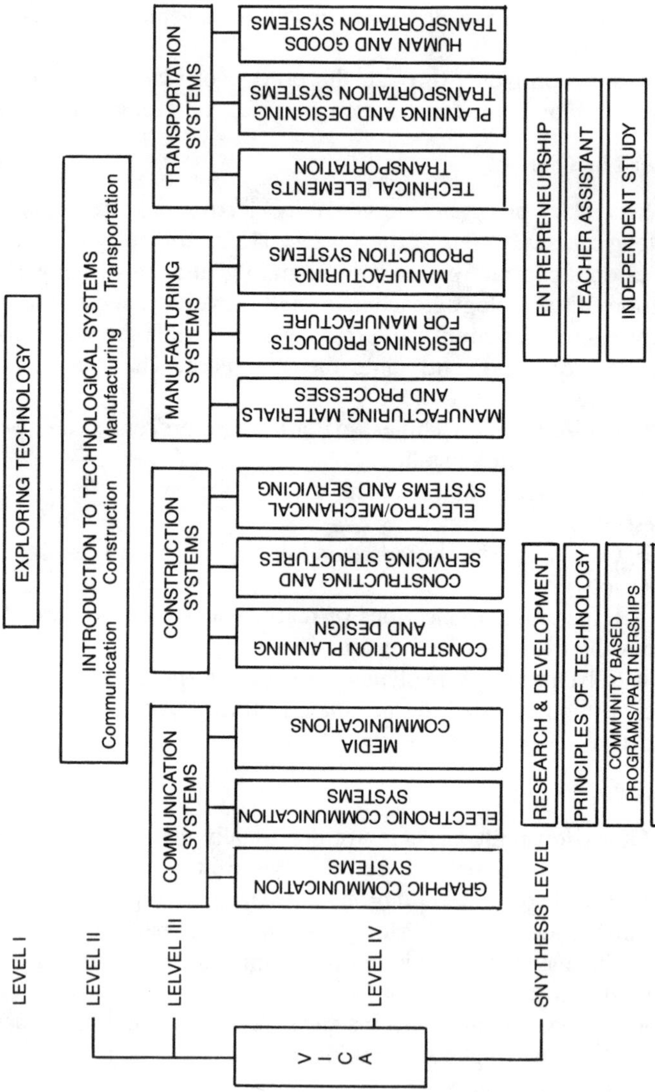

NOTE: This is a large school program model. The guide contains models more adaptable.

North Dakota, and Wisconsin. Wisconsin, for example, proposes a slightly different model for small, medium, and large schools. Figure 10.3 shows the large-school model for secondary schools. In this model, the Level I and II courses are proposed for junior high school, the Level III courses for early senior high, and the Level IV and Synthesis Level courses for the last two years of high school.

Content Selection Methods

Curriculum developers use several methods to identify and structure content for technology education programs. These include the *conceptual, behavior analysis, problem-solving,* and *systems* methods. Use of a particular method for content selection has significant impact on the structure of courses included in a school's program.

The Conceptual Method

The conceptual approach organizes technology into categories and hierarchies, creating a taxonomy of content (see Figure 10.4). This taxonomy shows where a subconcept fits into the discipline, and how subconcepts interrelate. These subconcepts can be studied at any level, from elementary to postdoctoral.

The conceptual method promotes inclusiveness and ensures a holistic study of technology. The goals of the program, rather than the concepts themselves, dictate the nature of the study. This follows the principle of readiness proposed by Jerome Bruner in *The Process of Education* (1960). DeVore provides an example of a conceptual approach in *Structure and Content Foundations for Curriculum* (1973, pp. 12-15).

The Behavior Analysis Method

An alternative approach structures the curriculum around the behaviors needed to function in a technological world. These include tasks performed in the workplace, as well as the "life tasks" of a citizen, consumer, decision maker, and home owner (Bensen 1980, p. 12).

Using this method, a teacher might organize learning experiences around the tasks necessary to maintaining a home. These include not only the knowledge and skills used for maintenance, but the aesthetics of the dwelling and the landscape surrounding it. Students would learn how to make a "best buy" given the circumstances of the persons living in the home.

The Problem-Solving Method

Schools using the problem-solving method for content selection consider "process as content" an important dimension of a learner's experience. This requires providing both *foundation* instruction, so that students know

Figure 10.4. Illustrative Conceptual Model of Technology (DeVore, pp. 12-15)

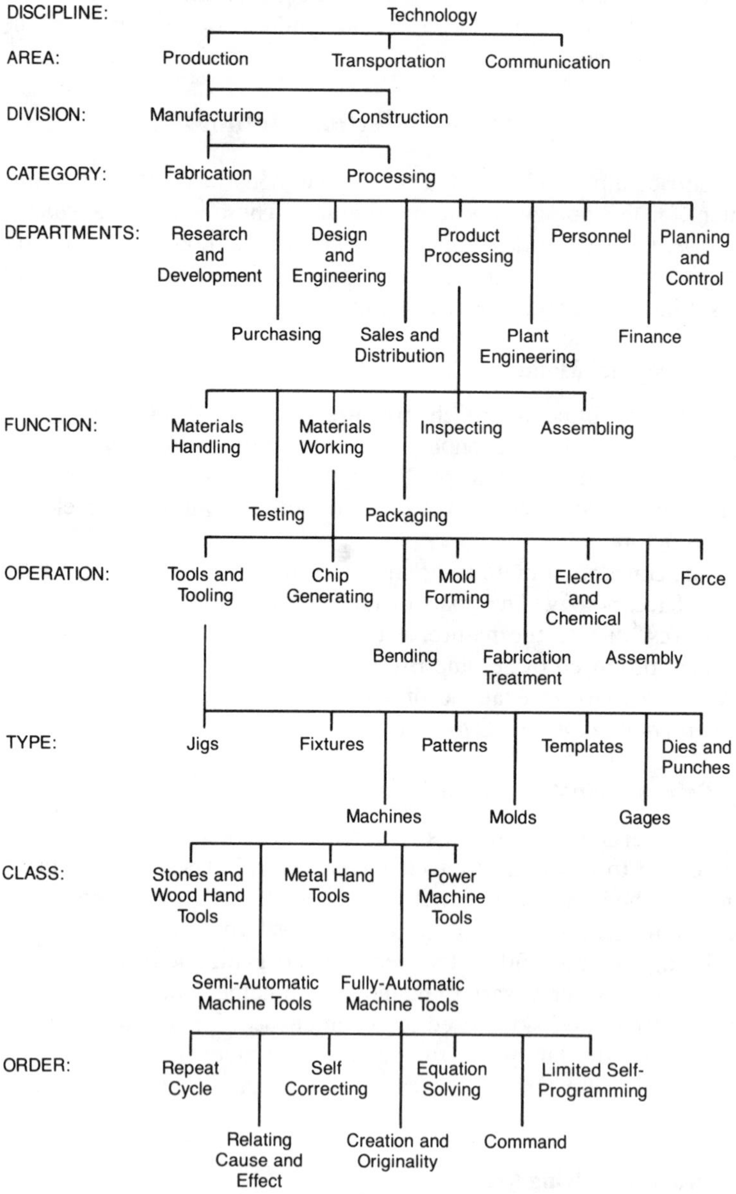

Figure 10.5. Instruction in Technology To Promote Process-as-Content

FOUNDATION INSTRUCTION	PROCESS INSTRUCTION
• Introduction to materials and processes	• Problem solving
• Overview of technical systems	• Engineering solutions
• Use of tools, machines & equipment	• Research & experimentation
• Use of experimentors, testing devices, etc.	• Designing & development
• Procedures, diagnostics & practice exercises, etc.	• Inventing
	• Values/judgments
• Etc.	• Etc.

the tools for solving problems, and *process* instruction, so that they can fully develop their capabilities. Figure 10.5 shows examples of these types of instruction.

One prominent problem-solving model is the Maryland Plan, developed and implemented by Maley and his faculty at the University of Maryland (Maley 1973). This program identifies major technological themes, such as transportation, communication, production, and materials, and studies them using a timeline.

The Systems Method

The systems method is one of the most popular ways to identify and structure content in technology education. Figure 10.6 shows a frequently used systems model developed through the Jackson's Mill Project (Snyder and Hales 1981). This model is further developed into four subsystems: communications, construction, manufacturing, and transportation. Figure 10.7 shows the manufacturing subsystem.

Students in a manufacturing course form a company, conduct market research, sell stock to raise capital, design and build prototypes, engineer the manufacturing system, construct jigs and fixtures, write software for controllers, interface robots on the production line, produce and package their product, sell it, conduct consumer satisfaction research, liquidate the company, and pay off stockholders. Manufacturing courses are taught at all levels, from early elementary to university, with the appropriate level of sophistication.

The British School Technology Project has developed a systems model that focuses on using systematic problem solving in any technological endeavor (Figure 10.8).

Learning Activities

The value of a technology education program rests on the quality of the learning activities it provides. Learning through involvement enhances both motivation and retention.

Figure 10.6. Curriculum Interaction Model

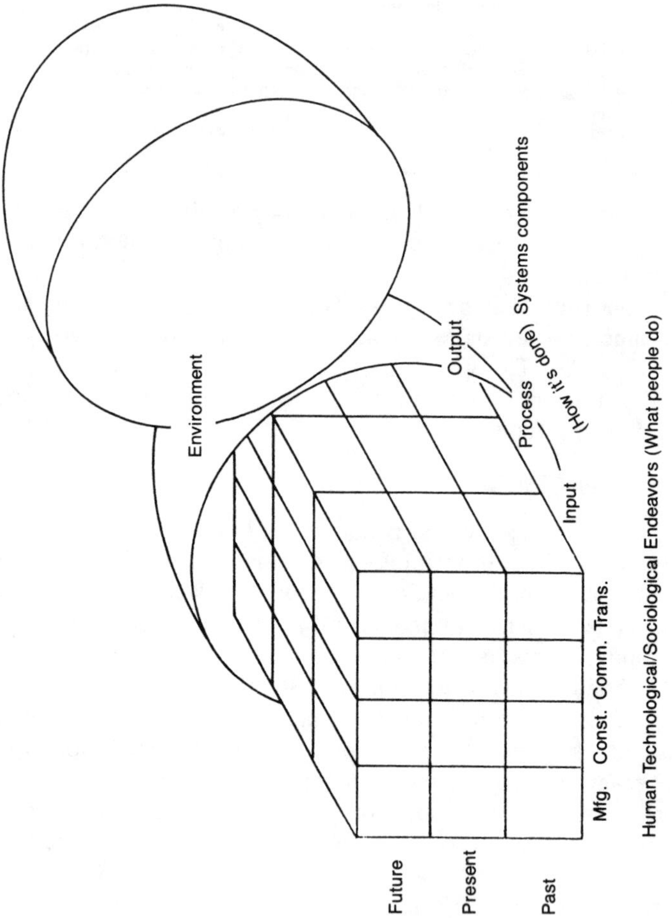

Figure 10.7. Managed Manufacturing System

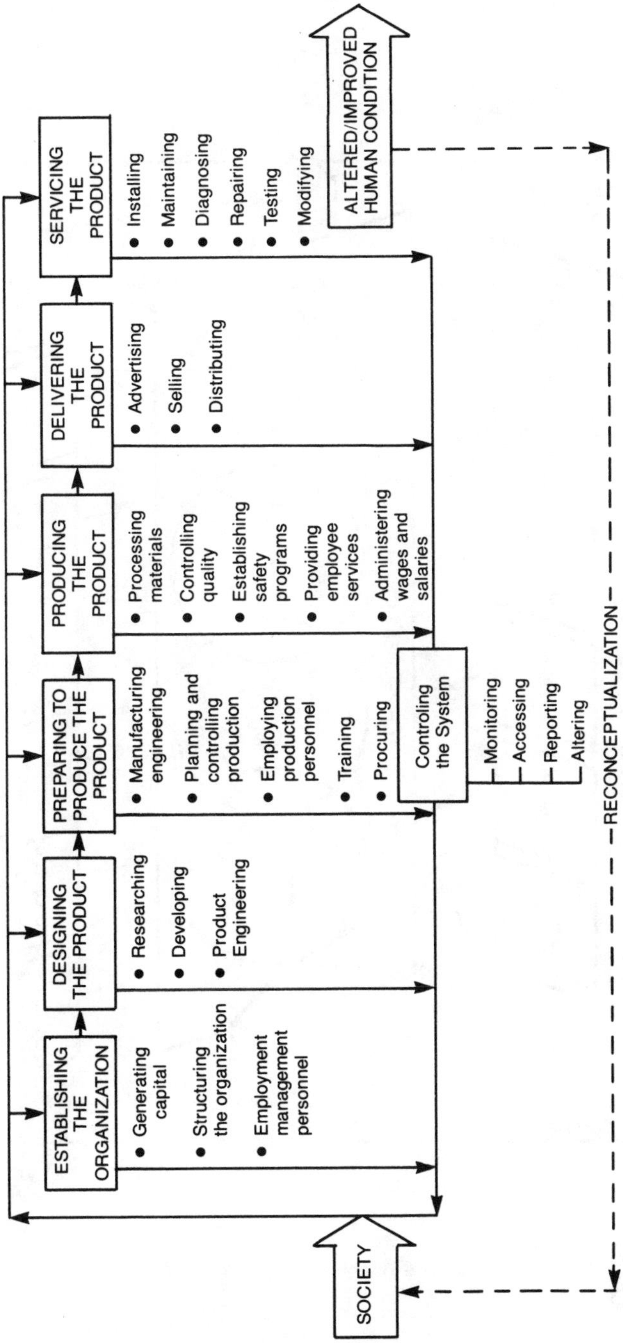

Figure 10.8. Technology is the Disciplined Process of Using Scientific, Material, and Human Resources to Achieve Human Purpose

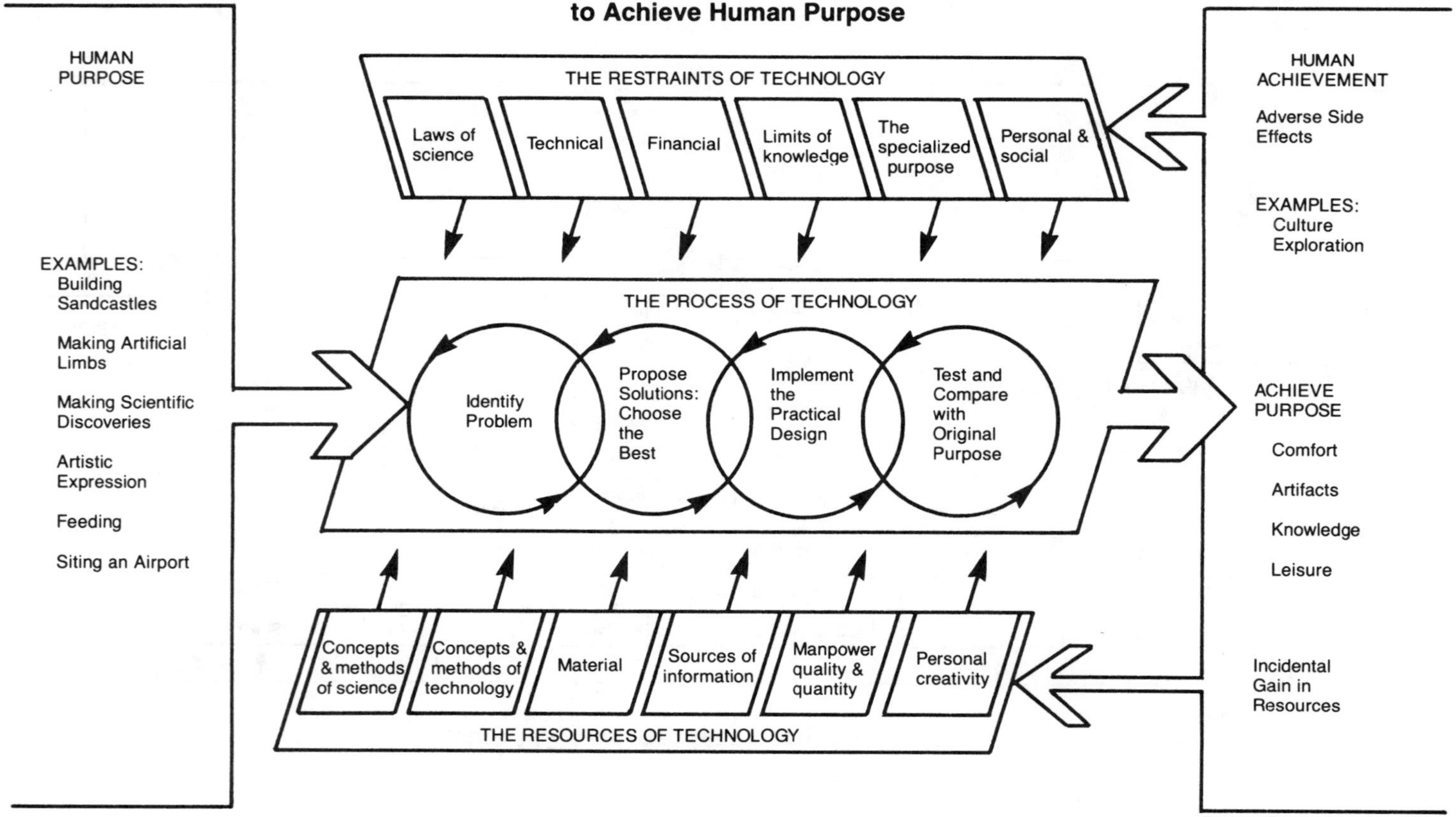

Project Technology Jan. 1970

Figure 10.9. Sample Elementary Technology Education Learning Activity ("Technology and You")

Activity 2. BLOWING IN THE WIND

With a student team you invent a device that uses wind power to lift weights.

Your team will need:

"Blowing in the Wind" specifications (following)
Checklist for individual contributions to team, one copy
Blow hair dryer
Metric ruler or tape
Paper clips
Clothes hanger
A variety of materials of your choice, such as
- Aluminum soft drink cans
- Dowels of various sizes
- Coping saw, screwdriver, pliers
- String, wire
- Spools
- Small brackets
- Pieces of plywood

Humans have found throughout history that the abilities of a group of people add up to more than the sum of their individual talents.

Some people are good at certain skills and weak in others. We add to each other's strengths and make up for many weaknesses when we work together.

Most new knowledge and new inventions today come as a result of many people putting their skills together.

In this activity, you are to work in your team of four students.

Your team's mission: Build a device that will lift weights using only the power of the wind created by a blow hair dryer. In other words, you are to invent a WIND-POWERED CRANE!

- Join your 4-member team. Your success in this activity and your grade will depend on your team cooperation.

  Every individual on the team is responsible for the team's success. You will sink or swim together!

  NOTE: One group of four will serve as patent officers. Your teacher will give you your instructions.

  ROLES

- Read over the role descriptions in Activity 1-3. Adapt them for this activity. Group members may either choose their roles or draw them at random. Make sure everyone understands all the roles and for what jobs each person is responsible.

  GROUP SKILLS

- You will need to use all the group skills carefully if you are to succeed with your invention. The best group skill to practice will be "Everyone listens to others." If your group . . .

Figure 10.9 shows an elementary-level learning activity that promotes problem solving using everyday tools and materials. The freedom to experiment, as students test their solutions, stimulates an exciting learning environment. At the end of the activity, the teacher carefully analyzes the results and makes connections to science, math, and social studies. Requiring students to prepare an "invention log" or final report helps develop language skills.

The Future

Technology education has developed so rapidly during the past five years that it is difficult to project where the movement will be five years from now. With the technology base for the field doubling during the time a student is in high school, program offerings will certainly become even more dynamic and exciting.

References

Bensen, M. James. "Selecting Content for Technology Education." In *Program Proceedings for Symposium '80: Technology Education*. Charleston, Ill.: Eastern Illinois University, Spring 1980.

Bruner, Jerome S. *The Process of Education*. New York: Random House, 1960.

DeVore, Paul W. *Structure and Content Foundations for Curriculum*. Washington, D.C.: American Industrial Arts Association, 1973.

Face, Wesley, and Eugene Flug. *The American Industry Project*. Menomonie, Wis.: The University of Wisconsin-Stout, 1966.

International Technology Education Association. *Technology Education . . . The New Basic*. Reston, Va.: ITEA, 1986b.

Johnson, James R. "The Technology Panel Report," Draft Version V, Project 2061 (unpublished manuscript). Washington, D.C.: American Association for the Advancement of Science, 1986.

Maley, Donald. *The Maryland Plan*. New York: Bruce, 1973.

Snyder, James, and James A. Hales. *Jackson's Mill Industrial Arts Curriculum Theory*. Charleston, W.Va.: West Virginia Board of Education, 1981.

Towers, Edward R., Willis E. Ray, and Donald P. Lux. *A Rationale and Structure for Industrial Arts Subject Matter*. Columbus: The Ohio State University, 1966.

Warner, William E., et al. *A Curriculum to Reflect Technology*. Columbus, Ohio: Epsilon Pi Tau, 1937.

11. Reconceptualizing the Home Economics Curriculum

Joanna B. Smith

HOME ECONOMICS IS THE ONLY CURRICULUM AREA THAT FOcuses on the family and prepares students for family and home living. The field of home economics includes content areas such as consumer education and resource management; housing, furnishings, equipment, interior design and care; individual and family development; nutrition and food; and textiles and clothing. From the passage of the Smith-Hughes Act in 1917, vocational home economics programs have focused on the occupation of homemaking. Today, federal legislation designates these programs as consumer and homemaking education.

In 1963, new vocational education legislation called for the use of federal funds for what are known as home economics *occupations* programs (Blankenship and Moerchen 1979). Thus, the mission of home economics has been broadened to include the objectives of both homemaking and wage-earning programs. These two types of programs have different settings, techniques, and instructional objectives (Hill et al. 1979), but they are related. Food service occupations call on the same principles of nutrition and food preparation as are used at home. Similarly, the principles of human development, care, and guidance are the same whether one is caring for family members or working in a daycare center or nursing home.

Home Economics in the '60s

In 1967, the American Home Economics Association published *Concepts and Generalizations: Their Place in High School Home Economics Curriculum Development,* the report of a national effort to define the structure of home economics using a conceptual approach. For many years the report was a source of the recurring themes in the major subdivisions of home economics. The publication was particularly relevant in 1967, a time when leaders in most subject fields sought to determine the fundamental structure of their disciplines.

Concepts and Generalizations is now out of print and, more importantly, out of date. The factors that affect home economics—families, their potential and their problems; learners and their development; the knowledge base on which the subject depends—have changed drastically since 1967 (Knorr 1986). Demographic projections of the composition of the workforce, for example, are the basis for a new emphasis on preparing learners to balance their work responsibilities with their roles and functions as family members. The quality of life at home is recognized as a factor in productivity of the worker.

As a result of these changes, there is a great deal of variety in the content of courses offered under the rubric of home economics. The diversity in today's programs is a result of a number of factors, including state mandates. A major influence, however, is the individuality of teachers coupled with their strong motivation to address the needs of individuals, families, and society in the local setting. Also, home economics is not a required high school subject. It is not on lists of college entrance requirements, even for students who go to college to prepare for a home economics profession. Such requirements, which tend to produce consistency in curriculum, have not existed for this subject.

Reconceptualizing Home Economics Content in the '80s

A steering committee for a national project—supported by the Home Economics Division of the American Vocational Association, the American Home Economics Association, and the Home Economics Education Association—to reconceptualize the home economics curriculum at the secondary level is now under way.

The project will produce a document, to be published in 1988, that sets forth concepts that are distinctive, but not necessarily exclusive, to the high school home economics curriculum. The committee is consulting experts in all related areas and gathering information at national forums. The following sections describe some of the issues affecting the selection of content for home economics.

Identifying Content by Task Analysis

One way to determine curriculum content is through task analysis. Study of a particular cluster of occupations yields a list of tasks, which becomes the basis for course design and evaluation of student progress. Advice from employers and skilled workers is sought to verify the task list and to suggest changes to ensure that students are adequately prepared for employment. Notable examples of use of this technique are the Colorado Curriculum Project (Brink et al. 1986), the V-TECS Consortium Project

(Downey and Kizer 1986), and the Texas Curriculum Project (Glosson 1986).

Although the competency-based model has been mandated for state developed curriculum in many states, it is frequently criticized for its dependence on current practice and lack of attention to futuristic goals. Another serious criticism relates to the difficulty of identifying competent workers in the occupation of homemaking. What consensus exists for the definition of competence in furnishing and organizing a home, managing resources, or nurturing children?

Teaching the Basics in Home Economics Courses

Another consideration in determining the content of home economics courses is their role in teaching basic skills. Recent demands for school reforms have been based on the popular view that schools have failed by straying from teaching reading, writing, number skills, and large amounts of information. Many reforms have increased the requirements for courses in English, mathematics, science, and social studies. The time left for home economics and other elective subjects has been reduced, and advocates of home economics are hard pressed to justify continuing these electives in the curriculum. That justification is sometimes found in the contribution a subject area can make to teaching the basics.

Home economics has long claimed to teach the basics—or at least to strengthen students' functional knowledge of the basics—by providing experiences in their practical application. The new emphasis on basic skills (Smith 1987) can be seen in the acceptance of some home economics courses for credit in mathematics, science, and English. Generally, this is happening in states where it has been documented that the majority of topics covered in a given home economics course match those in a required course. For example, a science credit is awarded for Food Science or a mathematics credit for Consumer Education.

Because of this trend, home economics curriculum materials now frequently provide specific assistance to teachers in reinforcing the basics. Preservice and inservice courses for teachers include provisions for teaching and reinforcing the basics.

The basics, however, are the means by which home economics is learned and are not the goal of home economics education (Peterat and Griggs 1986). Teaching the basics may offer a temporary salvation for a course threatened with extinction, but, in the long run, home economics educators must maintain the integrity of their field and defend the value of its contribution to society.

Critical Thinking in Home Economics

The underlying premise for designing a futuristic curriculum is that thinking or reasoning skills are the educational basics for the 21st century.

Knowledge changes. Being able to acquire, manage, and use knowledge may be the only part of their education that students will find useful throughout their lives. Teachers who recognize this make an effort to use content to foster thought and reasoning rather than simply presenting content as a body of information to be learned.

Home economics educators are currently examining, debating, and applying ideas about developing higher-order thinking skills. Terms such as problem solving, critical thinking, and practical reasoning appear frequently in the literature.

While there is confusion and disagreement about the direction of the home economics curriculum, there is strong agreement that the acquisition of knowledge is not sufficient for functioning in a world primarily characterized by change. According to Glaser,

> A major factor contributing to the failure of our schools to do a more effective job of developing the attitudes involved in critical thinking has been a tendency for teachers to be too much concerned with having students memorize the accepted answers, and not concerned enough with guiding them in the processes and methods of arriving at well-founded answers (1985, p. 25).

In education as a whole, the question is whether to teach critical thinking as a separate course, to include it in instruction in all courses, or both (Ennis 1985). In home economics, one view is that content for now and the future is inextricably bound to special ways of knowing and processing information. A new curriculum component, practical reasoning, has been introduced into secondary home economics curriculum in some states. Since home economics offers the knowledge base needed to resolve home and family problems, adding practical reasoning—defined as reaching conclusions about what to do from knowledge available—as a content area is one way to help students develop good thinking skills in home economics (Laster 1987).

An issue being hotly debated by home economics educators is whether practical reasoning can be justified as a content area. An alternative view is that development of critical thinkers is primarily a matter of the way content is presented. Perhaps practical reasoning processes should be included in the content of courses for home economics *teachers*.

The Real Curriculum Makers

In fact, a major factor in determination of the home economics curriculum is the teacher. The formulation of desired learner outcomes, the selection of content, the delivery of teaching/learning activities, and evaluation purposes and strategies—all essential to the curriculum—are decided at the classroom level. Teachers are influenced, of course, by the thinking of leaders and researchers who advocate ideal curriculums, and by curriculum guides, rules of state and local authorities, and textbooks and supporting materials. Still, the individual teacher is given, or takes, a great amount of freedom within the classroom. It is the teacher's view of society; the teacher's understanding of learners and learning; the teacher's knowledge, skills, and beliefs about the relative merits of various learning activities that govern curriculum at the point of delivery.

The argument for the profound importance of the teacher's role is not an argument against curriculum development at higher levels, and certainly it is not an argument against the national project to reconceptualize home economics content. It is, however, an argument for continuing to express curriculum content as a framework of concepts.

A framework of concepts sets forth in a straightforward and understandable manner the content that is unique and exclusive to home economics, together with the content that is unique but not necessarily exclusive to home economics.

Concepts may be used in many ways. Believers in reinforcing the basics through home economics instruction can readily identify the concepts to use as vehicles, as can advocates of practical reasoning. Users of any curriculum model can apply that model to content expressed as concepts. The framework of concepts may be restated or expanded, but it is a starting point.

The forthcoming document delineating the content of home economics at the secondary level as a framework of concepts will not be the last word on home economics content, but it will satisfy the need to state what home economics is about for now and for the future.

References

American Home Economics Association. *Concepts and Generalizations: Their Place in High School Home Economics Curriculum Development.* Washington, D.C.: Author, 1967.

Blankenship, M., and B. Moerchen. *Home Economics Education.* Boston: Houghton Mifflin, 1979.

Brink, C., P. Apt, and D. Horell. "Occupation of Homemaking Task Analysis and Competency-based Design: Colorado Curriculum Project." In *Vocational Home Economics Education: State of the Field,* edited by J. Laster and R. Dohner. Peoria, Ill.: Macmillan, Bennett & McKnight Division, 1986.

Downey, J., and J. Kizer. "Homemaker Tasks-based Independent Modules: V-TECS Consortium Project." In *Vocational Home Economics Education: State of the Field,* edited by J. Laster and R. Dohner. Peoria, Ill.: Macmillan, Bennett & McKnight Division, 1986.

Ennis, R. "Critical Thinking and the Curriculum." *National Forum* LXV, 1 (1985): 28-31.

Glaser, E. M. "Critical Thinking: Educating for Responsible Citizenship in a Democracy." *National Forum* LXV, 1 (1985): 23-27.

Glosson, L. "Competency-based Consumer-Homemaking Design: Texas Curriculum Project." In *Vocational Home Economics Education: State of the Field,* edited by J. Laster and R. Dohner. Peoria, Ill.: Macmillan, Bennett & McKnight Division, 1986.

Hill, A. H., T. Shear, and C. Bell. *Coalition Statement: Vocational Home Economics Education.* Washington, D.C.: Home Economics Education Association, 1979.

Knorr, A. J. "Contextual Factors Impacting on Home Economics Curriculum." In *Vocational Home Economics Education: State of the Field,* edited by J. Laster and R. Dohner. Peoria, Ill.: Macmillan, Bennett & McKnight Division, 1986.

Laster, J. "Instructional Strategies for Teaching Practical Reasoning in Consumer Homemaking Classrooms." In *Higher Order Thinking: Definition, Meaning, and Instructional Approaches,* edited by Ruth Thomas. Washington, D.C.: Home Economics Education Association, 1987.

Peterat, L., and M. Griggs. "Reconsidering Practice: Home Economics in Personal and Educational Development." *Home Economics Forum* 1, 1 (1986): 7-9.

Smith, J. B. "Home Economics Places New Emphasis on Basic Skills." *Educational Leadership* 44, 8 (1987): 86.

12. Conclusion: Conceptions of Content

Ronald S. Brandt

THIS BOOK OFFERS BRIEF BUT AUTHORITATIVE ANALYSES OF most of the major content fields of the existing school curriculum.[1] The authors approach their task somewhat differently, partly because of the current situation in their respective fields. In mathematics, foreign language, the arts, technology, and health, they convey what appears to be a consensus position among specialists in their field as to what the curriculum should be. In English, social studies, and physical education, the authors present a more personal interpretation, reflecting their own values and professional judgment. (Their views may also be widely shared by their colleagues, but they present them in a more partisan manner, explicitly rejecting one or more alternative positions.) Finally, the authors of two chapters—those in science and home economics—report on current efforts to redefine their fields. The factors being considered, and the guidelines adopted so far, have implications for other curriculum areas as well.

Conceptions of Curriculum

In my introductory chapter, I summarized the conceptions of curriculum listed by Eisner and Vallance in the early 1970s and suggested that readers keep them in mind as they read. If you have done that, you have probably concluded that the conceptions are not discrete; most authors do not assume a single orientation to the exclusion of all others. Most do, though, tend to favor one approach.

In this chapter, I offer my interpretation of their positions. Bear in mind that although my analysis is based on what the authors wrote, it has not been confirmed by them, so it may not be completely accurate. Before

[1]There are conspicuous omissions. Several branches of vocational education are missing, as are speech, driver education, and others. No mention is made of reading, which, although a skill subject, also has content. These gaps are unfortunate, but our intent was not to be exhaustive; it was simply to survey most of the major curriculum areas.

presenting it, I want to suggest some modifications of the original scheme. Eisner and Vallance listed five orientations: academic rationalist, development of cognitive processes, curriculum as technology, self-actualization, and social reconstruction-relevance. They recognized two aspects of reconstruction-relevance: the adaptive branch, which focuses on preparing students to function in society, and the reformist approach, which prepares them to change it. They also listed structure of knowledge (which I consider different enough to be separate) as a subcategory of academic rationalism. I would also suggest an additional orientation—utilitarian—that is strongly reflected in most of the chapters in this book.

The authors of these chapters take the sensible position that schools should determine as carefully as they can what students will need to know and be able to do in the future, and then plan the curriculum accordingly. For example, Bragaw and Hartoonian say the significant question in planning a curriculum is "what students will be expected to achieve as a result." Rutherford and Ahlgren write that "to build an effective science curriculum, it is first necessary to identify what students should end up knowing." Met advises curriculum developers to determine the content of the foreign language curriculum by "first generating a list of communicative purposes, and then relating these purposes to the settings in which the language learner will be expected to function."

This straightforward approach is not easily reconciled with any of the Eisner-Vallance conceptions unless one extends social reconstruction-relevance beyond its original focus on active citizenship to include a broader range of adult functions, including earning a living. I prefer to construe that orientation more narrowly and classify preparation for other "real world" activities as *utilitarian*. The utilitarian view—that the choice of content depends on how it will be used—is not necessarily the same as the curriculum as technology approach, since that orientation refers more to the organization of schooling than to its intended outcomes.

The Author's Conceptions

The six conceptions I use, then, are cognitive processes, self-actualization, social participation, structure of knowledge, academic rationalist, and utilitarian.

Development of cognitive processes. While several authors refer to cognitive development as an important goal (it is specifically mentioned in the chapters on mathematics, social studies, and home economics, for example), none of the authors treats it as the primary goal of his or her subject area.

Self-actualization. Suhor in English and Bain in physical education give more explicit attention to personal experience than do the other authors. Bain takes the position that "the goal of education is to encourage critical reflection and self-awareness," and Suhor argues that "much of the student's store of personal experience is part of 'that which is to be processed'—part of the content of the English program."

Social participation. As might be expected, the authors of the chapter on social studies stress preparation for citizenship more than other authors. Bragaw and Hartoonian's views might occasionally even be characterized as *reformist*—"From earliest time, students need to deal with affluence, poverty, hunger, and unemployment, and major issues like welfare and well-being as part of local, state, and national policy"—but it is probably more accurate to describe their position as *adaptive*. Other subjects in which authors specifically recognize the role of curriculum in preparing students for social participation include physical education, technology, and science. Rutherford and Ahlgren, for example, note that "social issues of the day—population growth, environmental pollution, acid rain, waste disposal, energy production, and birth control" ought to receive attention in science education.

Structure of knowledge. Several authors describe their subject from a "structure of knowledge" position. Smith, for example, reports that she is involved in a national effort to "set forth the concepts that are distinctive, but not necessarily exclusive, to the high school home economics curriculum." The similar but more ambitious effort reported by Rutherford and Ahlgren to rethink the science curriculum also takes a structure-of-knowledge approach in that it begins with the field of science as a given.

Reflecting the influence of the 1960s curriculum reform movement, the arts and the technology chapters also embody an emphasis on structure. Lehman observes that each of the long-established disciplines of art, music, theatre, and dance "has its own content, language, and traditions." Technology, on the other hand, represents an attempt to build a partially new subject field on the foundations of an older one perceived as not fully up-to-date.

Academic rationalist. None of the authors takes a strictly academic-rationalist position, although Rutherford and Ahlgren acknowledge that orientation by listing "education for knowledge" as the first goal of science education: "Knowledge of the world around us—knowledge for its own sake, not for its utilitarian value—still remains a major purpose of general education." Other authors, however, specifically reject that idea. Suhor, for example, noting the preference of "traditionalists" for curriculums "rich in knowledge that every educated person should possess," argues that "such curriculums at elementary and secondary levels have been manifestly ineffective in producing adults who enjoy reading and who write with skill and verve."

Utilitarian. None of the authors takes an explicitly "curriculum as technology" approach either, although the straightforward ends-means viewpoint presented in several chapters might be considered a point of departure for such a position. For example, the chapter on foreign language proclaims the clear-cut objective of proficiency, defined as meaningful use of the language. This pragmatic approach, which I call "utilitarian," is surely an important determinant of curriculum content in most subjects. For example, the authors of the technology and home economics chapters represent this orientation when they list "task analysis"—dissecting what people in various jobs actually do—as one approach to designing curriculum.

Figure 12.1, then, is my analysis of the orientations presented in this book.

In summary, while most authors would undoubtedly concede the validity of each orientation to some degree (Rutherford and Ahlgren in science specifically recognize all of them), most emphasize one or another. Bain explicitly states a position for physical education compatible with the self-actualization orientation, noting that she has consciously chosen it over six competing models. Bragaw and Hartoonian in social studies and Suhor in English specifically reject academic rationalism. Instead, they advocate social participation and self-actualization. The other authors describe their subjects either from a structure of knowledge or a utilitarian perspective,

Figure 12.1. Editor's Analysis of Conceptions of Curriculum Represented in this Book

	Development of Cognitive Processes	Self-Actualization	Social Participation	Structure of Knowledge	Academic Rationalist	Utilitarian
Social Studies	+		**+**	+		
English	+	**+**				
Mathematics	+			**+**		
Science	+	+	+	**+**	+	+
Foreign Language						**+**
Arts		+		**+**		
Technology			+	+		**+**
Home Economics				+		**+**
Physical Education		**+**	+			
Health						**+**

Key: **+** indicates primary emphasis; + indicates another emphasis specifically mentioned or strongly implied.

although in some cases (home economics and technology), they also mention other ways to determine curriculum content.

If pressed, most teachers and curriculum leaders would probably choose, as I would, an eclectic approach similar to that taken by Rutherford and Ahlgren in the science chapter. Doing so has the advantage of recognizing that education in fact has multiple goals, none of which can be ignored. It has the disadvantage of accepting the need to deal continuously, at all levels and in all subjects, with competing claims for time and attention.

Factors Affecting the Selection of Curriculum Content

Three major considerations in choosing curriculum content are the nature of the society in which students are to live, the nature of students themselves (including the way they learn), and the nature of knowledge (Tyler 1949, Brandt and Tyler 1983). As a way to reflect on the recommendations of chapter authors, it may be useful to review their comments on these factors. This analysis is necessarily incomplete because the authors were asked to deal with a huge topic in very limited space, so they could not give much attention to discussion of such matters. Some (Lehman, for example) make no reference to them and instead use the available space for specific recommendations.

The Nature of Society

Technology. Several authors refer to rapidly changing technology as the primary factor requiring changes in the content of their field. Campbell and Fey, who note that computers and calculators are playing an increasingly important part in mathematics instruction, predict that these devices "will change *what* we teach as much as *how* we teach it." Technology, they say, will have a "profound effect on the content and organization of the mathematics curriculum." For example, since "computers have made the analysis of complex data sets relatively easy . . . it is now unthinkable that students should leave secondary school without a substantial introduction" to statistical methods in problem solving and decision making."

Bragaw and Hartoonian also cite technology as a major reason for restructuring the social studies curriculum. Technology, they say, will force more rapid policy decision making, and is contributing to a shift from representative democracy to participatory democracy.

Other societal changes affecting curriculum are at least partly indirect effects of evolving technology. Smith observes that home economics must adapt to redefined roles and functions of family members resulting from the changed composition of the workforce. Bain says that physical education must adapt to the "fitness boom," and Schlaadt calls for a stronger health curriculum because of "heightened public sensitivity to health issues."

Perhaps the best example of the impact of technology on the curriculum is the effort described by Benson to transform industrial arts into a field of study specifically encompassing all aspects of technology itself. This dramatic move exemplifies the continuing struggle by educators in all subjects to stake out the boundaries of their field so as to maintain a suitable role for it in contemporary and future society.

The Nature of Learners

An important factor in selecting content is the nature of those who are expected to learn it. Several authors mention the need for relevance to students' lives. Suhor, for example, comments that the English teacher "must find vital points of *connection* between the personal world of the student and the larger world of vicarious experience." Most authors, however, say relatively little about what today's students are like, probably because of the space constraints mentioned earlier, but perhaps also because, at the level of generality of a book like this, less can be said about particular learners.

All authors undoubtedly share a view of student learning that, although not always applied in classrooms, is so well accepted by educators that most authors probably felt it did not need to be made more explicit. This view, that meaningful learning requires active involvement, is nevertheless articulated by several authors, including Bensen, who stresses that hands-on learning activities enhance both motivation and retention. Suhor writes that "research has solidly demonstrated the value of classroom interaction of various kinds—inquiry teaching, scaffolding, reciprocal teaching, cooperative learning." Bragaw and Hartoonian observe that "the challenge for teachers is to promote the use of information . . . to help students create knowledge for themselves."

The Nature of Knowledge

The factor considered most thoroughly by most authors—understandably, since they were asked to speak from a disciplinary viewpoint—is the nature of knowledge in their field. Authors define the focus of their subjects in slightly different ways, and some point to overlaps with other subjects. Several also discuss, explicitly or implicitly, their conception of knowledge, including its relationship to information and to process.

Figure 12.2 presents a summary of the way the various authors define the focus of their subjects.

While each of the focuses in Figure 12.2 is appropriate, the list as a whole does not necessarily constitute the most rational scheme that might be defined for the organization of knowledge. Specifically, the various subjects are based on different principles, so there are numerous instances of overlap. Figure 12.3 reveals some of the interrelationships among the sub-

Figure 12.2. Authors' Characterizations of the Focus of Their Fields, as Paraphrased by the Editor

Subject	*Focus*
Social Studies	The study of how citizens in a society—past, present, and future—make personal and public policy decisions.
English	The ordering of personal and vicarious experience through language.
Mathematics	A language for expressing relations among quantitative factors in a situation.
Science	A body of developing ideas, a way of thinking and conducting inquiry, an outlook on the universe, and a complex social and cultural enterprise. Science is concerned primarily with understanding how the world works, technology with figuring out how to arrange things to happen in the way we want.
Foreign Language	Meaningful use of a foreign language.
The Arts	Education in the disciplines of music, art, theatre, and dance. Drama/theatre is the metaphoric representation of human behavior. Dance is expressive movement.
Technology	A comprehensive, action-based educational program concerned with technical means, their evolution, utilization, and significance with industry, its organization, personnel, systems, techniques, resources and products, and their social and cultural impact.
Home Economics	Preparation for family and home living.
Physical Education	The study and refinement of human movement.
Health	The development of health skills, attitudes, and practices that are conducive to well-being.

jects specifically mentioned by the authors. Rutherford and Ahlgren pinpoint relationships between the science curriculum and mathematics, on the one hand, and technology on the other. Social studies overlaps with science in two ways: in study of the history of scientific achievements and in consideration of such current issues as air pollution and atomic energy. English overlaps with social studies in similar ways: in the study of the literature of other eras and in speaking, listening, reading, and writing about current affairs. Health topics are dealt with not only in separate health classes but in home economics, social studies, and physical education classes as well.

The number of points at which the various subjects duplicate or compete with one another is probably increasing. Bragaw and Hartoonian point to "the creation of knowledge patterns that no longer fit neatly into Aristotelian and Germanic discipline structures." Many curriculum workers would probably welcome a reconceptualization of the entire curriculum, but for many reasons that is unlikely to happen in the near future. In the meantime, curriculum planners should attend to these intersections, not only to avoid redundancy, but because they present opportunities for curriculum articulation and integration.

Figure 12.3. Relationships Among the Content Areas Identified by Chapter Authors

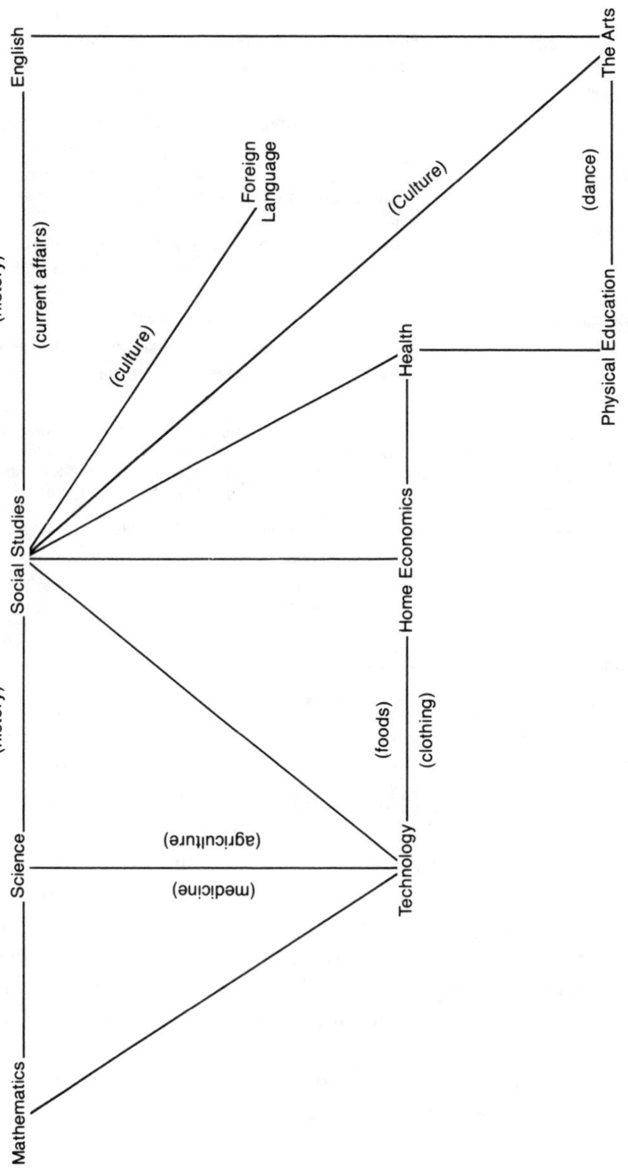

Knowledge and information. In chapter 1, I referred to accusations that educators tend to emphasize process to the detriment of content. I pointed out that, in terms of the framework proposed by Eisner and Vallance, the critics who take this position often represent an academic-rationalist view in which information is equated with knowledge. Several of the chapter authors explictly reject this view.

Bragaw and Hartoonian, for example, dispute the notion that information provided by a teacher or a textbook can be considered knowledge. Knowledge, they insist, is created by individuals and groups through a process of intimate involvement. Educators need to give themselves permission, therefore, "to let go of some information that we are now teaching and reallocate that time to deeper inquiries that will help learners build . . . connections."

Suhor agrees, asserting that "English programs have greatly overemphasized information. . . . Information is an essential but limited aspect of the study of English. . . . Students 'know' English when they 'do' English well." Met takes a similar position regarding foreign language instruction, which she says should be concerned with "what the learner *can do with language* rather than what the learner *knows about language*." Bain notes that "movement provides an essential form of direct knowledge that can be enhanced, but not replaced, by cognitive information."

Knowledge and process. The fact that these educators view knowledge as constructed by learners rather than transmitted by teachers helps explain the preoccupation with process that so distresses their critics. Even the proponents of this view recognize that it can be carried to excess. Suhor, who believes that reactions against information-heavy English programs "have correctly resulted in recommendations for engaging students in the actual process of language-making," concedes that the emphasis on process has resulted in "neglect of the kinds of knowledge that are appropriate in the English curriculum." Nevertheless, he is convinced that "our primary mission in elementary and secondary schools is to produce students who speak, listen, read, and write not only capably but with a joy that will have profound impact on their personal habits and will carry over to later phases of their lives."

Bain takes a similar stance, urging that in physical education, "knowledge must be presented as problematic and situated in a particular historical and social context, but must also be linked to the personal histories and experiences of students." Bragaw and Hartoonian advise that social studies content should help students "develop problem-solving skills from hypothesis formation to using probability and statistics." Campbell and Fey also stress the processes of learning mathematics because they believe that doing so is the only way to achieve the goals of mathematical understanding, interpretation, and application.

The main reason, then, that many educators find it hard to deal with questions of content apart from the processes of teaching and learning is that their conception of curriculum includes both. They prefer to start not with a "knowledge for its own sake" orientation, but with a set of goals that describe what students should be like after studying a subject. Viewing knowledge not as something to be handed intact from one person to another but as understandings developed through experience, they are necessarily concerned with the nature of that experience.

Still, educators need to ponder whether, in our concern with teaching and learning, we may in fact give less attention to substance than we should. If, as we sometimes say, the abundance of knowledge makes it impossible to learn everything, that is all the more reason we must be judicious about what we select for students to study. If Suhor is right that "curriculums that define the content of literature in terms of lists of works to be studied by every student do not serve the goal of producing lifelong readers and learners," schools can nevertheless specify the ideas, literary forms, and authors that are particularly important for students to encounter in their school careers, and can design curriculum to ensure that they do.

In the report of his study of U.S. high schools, Boyer (1983) makes a strong case for a well-constructed core curriculum that specifies what all students are expected to learn. Some schools have a coherent core program, but many do not. They have a set of required courses, but the relationships among the courses and the rationale for requiring them are obscure. One reason for this is that reaching consensus on what is essential, especially in secondary schools where each teacher is devoted to his or her own subject, is very difficult. In an ASCD-sponsored project (Roberts and Cawelti 1984), 15 high schools made headway by first defining specific "learnings" that all could agree were important and then reorganizing courses to incorporate them.

Aspiration vs. Reality

Having affirmed that well-chosen content is crucial, I must again emphasize the futility of trying to separate content from the way it is taught. From personal experience and from authoritative research such as Goodlad's (1984) *A Place Called School*, we know the extent to which much teaching is routine and enervating. From other research (Joyce, Showers, and Rolheiser-Bennett 1987) we have impressive evidence that when teachers properly use strategies that have been refined and tested, their students learn far more. And we should not have to squander our energy arguing the obvious fact that teaching skill does not necessarily accompany knowledge of subject matter.

Most of the authors in this book are in the uncomfortable position of envisioning a curriculum that they recognize is more aspiration than reality. Their concern is not with an arbitrary distinction between process and content but with the real problems of teachers and schools. Met, for example, confesses that "for the moment . . . proficiency-based curriculums exist more in the professional literature than they do in classrooms." Suhor worries that "many teachers are still uncomfortable in the role of discussion leader or orchestrator of classroom groups." Campbell and Fey observe that "the persistent challenge is to find ways to implement recommended changes—to close the gap between the ideals of professional practice and the reality of mathematics education in schools and classrooms across the country."

These educators want a curriculum with strong content—but they know it cannot be achieved except through processes powerful enough to ensure meaningful learning.

References

Boyer, Ernest L. *High School: A Report on Secondary Education in America.* New York: Harper & Row, 1983.

Brandt, Ronald S., and Ralph W. Tyler. "Goals and Objectives." In *Fundamental Curriculum Decisions*, edited by Fenwick W. English. Alexandria, Va.: Association for Supervision and Curriculum Development, 1983.

Goodlad, John I. *A Place Called School.* New York: McGraw-Hill, 1984.

Joyce, Bruce, Beverly Showers, and Carol Rolheiser-Bennett. "Staff Development and Student Learning: A Synthesis of Research on Models of Teaching." *Educational Leadership* 45 (October 1987):11-23.

Roberts, Arthur D., and Gordon Cawelti. *Redefining General Education in the American High School.* Alexandria, Va.: Association for Supervision and Curriculum Development, 1984.

Tyler, Ralph W. *Basic Principles of Curriculum and Instruction.* 1974 edition. Chicago: University of Chicago Press, 1949.

About the Authors

Ronald S. Brandt is Executive Editor, Association for Supervision and Curriculum Development, Alexandria, Virginia.

Andrew Ahlgren (Professor of Education, University of Minnesota, on leave) is Associate Project Director, Office of Science and Technology Education, American Association for the Advancement of Science, Washington, D.C.

Linda L. Bain is Professor of Physical Educaton and Associate Dean of Research, College of Education, University of Houston, Houston, Texas.

M. James Bensen is Dean, School of Industry and Technology, University of Wisconsin-Stout, Menomonie.

Donald H. Bragaw is Chief, Bureau of Social Studies Education, the State Education Department, the University of the State of New York, Albany.

Patricia F. Campbell is Associate Professor of Curriculum and Instruction, Department of Mathematics, University of Maryland, College Park.

James T. Fey is Professor of Curriculum and Instruction and Mathematics, Department of Mathematics, University of Maryland, College Park.

H. Michael Hartoonian is Social Studies Supervisor, Wisconsin Department of Public Instruction, Madison, and Adjunct Professor, University of Wisconsin-Madison.

Paul R. Lehman is Vice President, Music Educators National Conference, and Professor and Associate Dean, School of Music, University of Michigan, Ann Arbor.

Myriam Met is Foreign Language Coordinator, Montgomery County Public Schools, Rockville, Maryland.

F. James Rutherford is Chief Education Officer, Office of Science and Technology Education, American Association for the Advancement of Science, Washington, D.C.

Richard G. Schlaadt is Professor and Head, Department of School and Community Health, College of Human Development and Performance, University of Oregon, Eugene.

Joanna B. Smith is Vocational Education Specialist—Home Economics Education, Center for School Improvement and Performance, Indiana Department of Education, Indianapolis.

Charles Suhor is Deputy Executive Director, National Council of Teachers of English, Urbana, Illinois.

Reviewers

We are grateful to the following for their helpful comments on early drafts of one or more chapters.

David Ackerman, Winchester (Massachusetts) Public Schools
Daisy Arredondo, Consultant, Seattle, Washington
Gerald Bailey, Kansas State University, Manhattan
James Beane, Saint Bonaventure University, New York
Roger Bybee, The Colorado College, Colorado Springs
Theodore Czajkowski, Bellingham (Washington) Public Schools
Charles Dodson, Sapulpa (Oklahoma) Public Schools
David Ebeling, Monroe County (Indiana) Community Schools
Benjamin Ebersole, Hershey (Pennsylvania) Public Schools
Fenwick English, Lehigh University, Bethlehem, Pennsylvania
Katherine Ennis, University of Wisconsin, Madison
Gordon Floyd, Arkansas Department of Education, Little Rock
Meredith "Mark" Gall, University of Oregon, Eugene
Allan Glatthorn, East Carolina University, Greenville, North Carolina
Bernard Goffin, Monroe (Connecticut) Public Schools
Tom Howie, Huntington County (Maryland) Elementary Schools
Luther Kiser, Ames (Iowa) Community Schools
John T. Lambert, East Stroudsburg (Pennsylvania) Area School District
John F. LeBlanc, Indiana University, Bloomington
Susan Loucks-Horsley, The NETWORK, Andover, Massachusetts
Ruth Ann Lyness, Lincoln (Nebraska) Public Schools
David Martin, Gallaudet University, Washington, D.C.
Robert Mason, Mineral County (West Virginia) Schools
Carolee Matsumoto, Concord (Massachusetts) Public Schools
Jerry Patterson, Madison (Wisconsin) Metropolitan Schools
Gerald Ponder, North Texas State University, Denton
Mel Preusser, Douglas County (Colorado) School District
Arthur Roberts, University of Connecticut, Storrs
Vincent Rogers, University of Connecticut, Storrs
Sue Spangler, Millard Schools, Omaha, Nebraska
Georgea Sparks, Eastern Michigan University, Ypsilanti
Betty Steffy, Moorestown (New Jersey) Public Schools
Marilyn Suydam, The Ohio State University, Columbus
Stephen Willoughby, University of Arizona, Tucson
Marilyn Winters, California State University, Sacramento
Robert Yager, University of Iowa, Iowa City

ASCD Board of Directors as of November 1, 1987

Executive Council 1987-88

President: Marcia Knoll, Principal, P.S. 220 Queens, Forest Hills, New York
President Elect: Arthur L. Costa, Professor of Education, California State University, Sacramento
Immediate Past President: Gerald Firth, Professor and Chair, Department of Curriculum and Supervision, University of Georgia, Athens
Roger V. Bennett, Dean, College of Education and Allied Professions, Bowling Green State University, Bowling Green, Ohio
Donna Jean Carter, Superintendent, Independent School District 281, New Hope, Minnesota
Cile Chavez, Deputy Superintendent, Littleton Public Schools, Littleton, Colorado
Denice S. Clyne, Principal, Sand Lake School, Anchorage, Alaska
Corrine P. Hill, Principal, Wasatch Elementary School, Salt Lake City, Utah
Jean V. Marani, Supervisor, Early Childhood and Elementary Education, Florida Department of Education, Tallahassee, Florida
Stephanie A. Marshall, Director, Illinois Math and Science Academy, Aurora, Illinois
Loren E. Sanchez, Associate Superintendent of Instruction, Upland School District, Upland, California
Ann Shelly, Director, Teacher Preparation Program, Bethany College, Bethany, West Virginia
Bob Valiant, Assistant Superintendent, General Administration, Kennewick School District, Kennewick, Washington

Board Members Elected at Large

(Listed alphabetically; the year in parentheses indicates the end of the term of office.)

Alice Bosshard, Valdez City Schools, Valdez, Alaska (1991)
Rita Dunn, St. John's University, Jamaica, New York (1991)

Rita Foote, Traverse City, Michigan (1989)
Carl Glickman, University of Georgia, Athens (1990)
Delores Greene, Richmond Public Schools, Richmond, Virginia (1988)
Evelyn B. Holman, Wicomico County Board of Education, Salisbury, Maryland (1990)
Robert Krajewski, University of Texas, San Antonio (1989)
Richard Kunkel, National Council for Accreditation of Teacher Education, Washington, D.C. (1988)
Blanche J. Martin, E.S.R. Winnebago/Boone Counties, Rockford, Illinois (1990)
Anne Price, St. Louis Public Schools, St. Louis, Missouri (1991)
Lillian Ramos, Catholic University, Ponce, Puerto Rico (1989)
LaVae Robertson, Oak Elementary School, Albany, Oregon (1991)
David Robinson, Sheridan Public Schools, Sheridan, Arkansas (1991)
Thelma Spencer, Educational Testing Services, Princeton, New Jersey (1989)
Julia Thomas, Appalachian State University, Boone, North Carolina (1988)
Roberta Walker, District of Columbia Public Schools, Washington, D.C. (1990)
Lois F. Wilson, California State University, San Bernardino (1988)
Marilyn Winters, Sacramento State University, Sacramento, California (1990)
George Woons, Kent Intermediate School District, Grand Rapids, Michigan (1989)
Claire Yoshida, Naalehu High School, Keala Kekua, Hawaii (1988)

Unit Representatives to the Board of Directors

(Each unit's President is listed first.)

Alabama: Nancy Cotter, Talladega; Horace Gordon, Birmingham; Richard Brogdon, Auburn University, Auburn
Alaska: Dennis Daggett, Kenai Peninsula School District, Soldotna; Don McDermott, University of Alaska-Anchorage
Arizona: Bets Manera, Paradise Valley; Peg Moseley, Peoria Unified School District, Peoria; Darlene Haring, Scottsdale School District, Scottsdale; Larry McBiles, State Department of Education, Phoenix
Arkansas: Bobby Altom, Marshall Public Schools, Marshall; Jerry Daniel, Camden Public Schools, Camden
California: Ronald Hockwalt, Cajon Valley School District, El Cajon; Marilyn George, Kern High School District, Bakersfield; Bob Guerts, Sonoma Valley Unified School District, Santa Rosa; Yvonne Lux, Poway Unified School District, Poway; Dolores Ballesteros, Franklin-McKinley School District, San Jose; Dorothy Garcia, Colton Joint Unified School District, Bloomington; Bob Garmston, California State University, Sacramento

Colorado: Chuck Schwahn, Eagle County School District, Eagle; Mel Preusser, Castle Rock; Gary Gibson, Adams County School District #14, Commerce City

Connecticut: Tom Jokubaitis, Superintendent of Schools, Wolcott; Edward H. Bourque, Fairfield Public Schools, Fairfield

Delaware: Edith Vincent, Department of Public Instruction, Dover; Frederick A. Duffy, Lincoln

District of Columbia: Delores Hamilton, Banneker High School, Washington; Romaine Thomas, Ketcham Elementary School District, Washington

Florida: Evelyn Lynn, Ormond Beach; Virgil Mills, Ellington; Catherine Fleeger, School Board of Pinellas County, Clearwater; Eileen Duval, Tampa

Georgia: Wilma Biggers, Oconee County Schools, Watkinsville; Charles Sheperd, Georgia Department of Education, Calhoun; Gary Walker, Cartersville City Schools, Cartersville

Hawaii: Donald Young, University of Hawaii—CRDG, Honolulu; C.J. Baehr, Hawaii Interactive T.V. System, Honolulu

Idaho: Evelyn Cairns, Elementary Consultant, Boise; Lamont Lyons, Boise State University, Boise

Illinois: Sheila Wilson, Forest View Education Center, Arlington Heights; James Montgomery, Arlington Public Schools, Arlington; Carolyn Kimbell, Downers Grove School District #58, Downers Grove; Richard Hanke, Thomas Junior High School, Arlington Heights; Al Cohen, Wilmot Junior High School, Deerfield; Fred Osburn, School District #117, Jacksonville

Indiana: Sam Abram, Muncie Community Schools, Muncie; Ken Springer, Decatur

Iowa: C. Douglas Buchanan, West Des Moines Community School District, West Des Moines; Douglas Schermer, Briggs Elementary School, Maqudketa; Arnold Lindaman, North Scott Community School District, Endridge

Kansas: Kaye Tague, Emporia; Jim Jarrett, Kansas City

Kentucky: Robert Pettit, Davies County Board of Education, Owensboro

Louisiana: Joseph Pecarrere, Abramson Senior High School, New Orleans; Julianna Boudreaux, Associate Superintendent, New Orleans; Kate Scully, New Orleans

Maine: Scott Myers, Nezinscot Valley School District, Buckfield; Leon Levesque, Mt. Abram School District, Strong; Joyce Freeman, Bath

Maryland: Noel Farmer, Frederick County Schools, Fredericksville; Joan Palmer, Howard County Public Schools, Ellicott City; Richard Williams, Towson State University, Towson

Massachusetts: Isa Zimmerman, Lexington Public Schools, Lexington; Gary Baker, Acton Public Schools, Acton; Therese d'Abre, Dennis-Yarmouth Regional Schools, Yarmouth

Oregon: Carol Black, Eagle Point School District, Eagle Point; Thomas S. Lindersmith, Principal, Lake Oswego; Virginia Schwartzrock, Principal, Eugene

Pennsylvania: Ina Logue, Allegheny Intermediate Unit, Pittsburgh; Robert Flynn, McMurray; John Gould, Eastern Lancaster County School District, New Holland; John Lambert, East Stroudsburg School District, East Stroudsburg; Leo Gensante, Hollidaysburg Area School District, Hollidaysburg

Puerto Rico: Ramon Claudio, University of Puerto Rico, Rio Piedras

Rhode Island: Philip Streifer, Barrington Public Schools, Barrington

South Carolina: Edith Jensen, Lexington School District #5, Ballentine; Milton Kimpson, Columbia; Karen B. Callison, Union County Schools, Union

South Dakota: Donlynn Rice, Division of Education, Pierre

Tennessee: Betty Sparks, State Department of Education, Knoxville; Kay Awalt, Franklin Elementary, Franklin; Cindi Chance, K.D. McKellar School, Milan

Texas: Margaret Montgomery, Grapevine Independent School District, Grapevine; Bonnie Fairall, El Paso; Nancy Baker, Elementary Curriculum Coordinator, North Perry, Carrollton; Pat Mengwasser, Director of Language Arts, Austin; Charles Thacker, Assistant Superintendent, Carrollton; Charles Patterson, Assistant Superintendent, Killeen

Utah: Peggy Sorenson, East Sandy School, Sandy

Vermont: Lynn Baker Murray, Trinity College, Burlington; Raymond McNulty, Franklin North Eastern Supervisory Union, Richford

Virginia: Marion Hargrove, Bedford County Public Schools, Bedford; Evelyn Bickham, Lynchburg; Judy D. Whittemore, Superintendent, Grafton; Shelba Murphy, Consultant, Alexandria

Virgin Islands: Marva Browne, Virgin Islands Department of Education, St. Thomas; Anita Plasket, College of The Virgin Islands, St. Croix

Washington: Charles Blondino, Educational Service District #121, Seattle; Judy Olson, Staff Development Consultant, Fall City; Monica Schmidt, State Board of Education, Olympia; James Barchek, Enumclaw School District, Enumclaw

West Virginia: Robert P. Mason, Mineral County School Board, Keyser; Corey Lock, Marshall University, Huntington

Wisconsin: Patricia Koll, University of Wisconsin-Oshkosh, Oshkosh; Sherwood Williams, Green Bay

Wyoming: Lucien Trouchon, Platte County School District, Wheatland; Donna Connor, University of Wyoming, Rawlins

International Units:

British Columbia: Mary Ann Lyall, School District #57, Prince George

Germany: Candace Ransing, Assistant Superintendent, Frankfurt District, Frankfurt DSO
United Kingdom: Edward Brennan, Social Studies/Math Coordinator

ASCD Review Council

Chair: J. Arch Phillips, Kent State University, Kent, Ohio
Barbara D. Day, University of North Carolina, Chapel Hill
Donna Delph, Purdue University Calumet, Hammond, Indiana
Benjamin P. Ebersole, Hershey Public School District, Hershey, Pennsylvania
Delores Silva, Temple University, Philadelphia, Pennsylvania

ASCD Headquarters Staff

Gordon Cawelti, *Executive Director*
Ronald S. Brandt, *Executive Editor*
Sarah Arlington, *Manager, Annual Conference*
John Bralove, *Director, Administrative Services*
Diane Berreth, *Director, Field Services*
Helené Hodges, *Director, Research and Information*
Cynthia Warger, *Director, Program Development*

Francine Addicott
Patricia Bailey
Sylvia Bayer
Karla Bingman
Elizabeth Blaize
Joan Brandt
Dorothy Brown
Kathy Browne
Jeff Bryant
Colette Burgess
Sandra Chaloux
Aurora Chase
R.C. Chernault
Kathy Compton
Marcia D'Arcangelo
Marsha Davis
Chana Duckenfield
Perry Farmer
Anita Fitzpatrick
Delores Flenoury
Dorothy Haines
Dwayne Hayes
Sandy Hightower
Mary Hines
Harold Hutch
Consuella Jenkins
Jo Ann Jones
Teola Jones
Mary Keen
Michelle Kelly
Gina Kovarsky
Donna Lands
Amy Lashbrook
Indu Madan
Kelly Mattson
Gary Maxwell
Anne Meek
Clara Meredith
Frances Mindel
Ricky Mitchell
Nancy Modrak
Cerylle Moffett
John O'Neil
Lori Oxendine
Kelvin Parnell
Margini Patel
Ruby Powell
Janet Price
Lorraine Primeau
Yolanda Ramos
Melissa Reinberg
Mickey Robinson
Gayle Rockwell
Glenn Scimonelli
Beth Schweinefuss
Carol Shanahan
Bob Shannon
Carolyn Shell
Leslie Shell
Chris Smith
Lisa Street
Dee Stump-Walek
Michelle Terry
René Townsley
Patricia Verner
David Warden
Al Way
Marjorie Weathers
Cheryl Weber
Scott Willis